CW01307380

BMW Classic Coupés
1965-1989

OTHER TITLES IN THE CROWOOD AUTOCLASSICS SERIES

AC COBRA Brian Laban
ALFA ROMEO 916 GTV AND SPIDER Robert Foskett
ALFA ROMEO SPIDER John Tipler
ASTON MARTIN DB4, DB5 & DB6 Jonathan Wood
ASTON MARTIN DB7 Andrew Noakes
ASTON MARTIN V8 William Presland
AUDI QUATTRO Laurence Meredith
AUSTIN HEALEY Graham Robson
BMW 3 SERIES James Taylor
BMW 5 SERIES James Taylor
BMW M3 James Taylor
CITROËN DS SERIES John Pressnell
FORD ESCORT RS Graham Robson
FROGEYE SPRITE John Baggott
JAGUAR E-TYPE Jonathan Wood
JAGUAR XJ-S Graham Robson
JAGUAR XK8 Graham Robson
JENSEN INTERCEPTOR John Tipler
JOWETT JAVELIN AND JUPITER Geoff McAuley & Edmund Nankivell
LAMBORGHINI COUNTACH Peter Dron
LAND ROVER DEFENDER, 90 AND 110 RANGE James Taylor
LOTUS & CATERHAM SEVEN John Tipler
LOTUS ELAN Matthew Vale
LOTUS ELISE John Tipler

MGA David G. Styles
MGB Brian Laban
MGF AND TF David Knowles
MG T-SERIES Graham Robson
MAZDA MX-5 Antony Ingram
MERCEDES-BENZ CARS OF THE 1990S James Taylor
MERCEDES-BENZ 'FINTAIL' MODELS Brian Long
MERCEDES-BENZ S CLASS James Taylor
MERCEDES SL SERIES Andrew Noakes
MERCEDES W113 Myles Kornblatt
MORGAN 4/4 Michael Palmer
MORGAN THREE-WHEELER Peter Miller
PORSCHE CARRERA – THE AIR-COOLED ERA Johnny Tipler
RELIANT THREE-WHEELERS John Wilson-Hall
ROVER 75 AND MG ZT James Taylor
ROVER P5 & P5B James Taylor
SAAB 99 & 900 Lance Cole
SUBARU IMPREZA WRX AND WRX STI James Taylor
SUNBEAM ALPINE AND TIGER Graham Robson
TRIUMPH SPITFIRE & GT6 Richard Dredge
TRIUMPH TR7 David Knowles
VOLKSWAGEN GOLF GTI James Richardson
VOLVO P1800 David G. Styles

BMW Classic Coupés 1965–1989

2000C and CS, E9 and E24

James Taylor

THE CROWOOD PRESS

First published in 2014 by
The Crowood Press Ltd
Ramsbury, Marlborough
Wiltshire SN8 2HR

www.crowood.com

© James Taylor 2014

All rights reserved. No part of this publication may be reproduced or transmitted in any form or by any means, electronic or mechanical, including photocopy, recording, or any information storage and retrieval system, without permission in writing from the publishers.

British Library Cataloguing-in-Publication Data
A catalogue record for this book is available from the British Library.

ISBN 978 1 84797 846 2

Designed and typeset by Guy Croton Publishing Services, Tonbridge, Kent

Printed and bound in India by Replika Press Pvt Ltd

CONTENTS

	Introduction and Acknowledgements	6
1	COUPÉ CULTURE	8
2	2000 C AND 2000 CS	22
3	THE MAINSTREAM E9 COUPÉS	36
4	THE CSL AND THE RACING COUPÉS	64
5	DEVELOPING A SUCCESSOR	96
6	THE FIRST GENERATION E24s, 1976–1982	108
7	THE SECOND GENERATION E24s, 1982–1989	126
8	THE E24 IN COMPETITION	162
9	TUNED AND MODIFIED COUPÉS	174
	Index	191

INTRODUCTION AND ACKNOWLEDGEMENTS

BMW's big coupés of the 1960s, 1970s and 1980s were a major factor in the company's success in its fight for market share, not only in its native Germany but also in the UK and the USA, two of its major export markets. I have always liked these cars, and the opportunity to write about them was one I had no intention of turning down.

Nevertheless, the cars are quite rare in the UK today, and finding good examples to photograph was much harder than it should have been. I was greatly helped in my search by performance BMW specialists Munich Legends, who found me an excellent 3.0 CSL and a similarly special M635 CSi at short notice. Meanwhile, photographers Simon Clay and Craig Pusey managed to rediscover some long-forgotten shots of E9s and E24s in their archives, and Craig also found some old press and competition pictures from the days when these cars were new. I am grateful to both of them.

Further thanks go to BMW themselves, who over the years have provided a fine array of press and publicity pictures, many of which are also used in this book. Finally, I am extremely grateful to Doug Cain and to Mike Pugh in the USA – BMW enthusiasts both – who specially took some pictures of Doug's superb 3.0 CS that I saw during a visit to North Carolina in 2010.

James Taylor, Oxfordshire
April 2014

OPPOSITE: 1987 BMW E24 M6.

INTRODUCTION AND ACKNOWLEDGEMENTS

CHAPTER ONE

COUPÉ CULTURE

Between the 1960s and 1980s, any car manufacturer with ambitions to become a player in the prestige market in Germany had to include a big luxury coupé in its range. It is tempting to trace the tradition all the way back to the 1930s and the beginnings of Germany's Autobahn network, which allowed such cars to be enjoyed to the full. It is equally tempting to trace the style back to the elegant and luxurious French coachwork designs of the 1930s, which set the style for the whole of European high society. However, for the purposes of this book, there is no need to go back further than 1951 and the International Automobile Exhibition held at Frankfurt that April.

The Frankfurt show was a very important event for the German automotive industry. A significant number of companies had been put out of action by the six years of war that had ended in 1945. Many never recovered, but a handful did claw their way back to viability during the later 1940s. The country had been divided in two and even the average German in the West was unable to afford a car of any kind in those years. However, between 1947 and 1949 the car makers and accessory manufacturers did show their wares at the annual trade fair in Hanover, highlighting what Germany could offer overseas buyers. Even though the cars on show were mainly out of their reach, the event was always a major attraction for local visitors, who would visit to dream.

The BMW 327 Coupé of the 1930s was a strikingly beautiful car, and is seen today as an ancestor of the big coupés from the 1960s and 1970s.

COUPÉ CULTURE

The 1952 prototype coupé by Autenrieth on the 501 chassis was strangely bulbous, in the fashion of the times.

By the end of the 1940s, some semblance of order was beginning to return to the West German car market. Mercedes-Benz was building some extremely credible middle-class machines and was poised to re-enter the sports-car and prestige markets. BMW, by contrast, was still working on new designs, and by 1950 was testing prototypes of a little rear-engined two-seater, known as the BMW 331 and clearly inspired by the Fiat 500. By that stage, however, West Germany was preparing to move on. Planned for April 1951 was a brand-new event – a car show to be held in the halls of the trade-fair site in Frankfurt. Berlin, traditional host of the major annual motor show in Germany, also planned a revival of that event for that September. Although the Berlin event would be a last gasp and Frankfurt would take over as the major German show, it was clear that 1951 was going to be an important year.

For the German motor industry, Frankfurt 1951 acted as a call to arms. This was going to be an opportunity to show that it had left behind the problems of the war years and their aftermath. Here, they could show their latest wares – or, at least, the models they hoped to get into production soon – and demonstrate to the world that German engineering had undergone a renaissance.

Mercedes-Benz went all out to get its new six-cylinder 220 model ready for the show. BMW, meanwhile, had been looking at the possibility of producing other makers' designs under licence. Their fallback option was the little 331 model, but this was apparently vetoed by Sales Director Hanns Grewenig. His view was that BMW's limited production capacity was better suited to a small-volume car with high profit margins than to a small car that would have to be built in high numbers in order to generate good profits. He must also have realized that, if Mercedes-Benz did launch a new prestige model at Frankfurt in 1951, it was going to make a fundamental difference to the German car market and to the way German cars were perceived abroad. BMW needed to develop a prestige model, and quickly.

BMW abandoned work on the 331 and threw all their resources into developing a prestige saloon. Time and development resources were saved by using a further development of the pre-war BMW 2-litre engine. Although the new 501 that was announced at the Frankfurt Show in April 1951 was too heavy to equal the performance of the Mercedes-Benz 220, introduced at the same time, its 2-litre engine nevertheless made it a credible entrant in West Germany's prestige saloon class.

■ COUPÉ CULTURE

More commonly seen was the later Baur coupé body, seen here on a 502 chassis.

The importance of announcing the new model at Frankfurt was obvious: this was BMW's first post-war car. In practice, it would not be available for purchase for another 18 months – deliveries began in October 1952 – but BMW had laid claim to a slice of the prestige coupé market. Like Mercedes-Benz, BMW knew that that market would return. Lacking the resources to build their own coupé bodies, they turned to coachbuilder Autenrieth in Darmstadt and were looking at that company's prototype coupé for the 501 chassis during 1952. This coupé, and from 1955 one by Baur, became available for special order alongside the saloons. As the original 501 chassis developed into a V8-engined 502 in 1954, so these coupés and their cabriolet derivatives presented an attractive alternative to the established Mercedes-Benz six-cylinders.

The 503 Coupé

Hanns Grewenig, still BMW's Sales Director, could see the potential of developing a distinctive grand tourer on the 501 and 502 chassis, and in 1954 he gained approval for such a car. Designed by Albrecht Goertz, with the encouragement of European car importer Max Hoffmann in the USA, the styling made deliberate reference to Italian coachwork, but remained determinedly Teutonic. It was ready to be shown at the 1955 Frankfurt Motor Show, which now occupied the autumn slot that had originally been reserved for the Berlin event.

Based on a wide-track 502 chassis and featuring the most powerful 3.2-litre version of the V8 engine, with 160PS, the new model came as either coupé or cabriolet. Despite aluminium panels, it was no lighter than the rather over-bodied saloons, but a top speed of 190km/h (118mph) made it faster than the rival Mercedes-Benz 220S coupé – and that gave it a special prestige of its own. Unfortunately, it was also nearly 40 per cent more expensive than the Mercedes, at 29,500 DM versus 21,200 DM, and that price premium proved a big hindrance to sales both at home and abroad. The 503 went on sale in May 1956, and production ended in March 1960. Just 412 cars – 273 coupés and 139 cabriolets – had been built, and BMW had lost money on every one of them. The cost of building these cars by hand at a rate of around two a week was really more than BMW could absorb at a time when it did not have a big-selling volume car in production.

Nevertheless, the 503 had staked BMW's claim to a place in the prestige coupé market at home in Germany and also in the wider European market and in the USA. In that sense, it was a vitally important model for the company's future. Although it was not immediately replaced – BMW was going through a tricky period around 1960, and could not finance such loss-leading products – the idea of a new big coupé was never far from the thoughts of BMW management.

COUPÉ CULTURE

Neither of the earlier 1950s coupé designs had much appeal outside Germany, so a special and more modern-looking body was drawn up for the 503 coupé, with which BMW hoped to capture a slice of the big US market. This example has an interesting spoked style of wheel trim.

More common on the 503 was a plain hubcap, as seen here. The lady is Sonja Ziemann, a German actress of the period whose presence in the picture would have enhanced the car's appeal to wealthier buyers.

11

■ COUPÉ CULTURE

ABOVE: *Tiny numbers of 503 coupés were built with right-hand drive. This was one of just three for the UK, delivered new to the Frazer-Nash family who were then BMW importers.*

There was a cabriolet version of the 503, too. The ladies in this contemporary picture are clearly not only wealthy, but also stunned by the smartly dressed gentleman and his shiny new car!

12

COUPÉ CULTURE

The dashboard of the 503 was very much of its time, with a thick-rimmed white steering wheel and an under-dash handbrake that was probably intended to appeal to US buyers.

The glamorous coupés and cabriolets were all very well, but BMW had to make money somehow. This is one way they tried to do it, with the little Isetta bubble car. This one was a UK-market example – the revolving beacon on the roof was definitely not a standard fit!

13

■ COUPÉ CULTURE

Quandt money financed the BMW recovery in the 1960s, which was led by the 1500 saloon introduced in 1961. It was a clear statement of BMW's abilities.

The 3200 CS Coupé

Italian stylists were seen as the world leaders during the 1950s and had undeniably influenced the shape that Goertz had drawn up for the 503 coupé. It had certainly caught the eye of Helmut Werner Bönsch, who had joined BMW in 1958 to take charge of what would now be called product planning, alongside multiple other responsibilities, such as marketing, quality control, and analysis of competitors' vehicles. It was in this role that he came to examine a Lancia Flaminia coupé, the Italian manufacturer's obvious rival for the 503 and any car that might follow it. He was pleased to observe that its elegant Pininfarina body would fit on to the chassis of BMW's current 3200L and 3200S saloons, the latest derivatives of the V8-engined 502.

Looking for cost-effective solutions to the company's product needs, Bönsch put together a proposal to create a new coupé by buying in the Pininfarina design, adding a BMW front end, and fitting the modified body on to the big saloon chassis. The proposal did not meet with the approval of the Board, but one outcome was that Technical Director Fritz Fiedler was asked to find an Italian coachbuilder who would be able to design a new coupé body specially for BMW on the existing saloon chassis. As BMW still did not have large production facilities, any deal would have to include body production as well.

That limited the options, but the coachbuilder Bertone took the bait. During 1961, Nuccio Bertone drew up a new coupé to suit the 3200S chassis, and in September that year BMW displayed the result at the Frankfurt Motor Show. It was called the 3200 CS, and the first production models were available for delivery in February 1962. The bodies were built and trimmed by Bertone in Turin, and then transported by train to BMW in Munich for mounting to the chassis and for final assembly.

Once again, the BMW coupé was formidably expensive. At 29,850 DM, it was priced way above the directly competitive Mercedes-Benz 220 SE coupé, which could be had for 25,500 DM. BMW's thinking perhaps was that the 3200 CS fitted into the market between that car and the top-model Mercedes-Benz 300 SE, which was priced at 33,350 DM. The appeal of the BMW lay partly in its exclusivity, partly in the fashionable Italian styling that the Mercedes

COUPÉ CULTURE

Alongside the new 1500 saloon, BMW was still building its older V8-engined cars. The 3200 CS coupé turned to the Italian master Bertone for its body styling. This picture caught it in an unusually ungainly pose.

did not have, and partly in its performance. A 3200 CS took the same 14 seconds to reach 100km/h from rest as did the 220 SE, but it had a much greater top speed. A 220 SE peaked at 172km/h (107mph) and a 300 SE at 180km/h (112mph), while a 3200 CS was claimed to reach 200km/h (124mph).

Undeniably, the 3200 CS lacked something in the handling department; its chassis was, after all, essentially the same as that introduced back in 1951 for the 501 saloon. It was also available only as a coupé, although one cabriolet prototype was constructed. The Mercedes came in both open and closed forms. From some angles, the BMW also looked a little awkward, although from others it was extremely attractive.

The 3200 CS was announced at the same Frankfurt Motor Show as the new BMW 1500 saloon, the car that finally gave the Bavarian manufacturer a model capable of selling in large volumes and providing decent profits at the same time. That, too, had Italian influence in its styling, in this case from Michelotti. However, what visitors to that show would have noticed was a common styling element that had not before graced any BMW. It was a reverse curve at the bottom of the rear side window, a feature that would become a BMW styling trademark for the next 30 years or more.

Bertone's coupé design was also important in establishing a number of other characteristics that would be carried over to subsequent BMW coupés. In marked contrast to the heavy-looking roof design of the contemporary Mercedes coupé, it had a very shallow roof panel supported on thin pillars. It also had deep side windows, which were made to look even deeper by an optical trick: Bertone had added a deep, bright-metal sill panel below the doors, which helped to conceal the depth of the side panels and made the windows look larger by comparison.

If the 3200 CS did not make a massive contribution to BMW's revival in the early 1960s, it did at least ensure that the company was again represented in the prestige coupé class. It also sold roughly twice as well as its predecessor, with 603 being built before production ended in September 1965 – an average of 150 or so each year. The 503, in its closed coupé form, had been built at a rate of about 70 a year.

15

■ COUPÉ CULTURE

There was a pleasing sleekness about the 3200 CS from most angles, and the car would go on to inspire later BMW coupé designs.

COUPÉ CULTURE

The 2000 C and 2000 CS

Anxious to keep their position in the prestige coupé market, BMW had to think creatively in the early 1960s. Although the 3200 CS had its appeal, its positively ancient chassis meant that it could not reasonably attract buyers for very long. Something had to be found to replace it.

At this stage, BMW was committed to a new engine policy that was based on a single basic design: a four-cylinder known internally as the M10. The idea was that the engine should start life as a 1.5-litre, but that it could be progressively upgraded until it reached the 2.0 litres of its design capacity. The thinking was that, with variations of carburation, it could meet all BMW's foreseeable engine needs until the second half of the 1960s.

This engine was the one that would have to power the replacement for the 3200 CS, and there was no doubt that switching from a 3.2-litre V8 to a 2.0-litre four-cylinder in the prestige coupé class required a considerable stretch of the customer's imagination. The V8 had boasted 160PS; the four-cylinder, even in its most powerful 2.0-litre twin-carburettor form, could muster no more than 120PS. It was obvious to the designers from the start that the new coupé would not have the performance pretensions of the old.

On the other hand, it would not need to be anywhere near as expensive, and in that respect it would give BMW a credible alternative to the big Mercedes coupés. This time, there was be no outside consultant for the body; it would be designed in-house by BMW's own styling chief, Wilhelm Hofmeister, who borrowed elements of the Bertone design for the 3200 CS to come up with a light, modern-looking design. Production space was still a problem, but BMW solved that by arranging for the bodies to be built at the Karmann plant in Osnabrück.

Although they had their faults, the E120 models that went into production in 1965 as the 2000 C and 2000 CS were another important stage in the evolution of the big BMW coupés. In terms of sales, they were simply off the scale of previous attempts, selling an average of more than 2700 for each of the five years they were available – eighteen times as many as the 3200 CS had managed. The era of the laboriously hand-built BMW coupé was over. These cars were now mass-produced, even if there was an element of hand-finishing to achieve the quality that the market demanded.

Holding Operation: The BMW-Glas 3000 V8

BMW's carefully planned engine strategy for the 1960s envisaged the introduction of a six-cylinder companion to the M10 four-cylinder towards the end of the decade. The architecture of the two engines would share a number of characteristics, but the arrival of a six-cylinder would broaden the possibilities for the BMW model range.

In the meantime, the issue of production facilities had to be addressed. It was a problem that not only affected the big coupés, but would also prevent BMW from expanding their range to exploit the new possibilities that a six-cylinder engine would open up. Fortunately, it was solved during 1966, when BMW purchased the ailing Glas company, which had premises not far from Munich, in Dingolfing. Once the Glas site had been redeveloped, BMW's further expansion could begin.

While the new BMW assembly hall was being constructed at Dingolfing, the Glas workforce had to be retained so that BMW could count on experienced hands for their new factory when it was ready. In order to keep them occupied, BMW maintained two of the old Glas models in production as a short-term measure. One of them was a prestige coupé.

Like the old BMW 3200 CS, the Glas 2600 coupé embodied Italian styling, in this case by Frua of Moncalieri. As a low-volume model, built at a rate of fewer than 300 a year, it had been sold at a much higher price than the BMW 2000 C and 2000 CS, so it presented no threat to the sales of those cars. On the other hand, it did have some notable advantages for BMW. First, it gave the company a prestige coupé further up the market, where it could usefully hurt sales of the rival Mercedes-Benz products. Second, it announced BMW's intention to stay in that sector of the market, which the company certainly intended to do when the planned new six-cylinder coupés became available.

Newly presented with BMW badges and with the enlarged, 3.0-litre version of their V8 engine, which had been under development at Glas before the BMW takeover, the car became a BMW-Glas 3000 in autumn 1967. BMW had also built the car with Glas badges and the original 2.6-litre V8 engine for the first half of 1967, but production of the revised car lasted less than a year. However, it was important in the story of the big BMW

17

■ COUPÉ CULTURE

Italian styling led the world in the 1950s and 1960s, and BMW's rivals Glas turned to Frua for the design of their big V8 coupé. When BMW bought them out, the car remained in production for a while, now wearing BMW badges and with an enlarged engine. It was called the 3000 V8.

coupés, in that it paved the way for the arrival of the next generation of BMW's own cars, this time with the new six-cylinder engine.

The E9 Coupés

By the time the six-cylinder engine was ready to enter production, in 1968, the 2000 C and 2000 CS four-cylinder coupés had barely been in the showrooms for three years, and still looked fresh. There was no need to design a completely new body yet; Wilhelm Hofmeister's E120 design would do very well. However, the front end would have to be redesigned to accommodate the longer six-cylinder engine and, while this was being done, the body was also tidied up and modernized, taking on a deliberate family resemblance to the front end of the all-new BMW six-cylinder saloons that were to enter production at the same time. As before, the bodies were made by Karmann in Osnabrück.

Where the 2000 C and 2000 CS had been admired, albeit with reservations, the new six-cylinder coupés – known to BMW by the E9 designation – were immediately seen as masterpieces of design and as excellent value for money, even though they were much more expensive than the four-cylinder cars. They undercut the latest Mercedes coupés on price and out-performed them in every respect too. High cost deterred sales in the USA, but there was no lack of interest.

From 1971, the E9s took on a new 3.0-litre engine, half a litre smaller than the latest Mercedes-Benz V8 but still capable of out-running the coupés from Stuttgart. There was an even more powerful fuel-injected version, too. Coupé sales increased in the USA, even though Federal emissions regulations reduced the power output and the performance of these cars. By now, the 3.0-litre coupés were also making a name for themselves on the race tracks in Europe, and that was a place where their Mercedes rivals would never follow. Gradual development led to lightweight versions, and a 3.0 CSL (CS Lightweight) production derivative as well. Homologated under FIA regulations until 1979, the final racing models boasted 3.5-litre engines that would have an important influence on the next generation of BMW's prestige coupés.

Once again, sales increased, and over the seven model-years of E9 production they averaged more than 4300 cars a year world-wide – a 63 per cent improvement on their four-cylinder predecessors. Perhaps even more important was the fact that the big BMW coupé was now seen as a fixture in the prestige coupé class and had acquired a semi-legendary status, thanks to that hugely successful racing programme.

COUPÉ CULTURE

THE TRUE GRAND TOURING TRADITION HAS COME WITHIN ONE CAR OF EXTINCTION.

1938 BMW 328

1973 BMW 3.0 CS

1984 BMW 633CSi

Generations ago, a special breed of now-fabled automobiles roamed the landscape of Europe.

They were known as Grand Touring cars, and for good cause. They constituted perhaps the world's first automotive aristocracy—one distinguished by superlative performance, sumptuous luxury, and impeccable styling and craftsmanship.

Today they're distinguished by their scarcity.

Despite the indiscriminate manner in which the "GT" designation is often used, one car remains utterly faithful to the legacy.

The BMW 633CSi.

Its 3.2-liter fuel-injected engine has been called "the heart of a true blueblood" by Car and Driver. Its ability to cover vast expanses of terrain tirelessly derives from its ancestors—the six-cylinder BMW engines that dominated the 1,000-mile Mille Miglia over four decades ago.

Its internationally-patented suspension—another beneficiary of racecourse breeding and refinement—provides unrelenting adhesion over the most sinuous Alpine roads.

The 633CSi's comfort left one critic "surprised how little a role fatigue played in the day's passing," and results in part from leather bucket seats orthopedically contoured to the curvature of the spine.

Its sensuous styling speaks to those who think of cars in terms of generations, not model years. So does the way it's constructed: to tolerances as fine as 4/100,000ths of an inch.

Of course, the process of building a car to such uncompromising standards is necessarily slow. A fact that ensures the continued scarcity of authentic Grand Touring coupes.

The few that remain can be found at BMW dealers. Where you can test drive the car AutoWeek designated "the class of the field in a field of one."

THE ULTIMATE DRIVING MACHINE.

This was the way BMW reminded its US buyers of its coupé heritage in the mid-1980s. The 328 roadster was better known in the USA than the 327, and so stood in for the big coupé of the 1930s. In the middle is a 1973 3.0 CS, and at the bottom is a 1984 633 CSi.

■ COUPÉ CULTURE

The ultimate version of the E9 coupés was the 3.0 CSL, but not every car was delivered with the spartan interior and full bodykit of spoilers. This beautiful UK-market car was delivered in 1973, and was ordered with a specification that made it more viable as an everyday road car.

The E24 Coupés

Even though the E9 coupés still looked fresh by the middle of the 1970s, it had been obvious for some time that they would have to be replaced by a very different sort of car. The issue was neither outdated performance nor an outdated appearance; it was the increased emphasis world-wide on crash safety and on control of exhaust emissions. As a result, although many of the powertrain developments pioneered on the E9 coupés were taken forward into the new models, the big coupé range was redesigned from the ground up.

Designed in-house by BMW's own Paul Bracq, who had earlier been with Mercedes-Benz, these new coupés were known to BMW as E24 types. Once again, BMW declined to find room to build their bodies in their own factories, and sub-contracted the job to Karmann. Early cars for 1976 came with 3.0-litre and 3.2-litre engines, but the 3.0-litre gave way to a more powerful 2.8-litre in 1979 and a new 3.5-litre arrived in 1978. The cars emerged from a major re-engineering programme in late 1982 with lightened bodywork, improved suspension, and engine changes.

These coupés were very different in many ways from the E9s that had preceded them. Their market positioning harked back to that of the 3200 CS in the early 1960s, where prestige and luxury were paramount. BMW regularly used the E24s to showcase new technology, and their image was very different from the more hard-core, performance-oriented one that had been fostered for the E9s. BMW had positioned them as the flagships of the brand, and from the start they were as much about luxury as about speed.

Not that there was any shortage of performance, of course. Not only did the E24s have a successful racing career in Europe (see Chapter 9), but they also gave rise to the ultimate in big coupés from BMW's Motorsport division: the M635 CSi that was re-named M6 for the US

COUPÉ CULTURE

The ultimate derivative of the later E24 coupé was the M635 CSi, seen here in UK-market guise.

and some other markets. This had a 24-valve version of the 3.5-litre engine that could ultimately trace its ancestry back to the racing E9 coupés of the 1970s, and it took nothing less than a 5.6-litre V8 to produce a credible competitor from Mercedes-Benz.

BMW were able to keep these cars in production for far longer than any of their earlier prestige coupés – they remained available for no fewer than 14 years. In that period, they sold 86,216 copies – far more than any of their predecessors – and maintained an average annual figure of more than 6100, which was nearly 50 per cent more than the E9 models had achieved. It was a very long way from the 70 cars a year that the 503 coupé had managed in the late 1950s, and yet these much more numerous cars were still perceived as desirable rarities. That was a marketing triumph of which BMW could justifiably be very proud.

CHAPTER TWO

2000 C AND 2000 CS

When car enthusiasts talk about the classic BMW coupés of the 1960s, they almost invariably limit their discussion to the six-cylinder cars which appeared in 1968 and went on to score some notable victories on the race tracks. But there was another, earlier BMW coupé that actually sired these cars and is just as deserving of the 'classic' title. That car had a four-cylinder engine, was introduced in 1965, and is sadly all but forgotten today. Many enthusiasts even call it by the wrong name: even though there was a variant called the 2000 CS, that was not the name for the model. At BMW, it was known as the E120.

The Neue Klasse and Its Variants

To understand where the E120 coupé came from, it is necessary to look first at the BMW product strategy of the early 1960s. Thanks to investment from the Quandt family, the company had been able to effect a remarkable recovery from the doldrums into which it had sunk by the end of the 1950s. The barely coherent model range of big saloons, expensive sports models and economy cars gradually disappeared as those models reached the end of their production life, and in their place BMW staked their future on a new medium-sized saloon.

A subject of earnest discussion! This magnificent example of the 2000 CS now belongs to BMW's own museum. The bullet shape of the single wing mirror is another typical 1960s touch; it was thought to be more aerodynamic than conventional types and therefore more sporty.

2000 C AND 2000 CS

The M10 four-cylinder engine was a quite remarkable design that went on to form the basis of the legendary BMW six-cylinder of the late 1960s. It was designed by the company's Alex von Falkenhausen. All the carburettor versions looked the same, regardless of actual capacity.

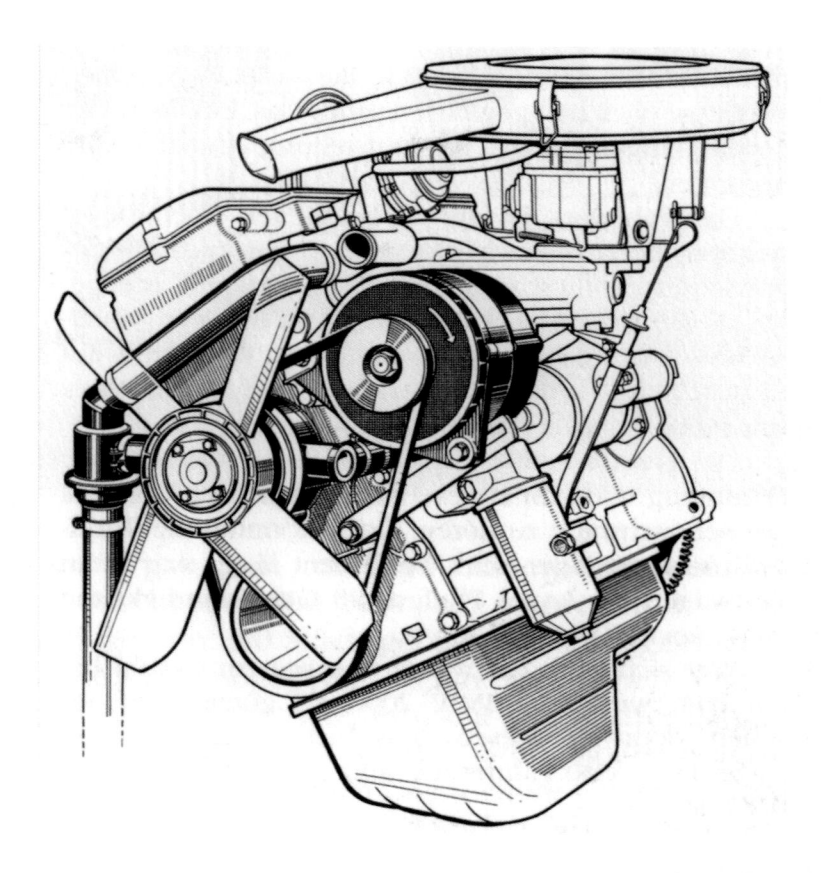

That new medium-sized saloon was called the Neue Klasse ('New Class'), and it took BMW in a new direction. It created something of a sensation at its launch in 1961, and even though there were problems in getting production under way, by the time the first examples began to reach customers, in the second quarter of 1962, public enthusiasm was undimmed. In many ways, the Neue Klasse – or E14 to the engineers and designers who had created it – represented a new beginning for BMW.

BMW had realized that they were too small to compete against Mercedes-Benz in what would now be called the upper-medium saloon market. They also knew that the market for economy cars had peaked and had begun to dwindle. So they had determined to pitch their new car right in the middle of the market. Their thinking was that, if it succeeded, it could serve as a base for expansion into other market sectors. For the moment, though, it was right to be cautious.

Introduced as a BMW 1500, with the 1.5-litre engine that that name implied, the new four-door saloon was a revelation. It had fashionable Italianate looks that had originated in the design studio of Michelotti in Turin; it boasted sharp handling and excellent brakes, thanks to the use of discs on the front wheels; and its engine was a gem. Known internally as the M10 type, it was a modern overhead-camshaft four-cylinder that had been designed under the leadership of Alex von Falkenhausen, BMW's long-serving engine design chief. Most importantly, von Falkenhausen had designed his new engine to be stretchable: the design allowed for both bigger bores and a longer stroke if these should be required in the future.

It was not long before bigger bores and a longer stroke were indeed required. BMW's timing had been fortuitous – at the very time when the 1500 saloon was introduced, the Borgward company that produced its most obvious domestic rival was going under. By 1962, when the 1500 became generally available, Borgward was no longer a player in the car market and BMW in effect had a clear run. As the profits rolled in, so they risked enlarging the engine to produce additional models – first to 1.8 litres, to make the BMW 1800 in 1963, and then to 1.6 litres, to make the BMW 1600 as a replacement for the original model in 1964. A more potent twin-carburettor version of the 1.8-litre powered the 1800 TI of 1964, and this was

■ 2000 C AND 2000 CS

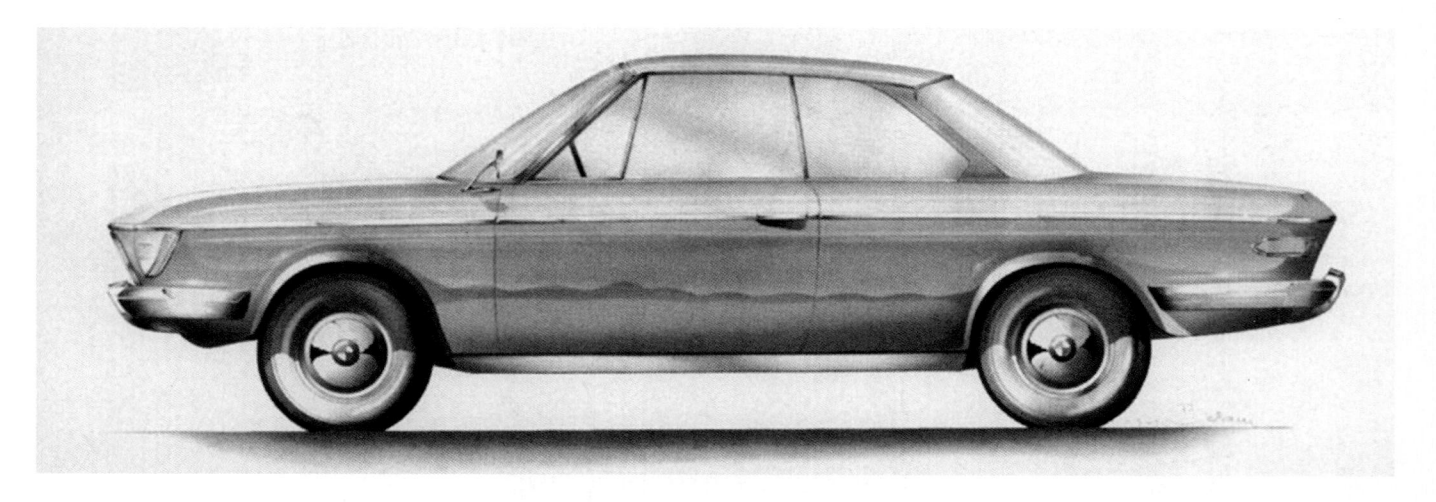

This was one of the very earliest concept sketches for the new four-cylinder coupé. Its lines are already assured, and the sill panel is already shown as being trimmed in bright metal, as on the 3200 CS. The reverse-sloped nose is already in place.

quickly followed by a special competition version called the 1800 TI/SA, which earned BMW a well-deserved reputation on the race tracks.

Von Falkenhausen had one more trick up his sleeve, and that was to enlarge the bore diameter one last time to produce an engine with a full 2-litre capacity. Although that engine would arrive in the Neue Klasse saloons in 1966, where it would create the new BMW 2000 model, BMW had other plans to implement first.

BMW had been building small-volume, rather expensive grand touring coupés since the early 1950s. The latest of these had entered production in 1962, a year after the Neue Klasse saloons, but it was really something of a place-holder model. Essentially, it married a new coupé body by the Italian styling house of Bertone to the platform and running-gear of the ageing 503. Although a fine car in its own right, it was old-style BMW and could not last in production for long against Mercedes' advanced new 220 SE coupé, which had set a new benchmark for the type in 1961. It was built laboriously and lovingly by hand, too, and in the new BMW company of the 1960s there was no place for such costly methods of manufacture.

Its replacement was planned as yet another variant of the Neue Klasse, although this time the saloon body would be discarded and there would be a completely new two-door coupé superstructure. The new coupé would also be the first BMW to have the 2-litre version of the M10 four-cylinder engine. To observers at the time, replacing a 3.2-litre V8-powered hand-built coupé with a 2-litre four-cylinder volume-built car might have seemed like madness, but there was method in that madness. First, taking the old V8 engine and the old 503 platform out of production would create valuable manufacturing space; second, the new coupé would use a large proportion of existing production components, which would reduce manufacturing costs; and third, by reducing the showroom cost BMW hoped to be able to sell their new car in larger quantities.

It is not clear exactly when work began on project E120 in Munich, although it seems that the idea of such a car can be traced back to 1961. Legend has it that a senior BMW man started thinking about it while driving back to Munich from the Frankfurt Show where the 1500 had been announced. The BMW archives certainly contain a sketch, dated 17 October of that year, which shows the essential outline of the car.

Nevertheless, serious work on the project probably had to wait until 1963, six months to a year after the 3200 CS had entered production; car makers usually begin work on a successor quite soon after a new model has gone on sale. By this time, it would also have been clear that the loss of the Borgward Isabella coupé had created a gap in the market that BMW could reasonably hope to fill. This time, the company had enough confidence not to turn to Michelotti or Bertone for help in designing the new car. Instead, they entrusted its appearance to Wilhelm Hofmeister, head of their own body design department since 1955 and the man who had dreamed up the original

2000 C AND 2000 CS

Straight away, this three-quarter view of an early E120 coupé shows the fly in the ointment. That unconventional nose embodied the latest ideas about faired-in headlamps and streamlining, but somehow it did not work aesthetically.

concept on the Autobahn between Frankfurt and Munich.

The style that Hofmeister drew up was strikingly modern. He borrowed the low belt-line of the Neue Klasse saloon with its chromed highlight strip, and he made sure that the body looked even lower by using a bright-metal sill panel below the doors, just as had been done on the 3200 CS. Using the same wheelbase as the saloons, he created long front and rear decks around a full four-seater passenger cabin, and he drew up a beautifully neat, rounded tail with horizontal light clusters that made the car look lower and wider than it really was. On top of this, he added a glasshouse that had truly huge windows – indeed, they were so huge that to some eyes they threatened to overbalance the styling. There were slim pillars front and rear, and frameless door windows.

Only at the front of the new BMW did Hofmeister's inspiration falter. BMW were planning to distinguish the eventual 2-litre version of the Neue Klasse saloon from its smaller-engined brethren by fitting rectangular headlight units in place of their round ones. The coupé had to fall into line with this thinking, and of course its nose had to be raked backwards in the prow-like shape that was a distinguishing feature of the saloons. Yet it also had to be distinctively different. This set of requirements must have presented Hofmeister and his team with a great deal of difficulty, and their eventual resolution of the problems has been controversial ever since it was first seen in public.

Hofmeister gave the coupé headlamp units that were horizontally arranged like those on the later 2000, but which incorporated turn indicator segments at their outer ends and curved upwards near the centre of the car. Between them, he set a version of the BMW trademark twin-kidney grille, and to make sure that enough air flowed through the engine compartment he created a row of cooling apertures behind and just above the front bumper. The rest of the front end was plain metal, painted in the body colour. The result was a 'face' for the new coupé that was like no other. If one of Hofmeister's aims had been to create an unmistakeable front end for the E120, he had certainly succeeded.

With sales of the Neue Klasse family booming, BMW's revival had perhaps come about rather more quickly than the company had expected. Even though the older models were gradually disappearing from production, this

■ 2000 C AND 2000 CS

BMW publicity favoured high-angle three-quarter rear views, because it undoubtedly showed the coupé styling at its best. The large glass area is immediately apparent, and so is the reverse curve at the base of the rear side window – a BMW trait. The lady is, of course, expensively dressed to represent the target audience for the 2000 CS.

2000 C AND 2000 CS

These side views make clear that the E120 had become longer and sleeker than it had looked in those preliminary design sketches. BOTTOM IMAGE: RUDOLF STRICKER/WIKIMEDIA

■ 2000 C AND 2000 CS

began to create pressure on manufacturing space. The decision was taken to sub-contract manufacture of the new E120 body and the assembly of the whole car to Karmann in Osnabrück, which was at the time perhaps the leading independent German body design and manufacturing plant. By Karmann's standards, the contract was a small one, calling for fewer than 3000 bodies a year. For BMW, it presented a new logistical challenge, because the engines and running-gear had to be transported from the company's Munich premises in the southern state of Bavaria to Karmann's factory in Lower Saxony, some 650km (400 miles) to the north, for assembly into cars.

The Model Range

BMW did not have a lot of options for positioning their new coupé in the German domestic market, which was where they expected to find the majority of sales. The big-engined coupé market was dominated by the Mercedes-Benz 220 SE, which could also be had in larger-engined form as a 300 SE; both versions could also be bought as a cabriolet. BMW's strategy was to target the 220 SE, whose 2.2-litre six-cylinder engine was only a little larger than their own new 2-litre four-cylinder.

The 2.2-litre Mercedes engine delivered 120PS, but the car was larger and heavier than the new BMW coupé, which slowed it down somewhat. It could be had with either manual or automatic transmission, and in manual form it had a top speed of 172km/h (107mph) and took 14 seconds to accelerate from rest to 100km/h (62mph). BMW built their sales strategy around this.

In single-carburettor form, with 100PS, their new coupé would reach the same 172km/h as the Mercedes and was quicker to 100km/h by a full second. With the single-carburettor engine and an automatic gearbox, the BMW had a slightly lower top speed but was still quicker than the Mercedes to 100km/h. Most importantly, BMW were able to bring their car to market at a whisker under 17,000 DM, which undercut by a huge margin the 23,500 DM that Mercedes were asking. Better yet, the twin-carburettor version of the 2-litre BMW engine offered the same 120PS as the six-cylinder Mercedes, delivered a higher top speed, of 185km/h (115mph), and made the new coupé a whole two seconds quicker than the Mercedes to 100km/h. And BMW were able to sell it for a mere 17,500 DM.

The E120 was drawn up as a three-model range. The single-carburettor car was called a 2000 C ('C' for coupé) and came with a manual gearbox for 16,906 DM or with

The tail was attractively executed, with strip-like lights blending into a textured rear trim panel. The overall effect was to make the car look wider and lower from behind. This Polish-registered example is actually a fairly rare 2000 C Automatic; note the distribution of the badging.
BEEMWEJ/WIKIMEDIA

an automatic for 17,750 DM. In between those two, and available only with a manual gearbox, came the twin-carburettor 2000 CS, priced at 17,500 DM. This was serious competition for the Mercedes, and no mistake – although the Stuttgart maker had an established reputation to set against BMW's still recent revival, and the 220 SE had the additional prestige of that six-cylinder engine. Mercedes' reaction was to increase the size and power output of their coupé's engine within a year of the BMWs' appearance on the market.

The twin-carburettor version of the new 2-litre BMW engine was a quite straightforward upgrade of the single-carburettor type. It simply had different pistons to give a higher compression ratio, and had a pair of twin-choke Solex carburettors in place of the single-choke Solex on the single-carburettor engine. The 40 PHH twin-choke carburettors were not new to BMW, either: they first appeared in 1964 on the 1.8-litre engine of the 1800 TI saloon. Once again, BMW were proceeding cautiously, sharing building blocks among their models to avoid complication and also to reduce buy-in costs through economies of scale.

The automatic gearbox was a new departure, though. No BMW of any kind had been offered with an automatic option, which made the 2000 C a pioneer. The transmission that BMW chose was made by ZF in Friedrichshaven, and was a three-speed type with a torque converter. Called the 3 HP 12, it was as much a leap in the dark for ZF as it was for BMW, as this was the first automatic gearbox they had put into production. That gave the BMW coupé a little extra cachet, too: it was seen to be pioneering new technology. Unsurprisingly, the success of the installation led on to automatic options for some models of the Neue Klasse saloon from 1966.

The Cars on Sale

BMW announced their new coupé in June 1965 with the planned three-model range. In practice, however, only tiny numbers of the single-carburettor car were made that year, and production of the twin-carburettor models remained in double figures, too. It was not until 1966 that production really got under way and the cars became generally available. By then, Mercedes had seized the high ground again, with the new 150PS 2.5-litre engine in their revitalized 250 SE coupé. Not that this detracted from the BMW's appeal: even though Mercedes had actually reduced the price of their new coupé, the car from Munich still looked like a bargain.

The distinctive shape that Wilhelm Hofmeister had created for the E120 range was not the only appealing feature. Those huge windows made the interior particularly light and airy, adding to the impression of space when sitting in what was in any case a real four-seater cabin. The rear seat was shaped as two individual armchairs, but in practice there was room to squeeze a third person in the middle. The upholstery came in hard-wearing vinyl, as in the Neue Klasse saloons, although velour cloth did become available as an extra-cost option.

Most attractive, although now strangely dated, was the style Hofmeister and his team had created for the facia. The instrument panel was essentially adapted from the Neue Klasse saloons, but it was set next to a full-width parcels shelf with a varnished wooden rail that ran right across the car, forming both a barrier to objects slipping off the shelf and a grab-handle for front-seat occupants. A vertical wooden panel formed the back of the shelf, and set into the centre of it were two adjustable air vents. More wood, on the centre bar of the two-spoke steering wheel, completed the effect.

On cars with a manual gearbox, the gear lever rose unceremoniously from the carpeted transmission tunnel, with only a rubber gaiter around its base. On the automatic car, however, there was a far more elaborate box-like construction underneath the centre of the dash, which contained the selector gate and its lever – and boasted yet more wood trim. These were early days for automatics in Germany, and the selector gate looks unfamiliar to modern eyes. It was marked R-1-2-A-O-P, representing Reverse, First, Second, Automatic, Neutral and Park.

As far as the single-carburettor 2000 C was concerned, demand proved to be overwhelmingly in favour of automatic versions; these were known in BMW literature as 2000 CA types, but were never badged as such. In fact, no manual versions of the 2000 C were built in 1966 as BMW focused on meeting demand for the automatic models. The greatest customer interest was nevertheless in the twin-carburettor models, which ultimately sold three times as well as the single-carburettor cars, a fact which certainly helps to explain why so many enthusiasts today think all the E120s were called 2000 CS models.

An additional attraction of the twin-carburettor cars was a red-and-silver plate reading '2000 CS' that was

■ 2000 C AND 2000 CS

The dashboard layout of this manual-gearbox car was both very modern for the time and typical of the 1960s. The two-spoke steering wheel gave a clear view of the neat and comprehensive instrument panel, and the knobs and switches were clustered together on the centre console for maximum visual appeal, even if they left something to be desired ergonomically. The dashboard rail and rear panel were, of course, made of real wood.

2000 C AND 2000 CS

attached to the body of the air cleaner, where it was visible only when the bonnet was open. This was an early instance of BMW's understanding of the value of detail and of the little touches that contribute to the pride of ownership. (Nevertheless, the plate may not have been on every 2000 CS; it does not seem to be on the car illustrated in the 1965 sales catalogue, which may admittedly have been a pre-production example.)

It was notoriously common practice in the German motor industry at the time to price cars in base condition and to charge extra for many items that in other countries were thought of as part of the standard specification. In Germany, the 2000 C and 2000 CS came with only one wing mirror (a streamlined 'racing' type called the Berlin and made by Talbot); a matching mirror on the passenger's side wing cost 27 DM extra. Electric door windows – the rear quarter-windows had electric operation as standard – were priced at 390 DM, and an electric sunroof cost a further 750 DM. A heated rear window cost 190 DM, and a lockable fuel filler cap was another item that could not be taken for granted. Even the anti-roll bars cost an extra 75 DM for the pair, and there were also fashionable whitewall tyres to be had, for 248 DM. Head restraints for the front seats could be had at a price, and a hazard warning light system cost the customer 85 DM. It was not hard to inflate the 17,000 DM base cost of an E120 coupé by a further thousand Deutschmarks or so.

BMW's primary market for these coupés had of course been in Germany, but the possibility of overseas sales had certainly not been neglected. By February 1966, the 2000 CS and automatic 2000 C were being advertised for sale in the USA, and it was also during 1966 that the first examples reached the UK. Interestingly, though, Karmann never made any right-hand-drive versions of the car for BMW. An October 1966 price list from the UK importers, BMW Concessionaires England Ltd (who were at Victoria Road, Portslade, Brighton), listed both the 2000 CS and 2000 CA for sale at the same price of £2950, made up of a base price of £2440 1s 9d plus £509 18s 3d Purchase Tax – but this was for cars with left-hand drive!

When right-hand-drive cars became available, probably not before 1967, the price had gone up to £3250, and that extra £300 paid for the importers themselves to convert the cars to right-hand drive. (Later in 1967, the price went up again, this time to £3365.) This bizarre arrangement continued throughout the production life of the E120, and the best figures available suggest that either 140 or 144 were treated in this way, the last being converted in 1970.

Export requirements did have an impact on the evolution of the E120 range. From 1 January 1968, all cars sold in the USA had to conform to a new set of Federal Motor Vehicle Safety Standards. Among those standards was a requirement for cars to use standardized headlight units so that a damaged or non-functioning light could be easily replaced. Whatever else could be said about the E120's headlamps, standardized they were not, and so BMW hastily redesigned them so that a pair of universal-fit round sealed-beam units could be fitted into a backing-plate that would fill the sculpted aperture on each side of the nose; the turn indicators meanwhile remained where they were. Cars sold in the USA during 1968 had this new design, although it did not last long there because the cars were dropped in favour of the new six-cylinder models that autumn. Cars destined for the UK also had the round headlights, probably from early in 1968. However, cars for other markets, including Germany, retained the original headlamp units until the end of production.

Another reason for the switch to twin round lamps in the UK market, where they were certainly not a legal

A Munich-registered car with a matching passenger's-side wing mirror, which came at extra cost. From this angle, that controversial nose looks a little more attractive, although the contrast between the vertical grille and the aggressively horizontal light units is still marked.

2000 C AND 2000 CS

Although somewhat the worse for wear when pictured at a classic-car auction, this 1968 US-market model is of interest because it has the twin circular headlamps used on some export cars.
MR CHOPPERS/WIKIMEDIA

necessity, may have been that they made the cars look more similar to the new 2800 CS coupé that was introduced that year. For all markets, the new six-cylinder car gradually took over from the four-cylinder 2000 C and 2000 CS, and the E120 range was reduced to a two-car range when the base-model manual car was taken out of production, in 1968. Yet there was clearly enough demand for the four-cylinder coupés for BMW to keep them in production – albeit in ever-declining volumes – until February 1970. This fact speaks volumes for the esteem in which the cars were held at the time, even when faster (and inevitably more expensive) derivatives were available.

The Professional Opinion

In the USA during the 1960s, public taste tended to lag a long way behind professional opinion when it came to cars. The public was used to its home-grown machinery and took a long time to be persuaded that European imports had anything to offer anyone except the enthusiast driver. As a result, when *Car and Driver* tested a 2000 CS in April 1966, it had to make its points quite forcefully.

'The BMW 2000 packs more luxury, comfort and over-the-road performance into a taut, sophisticated, beautifully-built package than anything available within its price range,' was the magazine's summary. The testers were particularly struck by the build quality, which was 'on a par with the Porsche and Mercedes', and with the way in which 'everything operate[d] with the precision of a key turning in a Yale lock'. Even that somewhat questionable dashboard layout appealed, and 'the use of walnut in the 2000 so impressed us with its taste and beauty that we couldn't imagine the car any other way'. The car was roomy, too: 'the 2000 is a full four-seater GT car [and] not a "two-plus-two" with occasional seats in the rear.'

On the road, the car was 'nearly fool-proof in a corner' and the gearbox was 'one of its most appealing features, with unbeatable Porsche-style synchromesh and a light, positive throw'. It was comfortable, too; in the opinion of the testers, it 'approache[d] the ride quality that only Mer-

ONE THAT GOT AWAY

Clearly thinking of emulating the Mercedes-Benz W111 two-door range of the 1960s, which consisted of coupé and cabriolet models based on the same design, BMW built a single convertible prototype of the E120. Sadly, the concept was taken no further, perhaps because of financial or build capacity constraints.

2000 C AND 2000 CS

BMW Classic's own 2000 CS is not just a pampered museum piece. Here it is in action in 2013 during a rain-swept 1000 Millas Sport, an event for classic cars in Argentina.

LEFT: Odd front end styling apart, the lines of the E120 coupé still look surprisingly modern today. RUDOLF STRICKER/ WIKIMEDIA

This picture highlights the fine sculpting of the front wing lines of the E120 as they meet the front panel just above the headlights. The air intake slots in the trim strip running above the grille add character, although they were not functional.

■ 2000 C AND 2000 CS

cedes ha[d] achieved in the past'. According to *Car and Driver*, 'the only area where the 2000 [did not] meet or exceed the competition [was] in straight-line performance'. In practice, comparing the four-seater BMW with cars like the Porsche 911 and Mercedes-Benz 230 SL two-seaters may not have been quite fair, but these sports models were the only real rivals that the magazine could find on the US market at the time.

There was, inevitably, a downside: 'The beholder's eye is inevitably drawn to those headlights. Oh dear.'

Road & Track also tested a 2000 CS in 1966, and reached some strikingly similar conclusions. They concluded that it was a car 'for the person who values finish, detailing, finesse and integrity over pretence, excesses and sure obsolescence…. It may not have as much performance as we like, but…. the rewards are worth the sacrifice.' They recorded 11.3 seconds for the 0–60mph sprint, which was not as good as the 10.6 seconds that *Car and Driver* achieved; BMW themselves claimed 12 seconds as the 0–100km/h (0–62mph) time.

The generous seating accommodation was a plus point for *Road & Track*: 'While it looks, feels and is sporty, it also happens to have fairly generous seating for four – and occasionally five – people. The term 2+2, as generally used today, wouldn't be fair to the coupé at all. There are simply no other comparable cars within $500 of the price.' Finally, the ride quality and roadholding came in for praise as well:

> To say simply that the suspension is effective would be an understatement…. On the worst surfaces, with potholes, dips and bumps, it's downright uncanny, for there doesn't seem to be an irregularity that can trip it up, even at twice the speed we'd dare go in a domestic sedan…. Combined with the impressive ride is equally impressive roadholding…. It's difficult to break loose a tire anywhere either in cornering or in acceleration, though the inside rear wheel lifts finally…. Put the ride, handling and steering characteristics together and you have the impression of a rather heavy, substantial vehicle, though not oppressively so.

TECHNICAL SPECIFICATIONS, 2000 C AND 2000 CS

Engines:
2000 C
Type M10 four-cylinder petrol, installed with a 30-degree tilt to the right
1990cc (89mm x 80mm)
Single overhead camshaft, driven by Duplex chain
Five-bearing crankshaft
Compression ratio 8.5:1
Single Solex 40 PDSI carburettor with automatic choke
100PS at 5500rpm
157Nm (115lb ft) at 3000rpm
2000 CS
As above, except:
Compression ratio 9.3:1
Two Solex 40 PHH twin-choke side-draught carburettors
120PS at 5500rpm
180Nm (123lb ft) at 3600rpm

Gearboxes:
Four-speed manual gearbox standard on both models, with single dry-plate clutch
Ratios 3.835:1, 2.053:1, 1.345:1, 1.000:1, reverse 4.18:1
Three-speed ZF automatic gearbox optional on 2000 C only
Ratios 2.56:1, 1.52:1, 1.00:1, reverse 2.29:1

Axle ratio:
2000 C   4.11:1
2000 CS   3.90:1

Suspension, steering and brakes:
Front suspension with McPherson struts and coil springs; anti-roll bar optional on 2000 C and standard on 2000 CS
Rear suspension with semi-trailing arms and coil springs; anti-roll bar optional on 2000 C and standard on 2000 CS
Worm-and-roller steering with 17.58:1 ratio
Disc brakes with 272mm diameter on front wheels; drum brakes with 250mm diameter on rear wheels; single hydraulic circuit on first cars; twin hydraulic circuits on all models from July 1968; vacuum servo assistance standard

Dimensions:
Overall length: 4530mm (178.3in)
Overall width: 1675mm (65.9in)
Overall height: 1360mm (53.5in)
Wheelbase: 2550mm (100.4in)
Front track: 1330mm (52.36in)
Rear track: 1376mm (54.17in)

Wheels and tyres:
5.5J x 14 steel disc wheels
6.95 x 14 cross-ply tyres; 175 S 14 radial tyres optional; four-ply radials on 2000 C and six-ply on 2000 CS; 175 HR 14 radial tyres optional on both models

Unladen weights:
2000 C	1200kg (2645lb)
2000 C automatic	1220kg (2689lb)
2000 CS	1200kg (2645lb)

PERFORMANCE FIGURES FOR 2000 C AND 2000 CS MODELS

2000 C	0–100km/h 13 sec
	Maximum 172km/h (106.8mph)
2000 C automatic	0–100km/h 14 sec
	Maximum 168km/h (104.4mph)
2000 CS	0–100km/h 12 sec
	Maximum 185km/h (115mph)

IDENTIFICATION NUMBERS FOR E120 MODELS

For clarity, identification numbers are shown here with a gap between the first three figures of the number and the last four. This gap is not present on the cars' identification plates.

2000 C (manual):	120 0001 to 120 0443
2000 CA:	100 0001 to 100 3249
2000 CS:	110 0001 to 110 9999

PRODUCTION FIGURES FOR 2000 C AND 2000 CS MODELS

	1965	1966	1967	1968	1969	1970	Total
2000 C	2		212	229			443
2000 CA	3	1611	1004	361	238	32	3,249
2000 CS	52	5581	2584	1051	698	33	9,999
Total	57	7192	3800	1641	936	65	13,691

Note: An alternative set of production figures sometimes quoted gives an overall total of 11,720 cars, made up of 2837 examples of the 2000 C and 8883 examples of the 2000 CS. These figures appear to be inaccurate. Figures from Karmann also differ, giving an overall total of 13,696.

CHAPTER THREE

THE MAINSTREAM E9 COUPÉS

BMW's road back to financial health was carefully planned from the earliest days of the Quandt takeover, but to those who were watching the company's progress in the 1960s it seemed as if the road was long and the going slow. For the first seven years, every new BMW product was based on the Neue Klasse platform and the M10 engine, but their plans were far more ambitious. From the middle of the decade, Munich's engineers were focusing on a move up market, which would take them into direct competition with Mercedes-Benz. For that, they needed a six-cylinder engine.

BMW's 'Silken Six'

Once again, the task of creating a new engine fell to Alex von Falkenhausen and his team; and, once again, progress was made cautiously. Although the new M30 six-cylinder engine was very different in many ways from the four-cylinder M10, it also retained many of that engine's characteristics. So once again the basic architecture was that of a crossflow cylinder head with a single overhead camshaft driven by roller chain and actuating the valves through rocker arms. Like the M10 engine, the new six-cylinder was

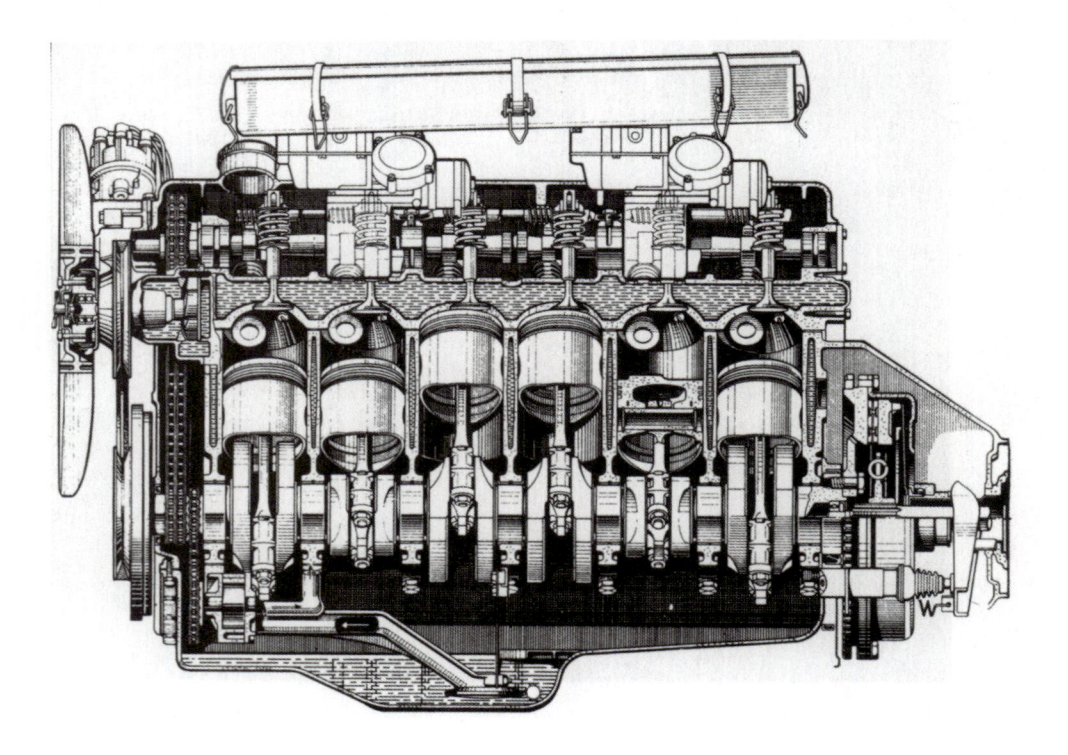

Cutaway drawing of the M30 six-cylinder engine issued by BMW when the engine was new, in 1968. Designed to power both the coupés and the new big saloons, it was an exceptional and yet simple design, smooth in operation and robust in service.

THE MAINSTREAM E9 COUPÉS

Early styling sketches showing that BMW always intended to retain the basic lines of the Wilhelm Hofmeister design for the E120 coupés. What they needed was a longer bonnet and a more attractive front end. Even at this stage, a wing vent was included to disguise the extra length.

■ THE MAINSTREAM E9 COUPÉS

also designed to be installed with a 30-degree slant to the right in order to allow for a lower bonnet-line.

Despite the similarities, this was very far from being a six-cylinder edition of the M10. In particular, von Falkenhausen's team had focused on improving combustion, and to that end had come up with a new design of combustion chamber. They called it the Dreikugelwirbelwannenbrennraum (triple-hemispherical swirl combustion chamber) – a word with which they would later both amuse and taunt the English-speaking press, especially in the USA. The new combustion chamber was constructed of three overlapping hemispheres, one around the inlet valve, one around the exhaust valve, and the third around the spark plug. This shape was designed to allow the flow of the air/fuel mixture to coincide more closely with the travel of the flame front. It was accompanied by carefully shaped inlet ports, where a metal rib on each valve guide gave the port area a uniform cross-section, resulting in better gas-flow characteristics.

Seven main bearings were expected by this stage in a six-cylinder engine, but von Falkenhausen's team went a stage further. To get the best possible balance and so eliminate vibrations, they added a pair of counterweights to each of the six crank webs. In combination with the excellent combustion characteristics, this made for an extraordinarily smooth-running engine. Commentators will probably never tire of calling it BMW's 'silken six'. It was, unquestionably, a tremendous achievement and one of the major foundation stones on which BMW's modern reputation has been built.

BMW had two tasks for its new six-cylinder engine. One of them was to power a new medium-size saloon that would be a direct competitor for the medium-size six-cylinder Mercedes. The M30 was therefore designed to be produced with swept volumes of between 2.5 and 3.0 litres, which was the size range in which Mercedes operated. The smallest, 2.5-litre, version was used for the new BMW 2500 saloon that would face the Mercedes-Benz 250 in the market-place, while an intermediate 2.8-litre size went into the new BMW 2800 that would sell against the Mercedes-Benz 280. The full 3.0-litre size was kept in reserve for later. The new saloons, coded E3 in Munich and designed to be deliberately more sporting in nature than their Mercedes counterparts, were announced in September 1968.

The second task for that new engine was to move the coupé range up a class, again to compete more directly with the Mercedes-Benz coupés. Here, BMW thinking was again directed towards a car with more sporting characteristics than Mercedes offered. There was no need yet for the coupé to be completely redesigned, as it would be only three years old by the time the new engine was announced. So the structure of the existing E120 coupés was modified – quite extensively, as it turned out – to take the six-cylinder engine. In order to compete most effectively with Mercedes, which had moved from a 2.5-litre engine to a 2.8-litre engine in their big coupés at the start of 1968, BMW chose to introduce their new car with no engine other than their new 2.8-litre. For the moment, the 2.0-litre 2000 C and 2000 CS models would take care of any demand for a less powerful coupé model.

Creating the E9

The longer six-cylinder engine demanded a longer engine bay, and the rest of the new car was developed around that. BMW gave it the new internal code of E9. To reduce the need for specially manufactured parts, they decided to use the whole front sub-frame and associated suspension from the six-cylinder E3 saloons, and it was this that determined the wheelbase of the new coupé. It went up from 2550mm to 2625mm, or just under 3 inches.

The new front suspension, which brought with it a slightly wider track, demanded some changes at the front end of the monocoque as well. In particular, there was now a new MacPherson strut layout with the struts inclined rearwards (at 14 degrees, 30 minutes); the hub was now mounted slightly behind the strut, so that the effective angle of slant was only 9.5 degrees. The new layout gave stronger resistance to nose-dive under braking, less castor action and therefore lighter steering, and greater horizontal compliance as well.

From the front bulkhead backwards, almost nothing was changed from the E120 design. In fact, it was hard to spot the additional length between the front wheel arch and the door without lining up a six-cylinder coupé alongside one of its four-cylinder predecessors. Wilhelm Hofmeister's styling team had made the difference that much harder to spot by adding a dummy air vent with three horizontal bright strips just behind the top of the wheel arch. That feature also served to make the new six-cylinder cars visually different from the four-cylinders they replaced, and to make them look more overtly sporting.

THE MAINSTREAM E9 COUPÉS

The treatment of the wing vents was masterfully resolved on the production E9 coupés, adding to the sleekness of their lines. This is an early 2800 CS.

The new front end was a major success. Here it is on a 1972-model 3.0 CS; the blue and white badge is that of the BMW Car Club of America.

39

■ THE MAINSTREAM E9 COUPÉS

ABOVE AND BELOW: The raked front panel was still in evidence, and those large indicators, if rather startling at the time, added distinction.

ABOVE AND BELOW: Sometimes, the simple solutions are the best. Twin round headlights gave the front end a family resemblance to other BMW models and removed the quirkiness of the E120 design.

40

THE MAINSTREAM E9 COUPÉS

The big visual change, however, came at the front. By the time Hofmeister's team began work on the revised coupé, they must have been well aware that the original front-end styling had not gone down well and that some sort of change was required. The solution they adopted was an elegant one: they gave the coupé a version of the wholly new front end that they planned to use on the six-cylinder E3 saloons.

The new front end featured a neat twin-kidney grille flanked by horizontal air intakes in the style pioneered by the Neue Klasse saloons, but with twin round headlamps in each flanking section. The twin round lamps may have been forced on the team by foreknowledge of the Federal requirement for standardized sealed-beam round headlamps but, if so, they were able to use the requirement to advantage. With slightly larger turn indicator lamps than were planned for the saloons, blacked-out side grilles and a different bumper as well, the new front end was both crisp and immediately recognizable.

There were some other, more subtle differences from the coupés that had gone before. The rather conservative-looking disc wheels with their chromed trims disappeared in favour of larger-diameter wheels made of aluminium alloy. These represented a new trend in the motor industry, mainly pioneered by Italian manufacturers. Alloy wheels were lighter than their steel equivalents and so reduced the unsprung weight that can play havoc with a car's ride quality. At this stage, they were exclusively associated with expensive and exotic sporting machinery, and so that had its own advantages on a car that was moving up-market from its predecessor. They also allowed for some stylish designs, and the cast-alloy wheels designed for the E9 certainly fitted that bill. Although fundamentally perforated discs, they had five radial 'spokes' cast into their faces, which added great distinction. To be on the safe side, because alloy wheels were still new territory, BMW also fitted them with chromed centre covers to conceal the securing nuts. The result was a triumph.

These larger-diameter wheels showcased another new trend in the motor industry – the move towards tyres with narrower sidewalls. The driving force here had been the stylists, who wanted to fill wheel wells with designs of their own making and not with boring black rubber bands. The 70-section tyres chosen for the new coupé (the sidewall height was 70 per cent of the tyre's width) represented the very latest in new technology, and again gave the new BMW coupé additional cachet.

There were a number of further small changes. The bright-metal sill panels of the E120 range were discarded in favour of black-painted panels with a slim horizontal bright trim strip. This helped the cars to look longer and lower in side profile. In addition, there was black rubberized paint on front and rear valances to resist stone chipping and the consequent early rusting problems. Both front and rear bumpers were rubber-faced, following another new trend that was intended to reduce minor impact damage such as that which occurs during parking manoeuvres. The rear bumper was provided with rubber-faced under-riders as well.

What was perhaps most surprising was that the E9 coupés did not take on the new rear suspension of the E3 saloons, or their rear disc brakes. Perhaps there had simply not been enough time or money for the associated re-engineering of the monocoque, which would nevertheless be done later for a model upgrade of the E9. As a result, the first versions of the E9 had what might be described as a hybrid specification, with the rear suspension and drum rear brakes of the E120 models. They did have the anti-roll bar that had been standard on 2000 CS models, but the overall result was that the flagship coupé could not boast the handling and braking improvements that had been made for the saloons, and it showed.

The 2800 CS (1968–1971)

The year 1968 was an important one for BMW. It was the first year in which the company had ever exceeded a production rate of 500 cars a day; the total production for the calendar year exceeded 100,000. By the end of the year, it was clear to observers of the German motoring industry that BMW had turned the corner. Its recovery was complete, and it was now set on a trajectory that would take it relentlessly ever onwards and upwards.

It was also the year that saw the E3 saloons and E9 coupés introduced together at the Frankfurt Motor Show in September. For the moment, the new 2800 CS coupé would be available alongside the four-cylinder 2000 C and 2000 CS models for some markets. BMW was still being cautious as it gradually clawed its way up the motoring hierarchy, but it was clear where the future lay.

The 2800 CS was marketed as a single model; it was notable that there was no 'lesser' model, such as the 2000 C had been. Instead, all models carried the 'CS' designa-

41

■ THE MAINSTREAM E9 COUPÉS

There was nothing wrong with the rear-end design of the E120, and so BMW did not change it for the E9. The early press pictures show a 2800 CS, and reveal how the Automatic badge was applied to the rear panel. The fog-guard lamp below the bumper was not a standard fit.

THE MAINSTREAM E9 COUPÉS

tion as an indication that Coupé and Sport characteristics were inextricably combined. The same designation was used whether the car had the standard four-speed Getrag manual gearbox or the optional three-speed ZF automatic. In the latter case, the big 2800 CS badge on the boot lid was complemented by a smaller script badge reading 'Automatic' on the tail panel underneath.

Standard equipment was quite comprehensive, with power assistance for the steering and the brakes, plus a limited-slip ZF Lok-o-Matic differential. However, there were still plenty of options to be had for extra money. These included electric front windows (as on the E120s, the rear side windows came with electric lifts as standard), a sunroof, air conditioning and a radio. Early examples of the 2800 CS came with the same driver's-side Talbot Berlin wing mirror that had been used on the E120s; a matching passenger's-side mirror again cost extra.

All this pushed the showroom price of the new car to a considerably higher level than that of its predecessors. The 2000 CS had been priced at 17,600 DM when last listed in Germany in August 1968. The new 2800 CS was announced a month later at 22,980 DM, although in practice volume production did not begin until December that year. This price increase of more than 30 per cent put the new model firmly into the premium coupé market, but BMW had carefully positioned it to undercut its direct rival from Mercedes-Benz. The Mercedes 280 SE coupé was at that time priced at 26,510 DM, with automatic an extra-cost option.

The cost savings came where they could not easily be seen. Once again, BMW avoided complication and its attendant cost on the assembly lines at Karmann by not building right-hand-drive examples of their new coupé. Every 2800 CS was built with left-hand drive, and cars for the UK – where the model created great interest – were converted to right-hand drive by the importers. This might have been one reason why UK-market cars retained the wooden dash rail of the four-cylinder cars; as completed in Germany, the 2800 CS had a dash rail covered in matt black vinyl.

Models for all markets had matt-finish wood veneer on the facia and the doors, and the standard steering wheel was a three-spoke item with dished centre and leather-trimmed rim that looked far more sporty than the two-spoke type used in the E120 cars. A wood-rim wheel cost extra. Also new for the E9s was a larger centre console

The dashboard of the 2800 CS was essentially the same as in the earlier E120 coupés, but it had been much improved with the addition of a more sporty-looking three-spoke steering wheel. The slightly awkward round vents in the dash of the earlier car had given way to a rectangular vent panel, and the centre console on this early automatic 2800 CS also shows a number of detail differences from the E120 design.

■ THE MAINSTREAM E9 COUPÉS

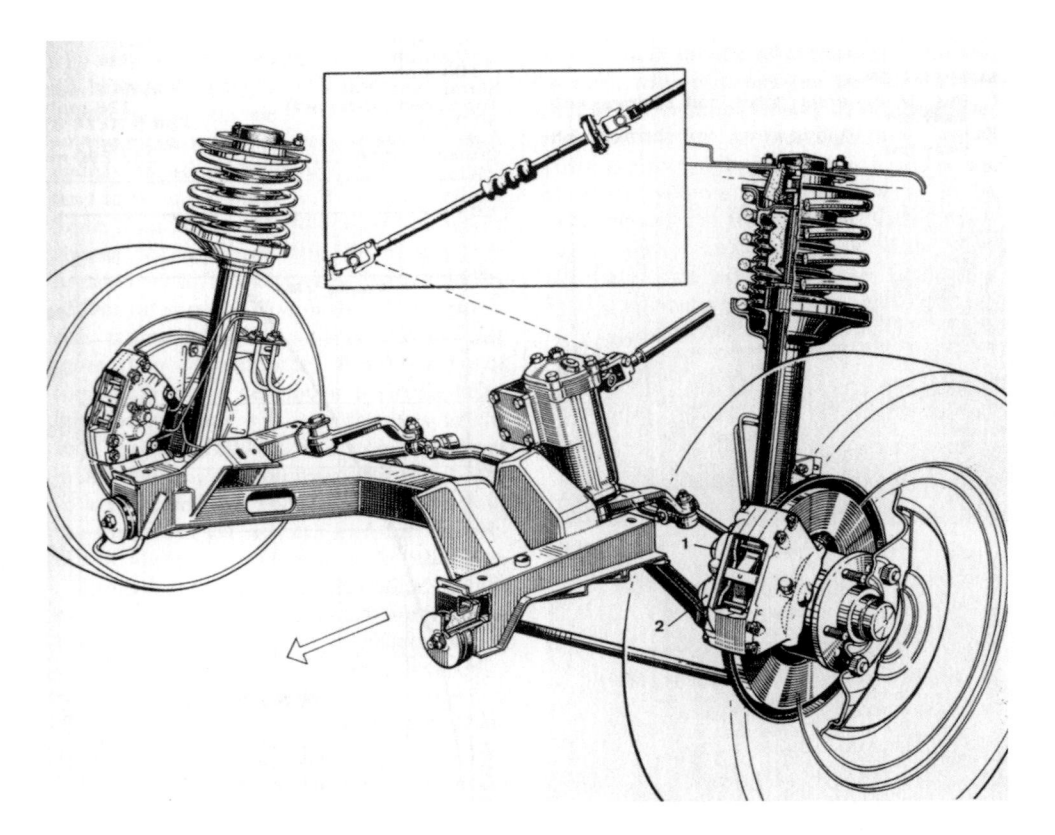

An early publicity picture showing the strut-type front suspension of the E9 coupés. Also highlighted here are the twin pistons of the front disc brakes.

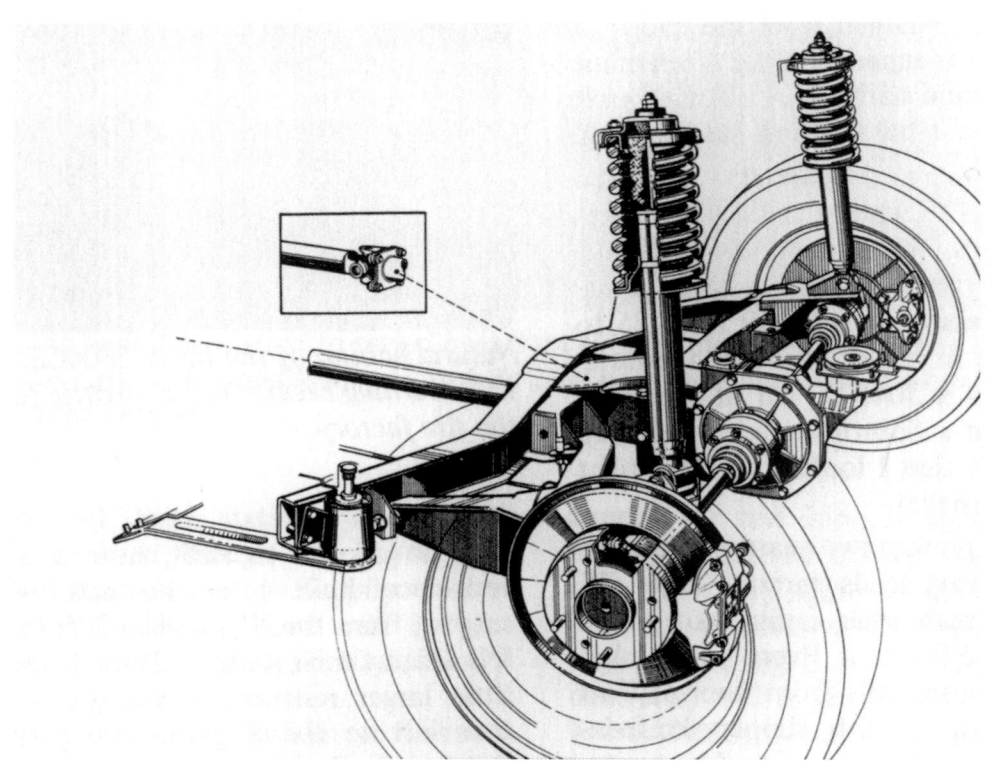

The rear suspension of the 2800 CS was carried over from the earlier E120 coupés. Although the new E3 saloons had an improved design, that would not reach the coupés until later.

44

THE MAINSTREAM E9 COUPÉS

The bodyshells were still constructed by Karmann, and were painted there as well. The evidence is a plate on the door hinge pillar.

A capacious and uncluttered boot was a major benefit on a car that purported to be a long-distance grand tourer.

■ THE MAINSTREAM E9 COUPÉS

The optional leather rear seats of this early 2800 CS are shaped and inviting. The side panels below the windows have textured cloth trim.

The BMW roundel on the rear pillars concealed an air outlet for the cabin ventilation system.

This right-hand-drive car has been fitted with a five-speed overdrive gearbox to reduce engine revs at cruising speeds.

THE MAINSTREAM E9 COUPÉS

The later US models had side-marker lights; this is the rear one on a 1972 3.0 CS.

that incorporated a useful parcels tray, embraced the gear lever, and included switches for the electric windows. Automatic cars still had a P-R-0-A-2-1 shift gate, now with a coloured-lights indicator in a housing above the steering column as well as on the gate itself. Those electric windows could often be maddeningly slow in operation – their fit was less than ideal, too, and many owners complained about wind noise above 50mph or so. One perhaps regrettable loss from the E120 was map pockets on the doors.

The seats had also undergone a transformation. The front pair were more comfortable, with deeper side bolsters that gave better support in hard cornering, while the rear bench had gone in favour of a pair of moulded armchairs with a centre armrest. Upholstery came in perforated vinyl (rather quaintly called 'artificial leather') as standard, but there were velour and leather options to be had at extra cost.

US sales of the new model began in 1969, and in that market the car was seen as expensive, at $8100 before extras. Nevertheless, the specification did include leather upholstery as standard, plus front-seat head restraints to meet US Federal regulations and side markers front and rear (a light in the amber front marker but a simple red reflector at the rear). A further FVSS-inspired change was made to the bumpers. Front and rear, they had stronger mountings than standard, and at the front the over-riders had larger, more pointed rubber facings.

In the UK, the car was not introduced immediately, but at the 1969 Motor Show it was listed with a price of £4594 19s 0d, made up of £3600 5s 0d base cost, plus £994 14s 0d Purchase Tax. This made it the most expensive BMW model and much more costly than a Jaguar E-type 2+2 (£2642 2s 6d all-in) and nearly as much as a Porsche 911S coupé (£4768 5s 3d, but of course with only two seats). Not surprisingly, sales were somewhat slow, hindered a little perhaps by the fact that BMW were still depending on an independent if enthusiastic franchise for its UK sales operations.

None of the drawbacks prevented the 2800 CS from becoming a big success for its makers. With few production changes along the way (door mirrors were standard by 1970, and so were head restraints), the Karmann works turned out an impressive 9399 examples in just under two and a half years of manufacture, which ended in April 1971. That works out at an average of 3760 cars for each of the 1969, 1970 and 1971 model-years – far more than the 2738 a year achieved by the E120 models over their five-year run and only just below their best-ever annual total in the 1967 calendar-year.

■ THE MAINSTREAM E9 COUPÉS

Autosport tested a left-hand-drive car for its issue dated 2 May 1969 and deemed it 'a much nicer car than the 2000 CS which it so closely resembles'. Indeed, the reviewer thought it 'a very desirable car, and far more practical than the majority of limited-production high-performance coupés'. Particularly impressive were the 'beautifully precise gearshift and ultra-light steering' and 'the smoothness and quietness of the engine'. Over in the USA, *Road & Track* in February 1970 thought the 2800 CS was 'a far more stable, balanced, totally usable car than any other we can think of'. The magazine's main reservation concerned the high price.

The 3.0 CS (1971–1975)

The next stage in the power race between BMW and Mercedes-Benz became clear in 1970. Mercedes announced their new 3.5-litre V8 engine that autumn, initially for the SL sports cars only but by 1971 for the big coupés as well. With 200PS, they had moved the game on significantly from the 170PS in BMW's 2800 CS model.

Although a new V8 engine was beyond BMW's resources, an enlarged M30 straight-six was not. At the Geneva Show in March 1971, new coupés and saloons were announced with a 3.0-litre engine that boasted 180PS. Although the paper figures were down in comparison with Mercedes, performance figures were not. A 280 SE 3.5 coupé took 10 seconds to reach 100km/h from rest and peaked at 210km/h. The new BMW 3.0 CS could reach 100km/h in 9 seconds and power on to 213km/h.

The 3.0-litre version of the M30 engine had almost certainly been planned right from the start; BMW had simply kept it in reserve until it was needed. The capacity increase was achieved quite simply by overboring the block to give the same 89mm dimension as was used in the 2.0-litre M10 four-cylinder engine, with which the bigger version of the M30 shared an 80mm stroke.

The bigger engine also pumped out more torque – its 189lb ft had been considered too much for the existing ZF gearboxes – so BMW switched to a stronger four-speed manual made by Getrag for the 3.0 CS, with lower second- and third-gear ratios. Out, too, went the three-speed ZF automatic, and in its place came a stronger Borg Warner Model 12 three-speed type, built at its maker's factory in Britain. On the automatic models, the identifying badge was now positioned on the left-hand edge of the boot lid

A publicity picture of a 3.0 CS, obviously intended to evoke the car's commanding presence, and showing it from a particularly flattering angle. Note how the BMW grille is still in bright metal, to make it stand out from the black flanking grilles that incorporate the headlamps.

rather than underneath the model badge where it had been for the 2800 CS.

To cope with the higher speeds of the 3.0 CS, the braking system had also been thoroughly overhauled. There were now ventilated disc brakes on all four wheels, with twin ATE servos for the dual hydraulic circuits. The 3.0 CS also switched to VR-rated Michelin 195/70 radial tyres from the HR-rated tyres of the 2800 CS. However, despite the change to an all-disc braking system, the old E120-type rear suspension was still in place, so the rear track of the 3.0 CS was narrower than the front track, as it had been on the 2800 CS.

THE MAINSTREAM E9 COUPÉS

This was how the 3.0 CS was advertised to US buyers. The background suggests a wealthy lifestyle, while the car has the side-marker lights demanded by US legislation.

Karmann was still handling assembly of the E9 coupés, as indeed it would until their production ended in 1975. As for the 2800 CS, the 3.0 CS was built only with left-hand drive, and cars for right-hand-drive markets had to undergo conversion by the local importers. In the UK, both manual and automatic versions of the 3.0 CS were sold at first, although from the spring of 1972 only automatic models were brought in, following a policy change at the importers.

Changing regulations in the USA were proving challenging for all the manufacturers who sold cars there in the early 1970s. BMW recognized the value of the US market, and of hanging in there until easier trading conditions returned, so the 3.0 CS was prepared with that market in mind in both manual and automatic forms. The two versions were different enough from the mainstream 3.0 CS models (usually referred to as 'European specification' cars) to have their own chassis number sequences. BMW even had to fit washers in the front suspension towers to raise the body so that the 3.0 CS met US regulations for headlamp height.

Federal-specification engines were less powerful than their European equivalents, although the efficiency of the BMW combustion chamber did mean that no add-on air pumps or post-combustion cleaning equipment were needed. Instead, the engines had a lower compression ratio to cope with the unleaded fuel that was now mandatory in North America. The European engines, by contrast, needed 100-octane leaded fuel to run without problems. There was also a lower-geared final drive to aid acceleration.

Performance did suffer, and the Federal-specification cars needed 10 seconds to reach 60mph as against the 8.0 seconds that *Autocar* recorded in its July 1971 road test of a manual-gearbox UK-specification car. Their lower maximum engine speeds also caused them to run out of steam earlier, and left them with a 125mph top speed that did not compare well with the 132mph that *Autocar* had recorded. That was one reason why the US cars were delivered with skinny 175 x 14 radial tyres instead of the 195/70 size favoured on European models; another was that BMW feared problems with availability of the new low-profile tyres in the USA.

Federal regulations continued to dictate changes in specification. For 1973, the US-model 3.0 CS gained stronger bumper mountings, to help it meet the 5mph crash regulations; as a result, the bumpers stood 3 inches further away from the body than on European cars. An exhaust-gas recirculation or 'smog' pump was also fitted, to reduce exhaust emissions. For 1974, huge and heavy rubber-faced bumpers had to be fitted, which did nothing for the overall appearance of the cars. No more US-model E9 coupés of any sort were built after the end of 1974 because the car would not pass the 1975 crash-test requirement – this involved the car being dropped on its roof to test its ability to withstand a severe rollover accident.

More than 10,000 examples of the 3.0 CS were built for world-wide markets between 1971 and 1975, giving an average of just over 2500 a year for the four model-years of their production. This figure was rather lower than the

49

■ THE MAINSTREAM E9 COUPÉS

Pictures taken from a BMW sales brochure of the time, showing the standard cloth upholstery in a 3.0 CS. Also clear is the distinctive grip of the manual gear shift.

THE MAINSTREAM E9 COUPÉS

Leather trim was standard in the USA, and so were front-seat head restraints. This 3.0 CS has also been fitted with an Alpina steering wheel.

■ THE MAINSTREAM E9 COUPÉS

ABOVE, BELOW AND OPPOSITE PAGE: *The US-model cars came with side-marker lights to meet local regulations. Doug Cain's beautiful 3.0 CS has the Alpina alloy wheels and bright metal arch extensions used with the wider tyre option. Also visible here are the front-seat head restraints that had become mandatory in the USA.*

2800 CS models had achieved for one main reason: from the autumn of 1971, the 3.0 CS was no longer the only version of the E9 coupé on sale, as BMW began to broaden its model range.

When *Autocar* tested a 3.0 CS for its 15 July 1971 issue, it reported that the car 'scores over some of its competitors in being more compact and practical as a town car, while still very fast and manageable as a min road express'. It was praised for being 'exceptionally economical overall' and for the fact that there was 'excellent response always immediately available in top gear'. The magazine highlighted the car's 'incredibly sweet, free-revving six-cylinder engine', but pointed out that it would run on badly if five-star fuel was not used.

Two years later, there was an interesting reflection from *Road & Track* magazine in the USA, which had tested a California-specification car for its issue of July 1973:

> *This year's tightened limit on oxides of nitrogen in the State of California has taken its toll... fuel economy isn't what it used to be and the exhaust-gas recirculation plus retarded spark at low engine speeds render what was once a beautifully responsive engine somewhat reluctant in around-town work. When driven hard, though, it frees up and goes almost as well as ever.*

Going 'almost as well as ever' meant achieving 0–60mph in 10 seconds and a maximum of 125mph.

The 3.0 CSi (1971–1975)

Any observer at the Geneva Show in March 1971 who thought that BMW had shot its bolt with the 180PS 3.0 CS and was no longer aiming to equal Mercedes' power outputs was gravely mistaken. The 3.0 CS was merely a taster of what was to come. BMW was saving a 200PS model for that autumn's Frankfurt Motor Show, when it would have maximum impact in the German domestic market.

The new 3.0 CSi, sold alongside the 3.0 CS as a supplementary model of the E9 range and at an even higher price, equalled the latest Mercedes V8 in terms of power. That car was an all-new model called the 350 SLC, which also boasted 200PS from a fuel-injected engine, in this case with an extra half-litre of capacity. The BMW 3.0 CSi was still faster, capable of 220km/h with the same 8.0-second 0–100km/h sprint time as the 3.0 CS. The latest Mercedes had a maximum speed of just 212km/h, with a 0–100km/h time of 9 seconds in manual form or 10 seconds with an automatic gearbox.

Needless to say, the new 3.0 CSi was even more expensive than its predecessor. As John Bolster put it in *Autosport* magazine for 22 June 1972, the similarly engined 3.0 Si four-door saloon was 'merely expensive', but the two-door coupé was 'a prestige car for the very wealthy'. Power-assisted steering was now part of the standard specification, and in the UK a 3.0 CSi cost £5345 inclusive of Purchase Tax and without extras. In its native Germany, the car was priced at 30,650 DM by mid-1972, some 1700 DM or nearly 6 per cent more than the 3.0 CS in manual-gearbox form.

What made the difference between the 3.0 CS and 3.0 CSi was a fuel-injection system for the 3.0-litre M30 engine. Interestingly, BMW had chosen a Bosch system with electronic control in preference to the mechanical Kugelfischer system introduced at the same time on their four-cylinder engines. This Bosch system was called the Jetronic, although it was retrospectively known as the D-Jetronic type. The D stood for Drück or 'pressure', and was introduced after the K-Jetronic system with its continuous (*kontinuierlich*) fuel flow was introduced in 1973. The control box for the injection system was tucked away under the right-hand rear seat, where it could not be affected by underbonnet temperatures.

With slightly more radical ignition timing than on the 3.0 CS, the injected engine offered much more than its extra 20PS suggested. Most important were increased flexibility and the elimination of the stuttering to which the twin-carburettor engines were sometimes prone under sudden and hard acceleration. The injection system also needed no maintenance, unlike the Solex carburet-

■ THE MAINSTREAM E9 COUPÉS

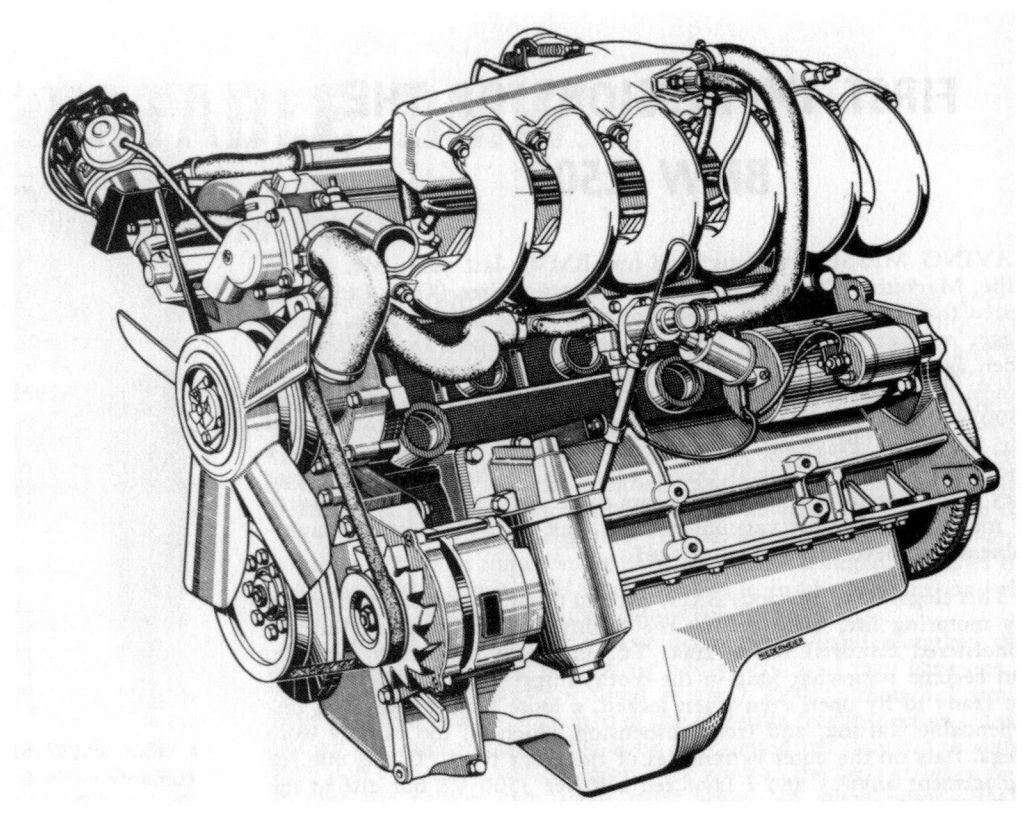

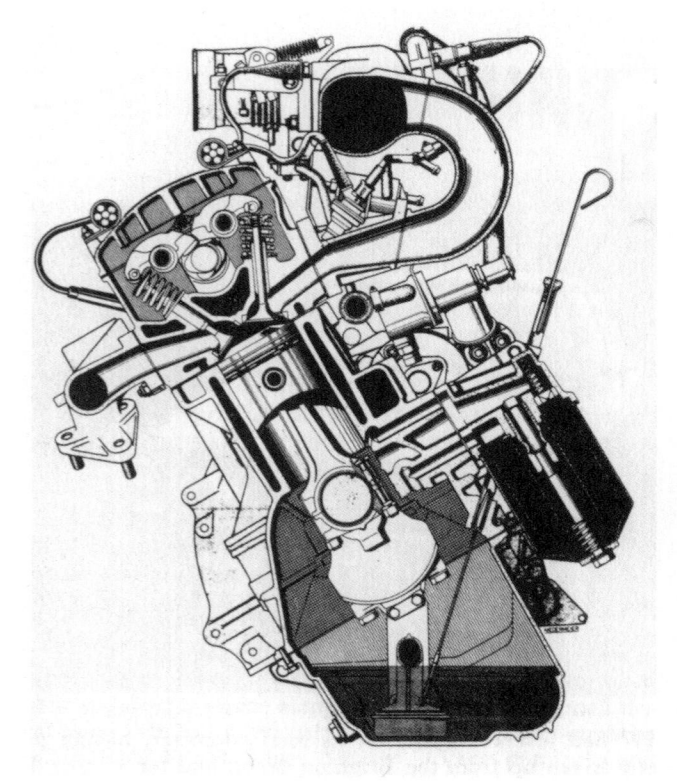

When fitted with fuel injection for the 3.0 Si models, the enlarged M30 engine sported a large tubular inlet manifold. The ultra-efficient cross-flow design of the engine is clear in the front cutaway view.

tors, which did need to be tuned and balanced at regular intervals. More torque allowed BMW to specify a taller rear axle ratio of 3.25:1, and this in turn had a beneficial effect on fuel consumption – unless, of course, a driver made regular and enthusiastic use of all the extra performance that was now available.

The 3.0 CSi was available only on the European continent in 1971, but with its arrival came a major change of policy: cars for right-hand-drive markets would be built with the steering wheel on the right and would no longer be converted by the importers. Although pre-production samples were available by summer 1972, production of right-hand-drive cars did not begin until January 1973. Right-hand-drive markets – notably the UK – took both manual and automatic variants, but left-hand-drive markets had to make do without an automatic option. After just two had been built in 1972, the model was dropped. As for the USA, that market was denied the 3.0 CSi altogether.

54

THE MAINSTREAM E9 COUPÉS

The engine bay of the 3.0 CS was always beautifully presented. This example is on a 1972 US-market car.

■ THE MAINSTREAM E9 COUPÉS

An overhead view showing one of the later 3.0-litre models. Note how the side vents, bonnet vents and wiper arms are now black. That door mirror is very much a 1970s design and the wheels are the optional Alpina multi-spoke type.

THE MAINSTREAM E9 COUPÉS

Britain took enthusiastically to the E9 coupés, more so after BMW set up its own UK branch and built the cars with right-hand drive. This is a 1974 3.0-litre car, with the blacked-out grilles of the later models. Those are the standard wheels.

The 3.0 CSi remained in production at the Karmann plant until 1975, and was withdrawn at the same time as the 3.0 CS. In four model-years of production, it sold a total of 8359, which gives a model-year average of 2090. Most importantly, perhaps, those strong sales made clear to BMW that it was performance that their customers sought – the more of it, the better.

The man who road-tested a CSi for the short-lived UK magazine *Competition Car International* in September 1974 liked it:

> I really enjoyed the CSi... and I reckon it must be close to the ideal all-round road car... acceleration is very impressive... if you need the power, it's there instantly.... The engine is smooth and effortless, the driving position very comfortable, the roadholding reassuring, and there is a very solid, well-constructed feel.

From 1973, black plastic was used on the side air vents.

57

■ THE MAINSTREAM E9 COUPÉS

The 2.5 CS (1974–1975)

Committed to a policy of increasingly high performance, BMW were caught on the hop by the 1973 Fuel Crisis. When fuel prices shot up as a result of the Arab oil embargo and fuel was, albeit briefly, rationed, the Munich manufacturer realized that it had to make changes to its product range in a hurry. The crisis was relatively short-lived, but it certainly had an impact on the development of the cars that were being drawn up in the second quarter of the 1970s as eventual replacements for the E9 range. It also forced BMW to produce a less thirsty variant of the E9, in a bid to maintain sales during the model's run-out period.

The new variant was called the 2.5 CS and was introduced in mid-1974. The 3.0 CS, 3.0 CSi and the 3.0 CSL models (see Chapter 4) all remained in production alongside the newcomer, which lasted for just one model-year. For BMW, it must have been relatively easy to develop – the major novelty was that the twin-carburettor 2.5-litre version of the M30 engine from the 2500 saloon was dropped into the engine bay in place of the 3.0-litre type.

With 150PS and 156lb ft of torque, the 2.5-litre engine was never going to give the performance of the 3.0-litre cars, but needs must when the Devil drives. Other car makers were being forced to take similar measures: Mercedes-Benz introduced a six-cylinder 280 SLC version of their grand touring coupé at the same time. The race at this time was not for more and more performance; it was to maintain as much performance as possible while reducing fuel consumption as much as possible. A 280 SLC could reach 205km/h and took 10 seconds to reach 100km/h from standstill, or 11 seconds with an automatic gearbox. The 2.5 CS was not quite as quick, with a 201km/h maximum and 0–100km/h in 10.5 seconds. The Mercedes used slightly less fuel, too, but the BMW was massively cheaper to buy, at 28,550 DM compared with the 37,200 DM of the Mercedes.

To get the price down this low, BMW had reduced equipment levels. From the outside, the lack of over-riders and the steel disc wheels with saloon-type trims and narrower 175 HR 14 tyres betrayed the cost savings. The

The 2.5 CS was essentially an economy version of the model, introduced to help sales after the fuel price rises of 1973–1974. It was the only version of the E9 range to have steel disc wheels as standard – although the full-size wheel trims actually suited the car rather well.

58

PRODUCTION FIGURES FOR E9 MODELS

	1968	1969	1970	1971	1972	1973	1974	1975	Total
2.5 CS							272	328	600
2.5 CS Auto							101	143	244
2800 CS	138	2534	3335	276					6283
2800 CS Auto		787	1089	73					1949
2800 CS USA		43	415	183					641
2800 CS US Auto		36	403	87					526
3.0 CS				1974	1172	779	267	263	4455
3.0 CS Auto				520	1215	1169	355	408	3667
3.0 CS USA				132	411	450	375		1368
3.0 CS US Auto				60	377	314	438		1189
3.0 CSi				1061	2999	2741	579	555	7935
3.0 CSi Auto					2				2
3.0 CSi RHD						66	128	13	207
3.0 CSi RHD Auto						69	139	7	215
3.0 CSL				169	252	287	40	17	765
3.0 CSL RHD					349	151			500
Totals	138	3400	5242	4535	6777	6026	2694	1734	30,546

Overall model totals:
2.5 CS   844
2800 CS   9399
3.0 (all types) 20,303

US sub-totals:
2800 CS   1167
3.0 CS   2557   (Total E9 coupés for USA: 3724)

rear side windows were fixed in place, there was no power assistance for the steering, and the final drive had the 3.64:1 ratio that had been employed to help Federal models overcome the power losses from their emissions-reduced engines. As the 2.5-litre engine was no longer homologated for the USA, the 2.5 CS was not made available there. Even though an English-language sales brochure was produced, there were never any right-hand-drive cars and the 2.5 CS was not sold in the UK, either. Just 844 examples were sold world-wide in the two years of production, some 75 per cent of them having the four-speed manual gearbox.

■ THE MAINSTREAM E9 COUPÉS

TECHNICAL SPECIFICATIONS, E9 MODELS

Engines:

2.5 CS
Type M30 six-cylinder petrol, installed with a 30-degree tilt to the right
2494cc (86mm x 71.6mm)
Single overhead camshaft, driven by Duplex chain
Seven-bearing crankshaft
Compression ratio 9.0:1
Two Zenith 35/40 INAT carburettors with automatic chokes
150PS at 6000rpm
156lb ft at 3700rpm

2800 CS
As above, except:
2788cc (86mm x 80mm)
170PS at 6000rpm
173.6lb ft at 3700rpm

3.0 CS and 3.0 CSL (1971–1972)
As above, except:
2985cc (89mm x 80mm)
180PS at 6000rpm
189lb ft at 3700rpm
US-specification engines with 8.3:1 compression, 170PS at 5800rpm and 185lb ft at 3500rpm

3.0 CSi
As for 3.0 CS and 3.0 CSL, except:
Compression ratio 9.5:1
Bosch electronic fuel injection
200PS at 5500rpm
272Nm (200lb ft) at 4300rpm

3.0 CSi (racing engine)
As above, except:
3003cc (89.25mm x 80mm)
Compression ratio 9.5:1
Bosch electronic fuel injection
200PS at 5500rpm
272Nm (200lb ft) at 4300rpm

3.0 CSL (1973-1975)
As above, except:
3153cc (89.25mm x 84mm)
Compression ratio 9.5:1
Bosch electronic fuel injection
206PS at 5600rpm
286Nm (211lb ft) at 4200rpm

Gearboxes:
Four-speed ZF manual gearbox standard on 2800 CS, with single dry-plate clutch
    Ratios 3.855:1, 2.08:1, 1.375:1, 1.00:1, reverse 4.13:1
Four-speed Getrag manual gearbox standard on all 3.0-litre models, with single dry-plate clutch
    Ratios 3.855:1, 2.202:1, 1.401:1, 1.000:1, reverse 4.3:1
Three-speed ZF 3HP 21 automatic gearbox optional on 2.5 CS and 2800 CS
Ratios 2.56:1, 1.52:1, 1,00:1, reverse ratio not known, with 1.94 torque converter multiplication
Three-speed Borg Warner automatic gearbox optional on 3.0 CS and 3.0 CSL
    Ratios 2.39:1, 1.45:1, 1.00:1, reverse ratio not known, with 2.0 torque converter multiplication

Axle ratio:
2.5 CS	3.64:1
2800 CS	3.45:1
3.0 CS and 3.0 CSL	3.45:1 (3.64:1 on US Federal cars)
3.0 CSi and later 3.0 CSL	3.25:1

Suspension, steering and brakes:
Front suspension with McPherson struts, coil springs and anti-roll bar
Rear suspension with semi-trailing arms, coil springs, telescopic dampers and anti-roll bar
Worm-and-roller steering; 18.05:1 ratio and power assistance standard on 2800CS, 3.0 CS, 1971–1972 3.0 CSL and 2985cc 3.0 CSi, optional on 2.5 CS and 1973–1975 3.0 CSL; 22.5:1 ratio with no power assistance standard on 2.5 CS, 1972–1973 3.0 CSi and 1973–1975 3.0 CSL
Disc brakes with 272mm diameter on front wheels and drum brakes with 250mm diameter on rear wheels of 2800 CS; all other models with 272mm ventilated disc brakes on all four wheels; twin hydraulic circuits and vacuum servo assistance standard

Dimensions:
Overall length:
4660mm (183.4in), except 1972–1973 3.0 CSi and 1973–1975 3.0 CSL
4630mm (182.3in) for 1972–1973 3.0 CSi and 1973–1975 3.0 CSL
Overall width:
1670mm (65.7in), except 1972–1973 3.0 CSi and 1973–1975 3.0 CSL
1730mm (68.1in) for 1972–1973 3.0 CSi and 1973–1975 3.0 CSL
Overall height: 1370mm (53.9in)
Wheelbase: 2625mm (103.3in)
Front track: 1446mm (56.9in) for standard cars
1426mm (56.1in) for 1972–1973 3.0 CSi
1470mm (57.8in) for 1973–1975 3.0 CSL
Rear track: 1402mm (55.2in) for 2800 CS, 3.0 CS and 1971-1972 3.0 CSL
1398mm (55in) for 2.5 CS
1422mm (56in) for 1972-1973 3.0 CSi
1426mm (56.1in) for 1973-1975 3.0 CSL

Wheels and tyres:
6J x 14 steel disc wheels for 2.5 CS
6J x 14 alloy wheels for 2800 CS, 3.0 CS and 1971-1975 3.0 CSi
7J x 14 alloy wheels for all 3.0 CSL and for 1972-1973 3.0 CSi
175 HR 14 radial tyres for 2.5 CS
195/70 HR 14 tyres for 2800 CS
195/70 VR 14 radial tyres for all other models

Unladen weights:
2.5 CS:	1400kg (3086lb)
2.5 CS automatic:	1420kg (3130lb)
2800 CS:	1355kg (2987lb)
2800 CS automatic:	1375kg (3031lb)
3.0 CS:	1400kg (3086lb)
3.0 CS automatic:	1420kg (3130lb)
3.0 CSL (1971–72):	1200kg (2645lb)
3.0 CSi (1971–75):	1400kg (3086lb)
3.0 CSi (1972–73):	1270kg (2800lb)
3.0 CSL (1973–75):	1270kg (2800lb)

PERFORMANCE FIGURES FOR E9 MODELS

2.5 CS	0–100km/h	10.5 sec
	Maximum	201km/h (124.8mph)
2800 CS	0–100km/h	10 sec
	Maximum	206km/h (128mph)
3.0 CS	0–100km/h	9 sec
	Maximum	213km/h (132mph)
3.0 CSL (1971–1972)	0-100km/h	8 sec
	Maximum	215km/h (133.6mph)
3.0 CSi (1971–1975)	0-100km/h	8 sec
	Maximum	220km/h (136.7mph)
3.0 CSi (1972–1973)	0-100km/h	7.5 sec
	Maximum	220km/h (136.7mph)
3.0 CSL (1973–1975)	0-100km/h	7.5 sec
	Maximum	220km/h (136.7mph)

■ THE MAINSTREAM E9 COUPÉS

IDENTIFICATION NUMBERS FOR E9 MODELS, 1968–1975

For clarity, identification numbers are shown here with a gap between the first three figures of the number and the last four. This gap is not present on the cars' identification plates.

2.5 CS

430 5001 to 430 5600	LHD manual, 1/74 to 12/75		600
431 5001 to 431 5244	LHD automatic, 1/74 to 12/75		244
		Total	844

2800 CS

220 0001 to 220 6283	LHD manual, to 12/72		6283
222 0001 to 222 1949	LHD automatic, to 12/72		1949
		Total	8232

US models

227 0001 to 227 0641	LHD manual , to 12/72		641
228 0001 to 228 0526	LHD automatic, to 12/72		526
		Total	1167

3.0 CS

221 0001 to 221 4006	LHD manual, to 12/72		4006
223 0001 to 223 2807	LHD automatic, to 12/72		2807
430 0001 to 430 0618	LHD manual, 1/73 to 12/75		618
432 0001 to 432 0860	LHD automatic, 1/73 to 12/75		860
		Total	8291

US models

224 0001 to 224 0975	LHD manual, to 12/72		975
225 0001 to 225 0738	LHD automatic, to 12/72		738
431 0001 to 431 0393	LHD manual, 1/74 to 12/75		393
433 5001 to 433 5451	LHD automatic, 1/74 to 12/75		451
		Total	2557

3.0 CSi

226 0001 to 226 6506	LHD manual, to 12/72		6506
435 0001 to 435 0207	RHD manual, 1/73 to 12/75		207
433 0001 to 433 0215	RHD automatic, 1/73 to 12/75		215
Sequence not known	LHD auto to 12/72		2
434 0001 to 434 1429	LHD manual, 1/74 to 12//75		1429
		Total	8359

3.0 CSL

227 5001 to 227 5429	LHD manual, 3003cc		429
227 5430 to 227 5539	LHD manual, 3153cc		110
228 5001 to 228 5500	RHD manual,		500
435 5001 to 435 5057	LHD manual, 3153cc, 1975		57
		Total	1096

Works competition cars
The works competition cars appear to have been numbered in a sequence ending in 227 6000. There were 21 cars in all.

THE MAINSTREAM E9 COUPÉS

The print is fading on the VIN plate of this car, but it is just possible to see that it is described as a 3.0 CS. In fact, the chassis number makes clear that it is a right-hand-drive 3.0 CSL; the CSL was not so designated on its chassis plate.

CHAPTER FOUR

THE CSL AND THE RACING COUPÉS

The 2000 CS was simply too underpowered to become a serious racing machine, but all that changed when the new six-cylinder engine arrived to turn the big BMW coupé into a 2800 CS.

Even so, it was not BMW who first took it racing. That honour fell to tuning specialist Alpina, who developed and campaigned a 2800 CS during 1969. Retaining the standard brakes with 13-inch wheels to suit Dunlop racing tyres and with barely modified suspension, the car had a blueprinted engine to which Alpina added three twin-choke Weber carburettors. Its 250bhp – or more, depending on who is telling the story – took it to a creditable but unspectacular ninth place at that year's Spa 24-hour event. BMW themselves, meanwhile, were simply too busy elsewhere to focus on the competition potential of the E9 coupé, and to some eyes they seemed to be losing interest in racing altogether: the works team was disbanded at the end of the 1969 season, and after 1970 they withdrew from their involvement in Formula 2 racing as well.

Nevertheless, tuners and privateers kept the faith. No doubt inspired by Alpina's example, several German privateers began to campaign 2800 CS cars during 1970, but unsurprisingly it was Alpina who made the headlines. BMW had asked them to keep the blue-and-white roundel represented in saloon-car racing while the factory devoted its competition efforts to Formula 2.

Now tuned to deliver 300PS with a lightened crankshaft and three twin-choke Weber carburettors, the Alpina coupés also had a patented Alpina auxiliary oil pump to prevent oil starvation in the wet-sump racing engine. Since

Alpina was among the pioneers of the E9 in motorsport. This is an early 2800 CS racer, pictured at the Spa circuit in Belgium.

THE CSL AND THE RACING COUPÉS

ABOVE: Without its additional spoilers, a CSL looked like any other E9 coupé from the front. This is the 'city-spec' 1973 car.

The multi-spoke Alpina wheels were standard wear on the 3.0 CSL, together with bright metal wheel-arch extensions.

■ THE CSL AND THE RACING COUPÉS

LEFT AND BELOW LEFT: These special side decals made sure that a CSL would be recognized for what it was. Alpina made up their own special version, with a cut-out reading 'Alpina 3.0 CSL'.

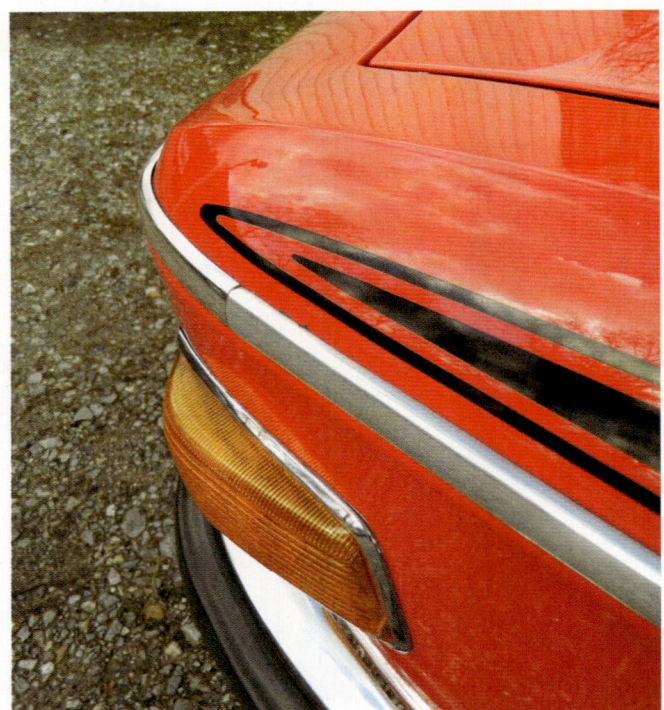

The CSL had its own special boot-lid badge.

THE CSL AND THE RACING COUPÉS

late in 1969, they had also been using five-speed ZF gearboxes. The Alpina 2800 CS cars were entered in a number of rounds of the European Touring Car Championship, where the main opposition came from Alfa Romeo. Wins at Salzburg and Spa showed that the big coupés had promise, but Alpina's cars were plagued by tyre problems throughout the season. Withdrawal from the German 'home' event at the Nürburgring event with tyre trouble was a bitter blow.

Alpina considered that 300PS was the best they could get on carburettors, and switched to fuel injection for 1971, using a Kugelfischer mechanical injection system with modified intake trumpets and modified combustion chambers to achieve 325PS. It was quick, but was raced before it was fully ready: at its first outing, for the Nürburgring 6-Hour race, the throttle linkage fell apart during the first lap. Tyres were now fatter, on 8-inch rims, and front apron spoilers arrived during the season. It was during 1971 that the Schnitzer team also began to use the big BMWs, claiming as much as 340PS. Ernst Furtmayer drove hard and well, but the only victory was at Zandvoort, where a Schnitzer car driven by Dieter Quester claimed victory after a straight fight with the Ford Capris that were now dominating European touring-car events. The big problem was weight: the BMW coupés were around 300kg heavier than the Capris, and the additional power was putting a huge strain on tyres, brakes and suspension. The only solution was a drastic weight-reduction programme, but that was not something the tuners could achieve on their own. For that, they needed the support of BMW.

The First-Series 3.0 CSL (1971–1972)

BMW were only too well aware of the weight problem, and they were already looking at it. Although the company seems to have kept its development work secret from the tuning companies in the beginning, a grand plan was in place. The idea was to develop a car suitable for Group 2 racing events, and that meant also building a number of cars for public sale that embodied some of the features specially developed for the racing versions. A first, prototype, example was used for a time by Sales Director Bob Lutz, and would later be tested by a number of magazines. Production of the real roadgoing 'homologation special' began in May 1971.

Brought to market with the name of 3.0 CSL (the L standing for *leicht*, or 'lightweight'), the new car was much more radical than it looked at first sight. Most obvious was the absence of a front bumper; the rear bumper looked standard but was painted matt black and was made of lightweight GRP instead of steel. A close look revealed that the rear side windows were made of lightweight Plexiglass, and a tap of the panels showed that they were made of aluminium alloy instead of steel. The interior had been changed, too, and featured lightweight racing-style buckets seats made by Scheel. The car looked so much like a standard 3.0 CS that BMW felt it necessary to advertise what it was by adding side decal stripes above the waistline, with the legend 'BMW 3.0 CSL' on each front wing. At the rear, there was a 3.0 CSL badge on the boot lid, too.

Overall, the changes saved a huge 200kg (440 lb) as compared with a standard 3.0 CS of the time. The comparison with the 3.0 CS is entirely valid, because BMW saw the first 3.0 CSL cars as modified 3.0 CS types, and numbered them within the standard 3.0 CS production sequences. They had exactly the same 2985cc twin-carburettor engine, with the same 180PS. Even so, a good number went to enthusiastic amateurs who had every intention of using them in motorsport. To anyone who did not intend to take one racing, the price of 31,950 DM – considerably more than a standard 3.0 CS of the time – was an enormous amount to pay for a car that took a second less to reach 100km/h from rest and was 2km/h (1.6mph) faster overall.

These CSLs with carburettor-fed engines were built over the spring and summer of 1971 and are now generally described as the first-series models. There were just 169 of them in all, and every one was built with left-hand drive. In principle, they could be ordered in any one of the colours approved for the standard BMW E9 range of the time.

The Second-Series 3.0 CSL (1972–1973)

Production of those first-series cars had begun too late for them to be homologated for the 1971 racing season. That had to wait until later in the year. Now that fuel injection had been announced for the 3.0 CSi that March, it was quite obvious that a fuel-injected engine would be among the homologated features. However, BMW commentators had not predicted another change that was

67

■ THE CSL AND THE RACING COUPÉS

Not every owner wanted the stripped-out interior associated with the CSL. This UK-market car from the second series was fitted with electric windows.

The engine of the roadgoing CSL looked much like that of the less powerful 3.0 CSi, with the same tubular inlet manifold. This is a right-hand-drive car.

These are the Scheel front bucket seats in a right-hand-drive CSL. Although there are receiver sockets for head restraints, none are fitted.

The rear seats of a CSL were of course upholstered to match those at the front. The mounting for the front-seat safety belt was the same as in other E9 models.

THE CSL AND THE RACING COUPÉS

The popular view is that every CSL came with the 'Batmobile' array of spoilers and wings, but that was not the case. This is a genuine CSL from 1973, without the bodykit.

incorporated on the road cars and was a direct result of BMW's racing plans.

This change was an increase in engine capacity to 3003cc. BMW achieved it through the simple expedient of increasing the bore size by a quarter of a millimetre – a change that would have been completely meaningless outside the context of the racing programme. It was, as Jeremy Walton noted in *Unbeatable BMW*, 'really a maximum rebore size'. What BMW wanted to do was to compete in FIA Group 2 events for cars with an engine capacity of between 3.0 and 3.5 litres. The existing production swept volume of 2985cc would have obliged them to compete in a smaller-capacity class, but that extra quarter of a millimetre just tipped the balance. Entering the class at its lower end, and with the knowledge that the M30 six-cylinder could be developed to give swept volumes up to 3.5 litres if necessary, BMW were playing for safety.

The details of the 1972 racing season are set out later, but the roadgoing CSLs took on the new engine capacity together with a Bosch D-Jetronic injection system from August 1972. These were the second-series cars, and they were built with both left- and right-hand drive. The right-hand-drive cars, intended mainly for the enthusiastically pro-BMW UK market, were actually the more numerous, with 500 examples built, compared with just 429 with left-hand drive.

Even though many of these second-series cars retained the original purity of the lightweight racers, a change had taken place in their audience. Ownership of a CSL was now seen as conferring status, and the desire for status had little in common with the desire for the spartan levels of equipment that helped save weight in a CSL. As a result, cars in both Germany and the UK were often ordered with standard-glass side windows in place of the lightweight Plexiglass items, with steel bumpers front and rear, and an interior that was little different from the more luxurious version standard in the contemporary 3.0 CSi. The lightweight panels ensured that these 'city-spec' cars still weighed less than a standard CSi, but the difference in performance was less marked. Indeed, some later UK cars were supplied with standard steel panels in place of the aluminium-alloy boot, bonnet and doors. Exactly what made them CSLs outside of the owner's imagination is hard to determine.

These cars were built for just one year, and production lasted from August 1972 to July 1973. Once again, they could be ordered in any of the standard colours from the

■ THE CSL AND THE RACING COUPÉS

Inside a 1975 3.0 CSL. Those racing bucket seats have been known to make entry and exit awkward for the less agile!

The body addenda all had a purpose on the racing CSLs, helping to manage the airflow around the cars at high speeds on the track. On the roadgoing cars, they were not so much for show as to meet homologation requirements. The rear roof spoiler and rear 'wing' are seen here.

THE CSL AND THE RACING COUPÉS

Note how there was also a reshaped trailing edge for the boot lid on the 'Batmobile' cars. The badges, of course, remained unchanged.

The front apron and wing aerofoil clearly visible.

Another view of the rear roof spoiler and 'wing'.

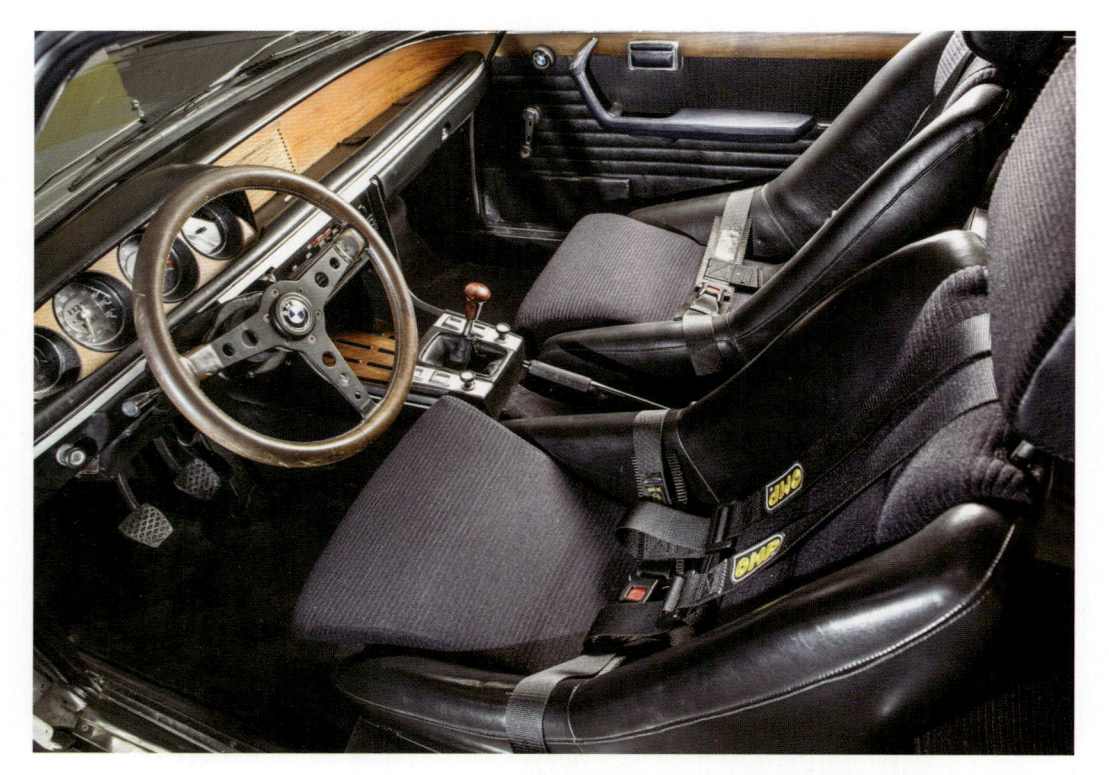

LEFT AND BELOW: The racing harnesses were not part of the standard CSL specification. The car has manual window lifts, so there are blanking pieces over the electric window switches on the centre console.

E9 palette. A total of 17, for example, were ordered in distinctly non-aggressive Ceylon metallic.

One very special car, probably a CSL rather than a standard E9 coupé, was built around 1972 for BMW works team driver Hans Stuck to use as his everyday driver. At the time, BMW were developing a 4.5-litre V12 engine, and the Stuck car is said to have been specially equipped with a prototype example. No doubt Stuck was expected to report back to the works periodically on how it was behaving. However, work on the V12 was suspended as a response to the Oil Crisis of 1973–1974, and the project was cancelled altogether around 1978.

72

THE CSL AND THE RACING COUPÉS

The Third-Series 3.0 CSL (1973–1974)

Matters never stand still in racing. As competition in the European Touring Car Championship and the German Touring Car Series hotted up, BMW was working on a further-developed CSL track car. Further changes to the roadgoing cars would be inevitable.

It was at the start of July 1973 that BMW Motorsport gained approval for what is known as an 'evolution' of the species. There were to be two major changes to the racers. First, a new crankshaft would give their engines a longer stroke of 84mm and an increased swept volume of 3153cc. Second, they would be fitted with a series of aerodynamic addenda, which would reduce speed-sapping drag and give more downforce at speed, to reduce the likelihood of lift.

BMW lost no time in applying these changes to the racers, and nor did they lose time in applying them to the roadgoing cars. From August 1973 there was a third series of CSLs. Still known as 3.0 CSL types, despite their 3.2-litre engines, these cars were supplied with a full aerodynamic kit of spoilers. There was a deep front apron, an aerofoil on the top of each front wing, a hoop spoiler at the rear of the roof and – most noticeably – a rear 'wing' spoiler between fins standing on each rear wing. It was these addenda that earned the third-series CSLs their nickname of 'Batmobiles', by analogy with the bewinged car driven by Batman in the 1960s TV series about the comic-book hero.

There was just one small problem: Germany had cracked down on dangerous protrusions in and on cars some years ago, and the rear spoiler of the 'Batmobile' bodykit offended against the new regulations. German cars were therefore delivered with the relevant parts packed into the boot and purchasers could choose to fit them at their own risk. All cars were built with left-hand drive, and all came in one of just two colours – Polaris Silver and Chamonix White – in each case set off by an array of stripes and decals bearing the triple colours of the

Decidedly eye-catching in its typically 1970s yellow paint, this right-hand-drive CSL was pictured on the 1997 Haynes Classic Rally in the UK.

73

■ THE CSL AND THE RACING COUPÉS

BMW Motorsport division. They came with a new set of wheels, too, this time multi-spoke types made by Alpina but bearing the BMW roundel on their centre caps. The wider tyres that accompanied them demanded wider wheel arches, a problem that BMW solved by fitting a bright-metal 'eyebrow' above each wheel. The interior always featured racing-style bucket seats in tandem with a smaller-diameter racing-style steering wheel.

The roadgoing 'Batmobiles' – seen as iconic machines these days – were never numerous. BMW built 110 of them, a figure way below the 1000 demanded by the FIA homologation regulations. But nobody seemed to mind too much; the other major contenders in touring-car competition at the time all bent the rules in one way or another, and motorsport enthusiasts expected nothing different.

The Fourth-Series 3.0 CSL (1974–1975) and Beyond

There was a fourth series of CSL, too, which continued the range into 1975. These were largely indistinguishable from the third-series cars, but they did have their own numbering sequence. There were just 57 of them, all once again with left-hand drive but not all with the tri-colour Motorsport stripes, despite a popular misconception to the contrary. By the time of their demise, the 'Batmobiles' were priced at 40,880 DM in Germany.

The last CSL 'Batmobiles' for public sale were built in the summer of 1975. BMW had no need to build any more, as the E9's replacement model, the E24 coupé, was now ready for introduction. Nevertheless, there would be further evolutions of the racing cars over the next four years.

ABOVE AND OPPOSITE: *This 1975 CSL has the full 'Batmobile' kit of body addenda: front apron, wing aerofoils, roof spoiler and rear 'wing' spoiler. These were the items most commonly left off the cars when they were used regularly on the road.*

THE CSL AND THE RACING COUPÉS

The Racing E9s

Once BMW had decided to take the CSL racing and put their weight behind it, the car became a huge success in motorsport. Between 1973 and 1979, CSLs won the European Touring Car Championship six times, missing out only in 1974 when the works racing programme was deliberately restricted. The legend of the racing CSL is based on its domination of touring-car racing in both Europe and the USA during those seven glorious years.

Nevertheless, it takes time to create a successful touring-car racer. The efforts of Alpina, Schnitzer and others, with the 2800 CS and later the original 3.0 CS, had pointed the way, but it was not until the lightweight cars became available that the E9 coupé's racing career really took off. Even though production of the CSL began in summer 1971, it could not be homologated for racing until the 1972 season; and it was not until the middle of the 1972 season that BMW established their new Motor-sport division to support competition work. In the mean time, the new CSL sat in a sort of limbo. Although it was available through the showrooms, it could not be raced in FIA events, as BMW's Dutch importers discovered when scrutineers rejected an example with which the Dutch hoped to race at an event in late 1971.

In theory, the early part of the 1972 racing season was down to the 2800 CS, by this stage running with what competition records describe as a 2996cc engine. One early CSL did slip through the net, however. In late 1971, BMW had commissioned Broadspeed in the UK to take a look at the car and make recommendations for its racing future, and had supplied the company with two prototype lightweight bodies, featuring lighter-gauge steel as well as the aluminium bonnet, boot lid and doors that would later become part of the standard CSL specification. Team Broadspeed decided to enter one of their wide-wheeled development cars in the ETCC round at Salzburg in April 1972. It was supposedly ballasted, but to this day nobody

THE CSL AND THE RACING COUPÉS

knows whether the Broadspeed '2800 CS' met the weight regulations. Driven by John Kirkpatrick, the car finished third behind a pair of Ford Capris, first of a swathe of 2800 CS cars that followed it home in fourth, fifth and sixth places.

The 1972 season was dominated in touring-car events by the Ford Capris, which won both the European Touring Car Championship and the German national championship. Alpina campaigned a coupé and so did Schnitzer; Jeremy Walton records that BMW had offered 10,000 DM for every ETCC win, plus 100,000 DM if either team won the title, and both teams were keen to take the money. However, their efforts were rewarded with just a single win, when the Schnitzer car (now producing a claimed 360bhp) won the Nürburgring 6-Hour event driven by the team of John Fitzpatrick, Hans Heyer and Rolf Stommelen.

Behind the scenes, a lot was happening. It was in May that BMW announced that Jochen Neerpasch, the man behind Ford's success with the racing Capris, would be moving from Cologne to Munich. With him would come chassis expert Martin Braungart. Neerpasch's task at BMW was to build up a works motorsport department (which would take the name of BMW Motorsport GmbH and was the forerunner of today's M Division). From here, BMW would tackle not only touring-car racing in Europe; the new division would also work with outside partners to raise BMW's racing profile. Among them would be March in Formula 2 events.

1973

High on the priorities list was the creation of an E9 coupé that would put the Ford Capris in their place on the tracks, and Neerpasch and Braungart got down to that task as fast as they could. It took four months to create the car they wanted, with a heavily revised suspension that allowed for larger wheels with fast-change centre-locks,

As the CSL developed on the tracks, so features such as widened rear tracks with lightweight arches to cover them became common. This is one of the Alpina-prepared cars; note the side exhaust pipe peeping out from under the door.

THE CSL AND THE RACING COUPÉS

new brakes designed in conjunction with ATE, a Getrag five-speed gearbox in place of the ZF type, lightweight magnesium castings for the bellhousing and gearbox, and a selection of axle ratios to suit different racing circuits. Meanwhile, in the engine department Paul Rosche's team created a new dry-sump 3.3-litre version of the six-cylinder engine, with a 92mm bore and 80mm stroke to give 3.3 litres.

The new car was ready for testing before the end of 1972, and was further developed over the winter of 1972–1973 with input from Hans Stuck and Dutchman Toine Hezemans, two of the three drivers whom BMW had engaged to drive the works CSLs for 1973. The third driver would be New Zealander Chris Amon. Rim widths were settled as 11.5 inches for the front and 13 inches at the rear, with BBS alloy wheels running on Dunlop racing tyres. There were four-piston disc brakes with alloy calipers, cooled at the front by ducting in the full-width spoiler. At the rear, those wide wheels demanded bodywork exten-

BMW engines specialist Paul Rosche was the man behind the dry-sump engine in the racing CSLs.

Brian Muir and Hans-Peter Joisten co-drove this bright orange Alpina-prepared CSL at the Spa 24-Hour race in July 1973. Tragically, Joisten and Alfa Romeo driver Roger Dubois were killed almost instantly in a three-car crash during the race's seventh hour.

77

THE CSL AND THE RACING COUPÉS

sions. On 1 January 1973, the 1973 'works' CSL and its new engine were homologated for FIA Group 2 events. The two cars that the Motorsport division planned to campaign were to run in dead white paint (white had once been the German national racing colour), set off by stripes in the three colours of the Motorsport division.

Meanwhile, the tuners were also intent on success with the big coupés. Alpina had signed up Austrian Niki Lauda and Australian Brian Muir, while Schnitzer had the Italian brothers Ernesto and Vittorio Brambilla and Frenchman Bob Wollek.

At Monza, the opening event of the ETCC, it was immediately clear that the Capris were again going to present a formidable challenge, even though failures put them out of the running. Both the BMW Motorsport cars were also eliminated by engine failures, leaving the Alpina car to win. At the second round, in Salzburg, engine failures again put the Motorsport cars out of contention. Concerned that the new 3.3-litre might have dangerous weaknesses, and anxious to prove the contrary in public, BMW now entered the coupés for the Le Mans 24-Hour event in June. The car, crewed by Chris Amon and Hans Stuck, retired after 160 laps, but the second car, with Toine Hezemans and Dieter Quester, carried on to the end to record an 11th overall placing. The main lessons from this event were associated with brake cooling, a problem later solved when ATE developed some fins to improve airflow over the discs.

Meanwhile, Neerpasch and Braungart had spotted an amendment in the FIA regulations that permitted evolutionary changes to existing models. One other problem that had surfaced was associated with the rear end of the CSL, which tended to break away under hard cornering. The two former Ford men reasoned that this could be countered by improving downforce on the rear wheels at speed with aerodynamic addenda, and worked flat out to develop a kit of spoilers that would do the job. They bought time in the Mercedes-Benz wind tunnel at

ABOVE AND OPPOSITE: *Alpina-prepared CSLs in action on the track.*

78

THE CSL AND THE RACING COUPÉS

Stuttgart (then the only one available in Germany) and developed what they wanted by 'knife and fork' engineering – simply trying different items in the metal until they found a design that worked. The next homologation deadline was 1 July, and on that day they gained FIA approval for the aerodynamic addenda which would later earn the CSL its 'Batmobile' nickname.

At the Nürburgring later that month, BMW claimed first and second places with CSL coupés driven by Hans Stuck with Chris Amon, and Dieter Quester with Toine Hezemans. The aerodynamic kit had worked. From that point on, the Capris were beaten, and the BMW coupés won every remaining event in that year's ETCC. Hezemans and Quester won at Spa, Zandvoort and Paul Ricard, and Hezemans finished the season with the European title. Hezemans also won the Touring Class at the Le Mans 24-Hours event. Ford's only revenge was a win in the German national series.

Back in the engine development department at Munich, meanwhile, Paul Rosche had been busy again. This time, he had come up with an even bigger engine, this time with a 3.5-litre (3498cc) swept volume. It had the crankshaft and 84mm stroke of the 3.2-litre type, but was bored out to 94mm. The new size was achieved only through Siamese bores, and Rosche admitted to some trepidation at the reduced cooling this brought; in the end, however, the new dimensions worked well. Still with only two valves for each cylinder, and with an 11.1:1 compression ratio, this engine achieved 370bhp at 8000rpm. It was ready for when the racing coupés needed it.

■ THE CSL AND THE RACING COUPÉS

1974

The 1974 racing season was characterized by two things. First, new regulations permitted engines to have four valves per cylinder, and of course BMW responded to that challenge with a 24-valve version of their 3.2-litre engine. Unfortunately, the second thing to characterize 1974 was a cutback in the budget of the Motorsport division. The whole motor industry lived through 1974 in the shadow of the Oil Crisis that had been triggered in the autumn of 1973, and the BMW Board was understandably keener to spend money on developing more fuel-efficient cars than on winning races.

Alpina and Schnitzer also lost interest in the big coupés. Alpina's policy had always been to use racing to develop new products for road cars, and at this stage they did not see how they could sell four-valve engine technology for road use. Using a 3.5-litre two-valve coupé, they did enter the first round of the 1974 ETCC at Monza, with drivers Harald Ertl, Rikky von Opel and Thomas Betzler. Sadly, the car retired with piston trouble, and the Alpina coupés disappeared from the ETCC. Schnitzer ran a single car, using drivers Vittorio Brambilla, Henri Pescarolo and Bob Wollek, but their heart was clearly no longer in it and that showed in their lack of results.

Meanwhile, the Motorsport division entered a few rounds of the ETCC, probably as much to wave the flag as for any other reason. Still sporting the 'Batmobile' addenda, the cars now ran in dark blue with the division's tri-colour striping, and their new 24-valve engines made them formidably quick. These now carried the M49 code at BMW and, unsurprisingly, had drawn on the design of the four-valve Formula 2 engine of 1970. The single overhead camshaft of the M30 engines had given way to gear-driven twin overhead camshafts, while there were lightweight cast-alloy Mahle pistons and titanium connecting rods. Fuel delivery was from a Kugelfischer injection system, and power was initially claimed to be as high as 435bhp at 8000rpm. The 24-valve engine made its first appearance at Salzburg, the second ETCC event of the season, in March 1974, and it was accompanied by enlarged rear wings that incorporated NACA cooling ducts. Stuck and Jacky Ickx took it to victory ahead of a pair of privately entered 3.5-litre CSLs.

At the Nürburgring in July, BMW entered two cars for the first time, experimenting with an ABS system developed by ATE on the car driven by Hans Stuck. Stuck was formidably fast but was forced to retire after a collision wrecked his suspension. His consolation was that his very first lap of the Nordschleife was achieved in just 8 minutes, 10.9 seconds – it was not only fastest lap of the day but also a new record for the circuit.

Meanwhile, a new name was emerging in the world of the BMW racing coupés. In Belgium, Team Luigi developed one of the 1973 cars into a Group 1 winner. Sometimes called the 'Francorchamps' car after the event for which it was designed, the car claimed victory in July at the Spa 24 Hours, crewed by Hughes de Fierlant, Pierre Dieudonné and Marc Demol.

1975

For the 1975 season, BMW left European racing to the tuners, focusing the works effort instead on the IMSA GT Championship in the USA. The remaining Group 2 24-valve CSLs were sold off in Europe, and four CSLs were shipped across the Atlantic for the American assignment. The team based itself at the premises of legendary NASCAR driver Bobby Allison, in Hueytown, Alabama. With it went German driver Hans Stuck, but there were also three new driver signings: Swede Ronnie Peterson (who was then driving for the Lotus Formula 1 team), American Sam Posey and US-based Briton, Brian Redman.

The IMSA regulations demanded new modifications to the cars. Weight limits were different, and allowed the cars to be lightened by removing side glass and interior trim; even the dashboard could go. There were fewer restrictions on wheel-arch extensions, too, so the CSLs gained wider arches front and rear. The cars ran with deeper front aprons but retained the aerofoils on the front wings and the hoop and 'batwing' spoilers at the rear. Further changes included aluminium wheel hubs and a reduced front axle weight, plus oil coolers for the gearboxes and differentials, and a new rack-and-pinion steering system that was both slick and accurate.

BMW claimed that the weight reductions and aerodynamic changes had the same effect as adding 50PS to the engine output. This was perhaps just as well, because the engines had to revert to 12-valve configuration to meet the IMSA regulations. In an exciting year, when the cars raced in a version of the striped white colours that European racegoers had seen in 1973, the BMW team claimed victory in no fewer than five rounds of the 17-round series: at Sebring, Laguna Seca, Riverside, Daytona and Talladega. Veteran CSL driver Hans Stuck was responsible for the last four (he was paired with Dieter Quester at Riverside), and Brian Redman with Allan Moffat drove the winning car at Sebring.

Back in Europe, meanwhile, BMW Motorsport's only CSL entry was at the Le Mans 24 Hours. Jochen Neerspach had given his blessing to an entry by Hervé Poulain with a car that had been specially painted by US artist Alexander Calder – this was the inauguration of the famous BMW 'Art Cars'. Poulain's co-drivers were Jean Guichet and Sam Posey, the latter of course fresh from racing CSLs in the IMSA series. In qualifying, the car showed promise as Sam Posey took first in class and 11th place in the field of 55 cars. In the actual race, the car was leading the GT class when a CV joint failed, nine hours into the event, and the team was forced to retire.

The major European events were meanwhile left to the tuners, who did not let the BMW name down. Alpina, supported by the BMW Faltz dealership in Essen, finished the season with the ETCC title, thanks to Siggi Müller and co-driver Alain Peltier. Schnitzer, also supported by BMW Faltz, showed up well in the German championship. This season, the cars ran 24-valve engines with power outputs as high as 470PS.

In Group 1 events, the 3.0-litre cars were by no means forgotten. Belgian team Luigi Racing entered two cars in the Spa 24 Hours, aiming to retain their 1974 title. Alain Peltier and Marc Demol set the fastest lap with a speed of 190.677km/h (118.48mph), but their car was eliminated after an accident. Nevertheless, the second Luigi car, driven by Jean Xhenceval and Hughes de Fierlant, pressed on to win the event, leading home another 3.0 CSL entered by the Atlas Racing Team and driven by Belgians Pedro Van Assche and Yvette Fontaine.

Meanwhile, Harald Grohs drove a Faltz-Alpina CSL to victory in the Deutsche Rennsport Meisterschaft. He took first at the Nürburgring in April, second at Diepholz in July and second again at the Nürburgring in August.

1976

By 1976, production of the CSL had ended, and BMW had begun to look to the future by introducing other models to its works team – notably the new 320. Nevertheless, the CSL's racing career was far from over yet. Even the

THE CSL TURBO (1976)

Something of a legend in its own right was the turbocharged CSL that BMW Motorsport developed for the 1976 season. It raced as a Group 5 car in just three events: the Silverstone 6 Hours in May, the Le Mans 24 Hours in June, and the closing round of the ETCC at Dijon in September. It failed to finish in any of these, succumbing to gearbox failures in the first two and to a differential failure at Dijon. Nevertheless, it was formidably quick: driver Ronnie Peterson reported a 284km/h (178mph) maximum on the Hangar Straight at Silverstone, and at Dijon the car qualified in first place, ahead of the Porsche 935 that eventually won the event.

For its first appearance at Silverstone, the car was painted white with the BMW Motorsport tricolour stripes sweeping up and over its tail. By the time of Le Mans, it had been transformed into the second BMW Art Car by American artist Frank Stella, and ran with its distinctive 'graph paper' livery. Driven by Brian Redman and Peter Gregg, it held third place overall for a time, but was eventually forced to retire with gearbox trouble. After withdrawal from racing, it became part of the Art Car collection in the BMW Museum.

The turbocharged engine was largely developed by Josef Schnitzer over the winter of 1975–1976, when he was working at BMW's Motorsport division. Retaining the standard 84mm stroke of the production cars, it had a 90mm bore to give 3195cc and was known to BMW as an M49/4 type. It had the four-valve cylinder heads, plus a pair of KKK turbochargers giving a boost of 1.3 bar. Output was a simply massive 750PS at 9500rpm, which amply explains the driveline failures.

The host car is believed to have been one of those that had seen service in the 1975 IMSA championship. It had a five-speed Getrag gearbox, and the front wheels had a 16-inch diameter with 12-inch rims while the rears were a 19-inch size with 14.5-inch rims.

THE CSL AND THE RACING COUPÉS

BMW works team competed with a CSL in 1976 – it was almost unheard of to do this with a car that was no longer in production. And if there were any doubts about the CSL's continuing viability as an endurance racer, the list of entries for the 1976 Le Mans 24 Hours race would have dispelled them. No fewer than seven CSLs were entered in the new Group 5 class, although only two of them actually completed the race.

Major regulation changes for the ETCC were intended to liven up the season's events, but their main effect in Group 2 was to deter entries from all the works teams except Jaguar. Luigi Racing in Belgium saw their chance and this year switched from Group 1 to Group 2. Competing with a 3.2-litre 12-valve engine (actually 3196cc from a 89.95mm bore and 84mm stroke), the Luigi car developed 340bhp at 7400rpm with a Kugelfischer injection system. Regulations required a four-speed gearbox, so a four-speed Getrag it was. Racing at 1050kg, and still with Batmobile-style spoilers, the Luigi car was on 16-inch wheels with 11-inch front rims and 12.5-inch rims at the rear.

From the start, Luigi Racing were favourites for the over-3000cc class, and they did not disappoint. Jean Xhenceval and Pierre Dieudonné took the BMW coupé to the Drivers' Championship, with wins at Monza and Mugello, although the manufacturers' title for 1976 went to Alfa Romeo. This was the third ETCC title for the big coupés, and more was to come yet, even though they were no longer in production.

Meanwhile, those revised FIA regulations had created a new category for Group 5 Special Production cars, and BMW's Jochen Neerpasch decided to put the big coupés into this. Build of four cars for the new season began in February 1976, and the CSLs were briefly tested at the Paul Ricard circuit. Among the new features were a front apron with a noticeably extended lower lip, and a rear wing that hung out further than ever behind the car on revised side supports. The rear wheel arches were also bigger than ever, covering rims that were 14 inches wide, while those at the front were now 12 inches wide. Goodyear tyres, tried during the 1975 IMSA series, were now standard wear.

Engine development was still forging ahead, and over the winter of 1975–1976 a great deal of work had been done by Josef Schnitzer, then doing a stint in the BMW Motorsport division. Key among his changes was the vertical mounting of the four-valve engine; moving away from the 30-degree slant that was always used in production allowed valuable changes to the inlet and exhaust systems. Power from the 3.5-litre, 24-valve engines, which retained Kugelfischer injection, now went up to 460PS at 8700rpm. The gearbox was once again a Getrag five-speed.

Three of the 1976 cars were built up with this specification, and with an initial weight of 1030kg. One was delivered to each of three racing teams – Alpina-Faltz, Schnitzer and British Hermetite – who would campaign them on BMW's behalf. The fourth car, meanwhile, was retained at Munich for development work on a new turbocharged engine, again led by Josef Schnitzer. It appears that this car may have started life as one of the 1975 IMSA racers.

The three CSLs put up a good fight against the better-prepared Porsches in the first few races, with the Schnitzer car having a slight edge. Later in the season its weight was quoted as being down to 975kg. Maximum speeds in fifth gear were as high as 260km/h (161mph). The hope was that the arrival of the turbocharged car in mid-season would boost BMW's Group 5 performance, but its astonishing turn of speed and Ronnie Peterson's experience were no substitute for reliability (see sidebar). Despite sterling efforts in the other three cars by drivers Brian Redman, John Fitzpatrick, Harald Grohs, Albrecht Krebs, Sam Posey, Dieter Quester and Tom Walkinshaw, BMW had to concede the Group 5 title to Porsche.

Over in the USA, BMW again suffered at the hands of Porsche in the 15-round IMSA championship. Lead driver was Peter Gregg, formerly a noted Porsche privateer, but he won only two races that season, at Daytona (in partnership with Brian Redman) and at Talladega. It was not enough to earn BMW of North America, newly named as sponsors of the car, any great honour.

1977

Amazingly for cars that had been out of production for nearly 18 months, the CSLs were still favourites in the European Touring Car Championship when the 1977 season opened. The major contenders were fielded by Alpina, who now had the Gösser Beer sponsorship and drove in that company's dark green livery, and by Luigi Racing.

THE CSL AND THE RACING COUPÉS

ANOTHER LEGEND: THE GÖSSER BEER CAR

The chassis number, 221365, of the well-known racing CSL that is usually known as the Gösser Beer car shows that it was probably built as early as 1972. However, it remained as a shell until February 1976, when it was built up as a complete car for use in the 1977 European Touring Car Championship. It went to Alpina, who obtained sponsorship from the Gösser beer company and raced the car in a distinctive green livery. With Dieter Quester as lead driver, it won five rounds of the 1977 ETCC and claimed overall victory in the Championship – a fourth win in the series for the BMW coupés. Quester's co-drivers during the season were (in alphabetical order) Vittorio Brambilla, Umberto Grano, Toni Hezemans, Patrick Neve, Gunnar Nilsson and Tom Walkinshaw.

The car was subsequently sold to Italian driver Martino Finotto, who raced it under the banner of the Jolly Club Team with co-driver Carlo Facetti. The car still survives and has been carefully restored as closely as possible to its mid-1970s condition.

The Gösser Beer racing CSL was prepared by Alpina, and is seen here with the racing team. In the racing overalls is driver Dieter Quester, and on the left in the front row is Alpina's founder, Burkard Bovensiepen.

■ THE CSL AND THE RACING COUPÉS

Team Luigi figured large in the CSL's racing career after 1975, and two of their later cars are seen accompanied by Ford Capri and Opel Commodore rivals.

ABOVE AND OPPOSITE: *This restored Group 2 car, which in an earlier incarnation raced in orange livery with Bosch sponsorship, now displays the iconic BMW Motorsport three-coloured stripes.*

THE CSL AND THE RACING COUPÉS

Note that this car has five-bolt wheels rather than the centre-lock variety favoured in the CSL's racing heyday.

■ THE CSL AND THE RACING COUPÉS

Racing cars evolve over time, and this one is no exception. It was built in 1968 as a 2800 CS with chassis number 2200093 and spent five months as a test vehicle with BMW. It subsequently became a racer, and by 1977 was listed as a full-specification 3.0 CSL and was being raced in Group 2 events. After a major rebuild at the start of the twenty-first century, it returned to racing in classic events.

THE CSL AND THE RACING COUPÉS

The instrumentation of a racing CSL was very different from that of the standard cars, giving the driver only the most important information. This is the restored Group 2 car, which of course has a substantial rollover cage as well.

■ THE CSL AND THE RACING COUPÉS

Large intake trumpets provide a ram-air effect for the injected 3.5-litre engine, and the front struts on the Group 2 racer are far from standard.

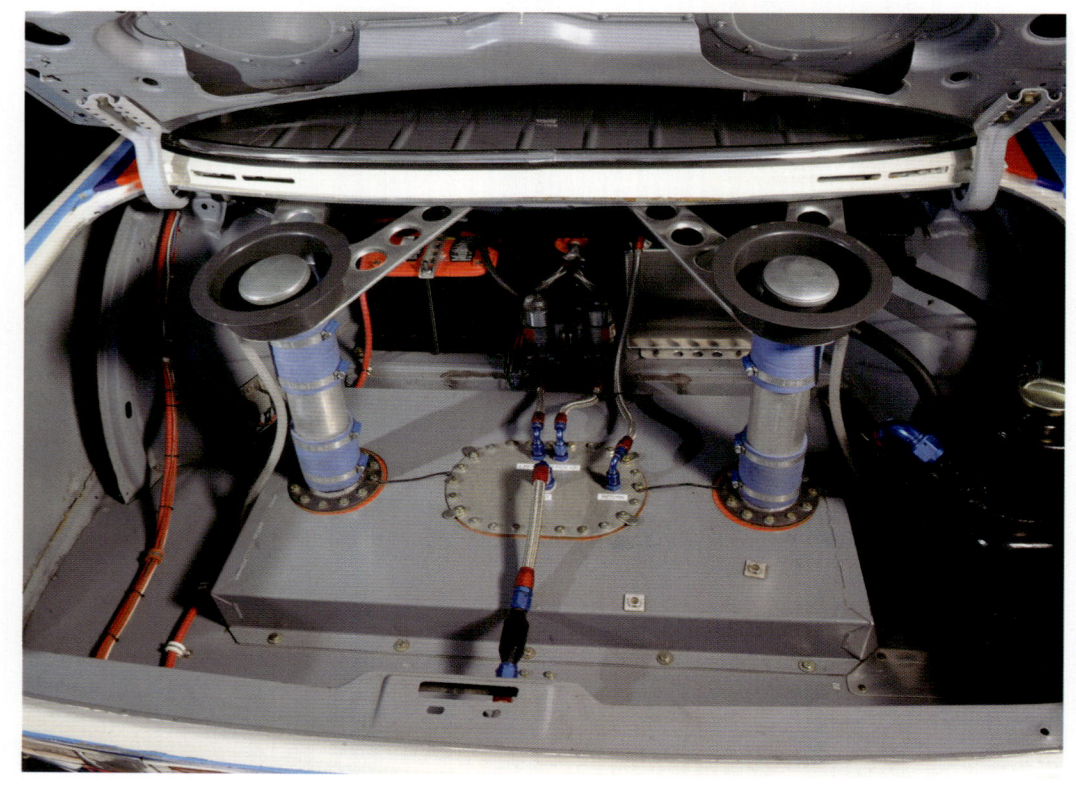

Twin fuel fillers, each with a wide neck, enabled pit crews to refuel a racing CSL in the shortest possible time.

THE CSL AND THE RACING COUPÉS

> ## A REPLICA RACER
>
> The 1977 ETCC-winning Alpina Gösser Beer car was built from a bodyshell numbered 221 1365, which strictly made it a standard 3.0 CS, despite the lightweight body panels with which it was supplied to Alpina by BMW.
>
> A replica car also exists. Built from car number 227 5492, it was created by a Dutch BMW enthusiast.

Luigi Racing campaigned three cars, of which two were new. In the successful 1976 3.0-litre car, Carlo Facetti was lead driver with Martino Finotto; Mohr and Umberto Grano joined the team for some events. Throughout the season, the Luigi cars placed well, and the Luigi drivers – Facetti, Xhenceval, Dieudonné, Finotto, Joosen and Grano – formed an orderly line-up behind the eventual ETCC winner at the end of the season. Interest was added at mid-season when Facetti took over preparation of the car he had been driving for Luigi Racing and continued to drive it in tandem with Finotto under the name of the Jolly Club. A win at Estoril in October was worthy, but made little difference to the overall results.

This was Alpina's year in the ETCC. As Jeremy Walton has explained, their Group 2 car was virtually a brand-new CSL, built up from one of the lightweight shells originally supplied to Alpina by BMW for Group 2 use. The engine was a 3.2-litre with the standard production 84mm stroke allied to an 89.8mm bore to give 3171cc (although figures of 3196cc and 3212cc have also been quoted). It started the season with a wet-sump lubrication system and 325bhp at a recommended maximum crankshaft speed of 8000rpm.

The regulations then in force demanded a four-speed gearbox, and Alpina fitted one that had ratios of 2.33:1, 1.47:1, 1.17:1, and a direct top. The alternator, meanwhile, was mounted at the rear and driven by a belt from the driveshaft. Other features were centre-lock wheels with a 16-inch diameter, and on-board air jacks. Overall weight was a claimed 1075kg.

Alpina had secured Dieter Quester to drive the car, but the early results were patchy. Engine troubles meant that it failed to finish in three of its first four races, although Quester won at Salzburg when partnered by Gunnar Nilsson. Then a mid-season regulation change permitted a return to dry-sump lubrication, and Alpina's fortunes changed too. Power went up to 340bhp. There were wins at the Nürburgring (with Nilsson again), at Zandvoort (with Hezemans as co-driver), at Silverstone (with Walkinshaw), and Zolder (with Patrick Nève). A fourth place in Jarama (with Walkinshaw) and a second at Estoril (with Umberto Grano) clinched the title for Quester and the big BMW.

Several teams entered 3.0 CSi cars for Group 1 events that year, although there were no spectacular results. A Team Luigi car driven by Michael Paulus, Claude de Wael, Jean Xhenceval and Jacques Berger achieved a front-row position at the Spa 24-hour event, although it did not cover itself in glory during the actual race.

1978

Driver Umberto Grano had fallen out with Luigi Racing during the 1977 season on a question of team tactics, and had immediately found a seat next to Dieter Quester in the Alpina CSL. For 1978, he was back with Luigi, once again racing their highly competitive 3.0-litre cars.

However, the 1978 season was a lacklustre one for the European Touring Car Championship. That the now elderly BMWs showed up so well in the final results was probably as much the result of sub-standard opposition as of the coupés' excellence on the tracks. Luigi Racing, now sponsored by BMW Italia, entered two cars and rarely finished outside the top three, although neither car finished at Monza or the Nürburgring. When the points were totalled up from that year's 12 rounds, Grano was the clear European Champion. Snapping at the heels of the Luigi cars all the time had been the Jolly Club CSL driven by Facetti and Finotto. This year, they were campaigning the 1977 Alpina car but their results were erratic. Wins at Monza, Salzburg and Brno were countered by too many retirements, and the car seems not even to have been entered in the final rounds of the championship.

■ THE CSL AND THE RACING COUPÉS

THE BMW ART CARS

BMW's Art Cars are now a well-known collection, but there were none before 1975. In that year, French driver (and auctioneer) Hervé Poulain had the idea of inviting a contemporary artist to use a car as a canvas. The artist he chose was Alexander Calder, who was also a personal friend, and the car he chose was a BMW 3.0 CSL that Poulain planned to drive in the 1975 Le Mans 24 Hours race.

Calder developed his design on a scale model of the 'Batmobile' car, later transferring it to the full-size machine. This was then shown in public during May 1975 at the Louvre Museum in Paris, in advance of the race that was held in mid-June. The car did not finish the race and was subsequently returned to BMW, who retain it to this day as part of their Art Cars collection.

Recognizing the publicity value of the first Art Car, BMW commissioned a second, this time a car that was earmarked for the 1976 Le Mans entry. The artist they chose was Frank Stella, and the car was the Motorsport division's unique turbocharged CSL. Stella's observations on the project were interesting:

The starting point for the Art Cars was racing livery. In the old days there used to be a tradition of identifying a car with its country by colour. Now they get a number and they get advertising. It's a paint job, one way or another. The idea for mine was that it's from a drawing on graph paper. The graph paper is what it is, a graph, but when it's morphed over the car's forms it becomes interesting, and adapting the drawing to the racing car's forms is interesting. Theoretically it's like painting on a shaped canvas.

This second car is also preserved in the BMW Art Cars collection.

(*continued opposite and overleaf*)

The first BMW Art Car was created from a CSL by Alexander Calder for Hervé Poulain. The two are seen here discussing a miniature version, and Calder is seen on the opposite page with the full-size car.

THE CSL AND THE RACING COUPÉS

The Alexander Calder car has to be seen in colour to appreciate the full effect of the artist's work.

91

THE CSL AND THE RACING COUPÉS

(continued from previous pages)

The Frank Stella CSL Art Car raced at Le Mans in 1976, and again at Dijon later that year. Here it lines up at the start in Dijon; Porsches from most of the visible opposition.

THE CSL AND THE RACING COUPÉS

The Frank Stella car is still part of the BMW collection, and is regularly displayed at the company's museum. DAVIDWIZ/WIKIMEDIA

US artist Frank Stella created the second BMW Art Car from a turbocharged CSL in 1976.

93

■ THE CSL AND THE RACING COUPÉS

Nearly five decades after their heyday on the tracks, the racing CSLs continue to command high prices among collectors. However, not all are quite what they seem. This car was actually built from a 3.0 CSi in 1981, and has been campaigned in Group 4 events wearing the legendary Team Luigi colours. It was sold at auction in 2012 by H&H Classics.

1979

Once again, the ETCC lacked sparkle in 1979. Every single one of the 13 rounds fell to a BMW of one sort or another, and the top two contenders were Luigi Racing (whose two CSLs regularly claimed at least one place among the first three) and the Jolly Club team of Facetti and Finotto, who were still campaigning the 1977 Alpina car.

In the final analysis, the ETCC title fell to Facetti and Finotto, with Luigi Racing's team of Xhenceval, Dieudonné and Van Hove in equal third place, and the other regular Luigi drivers Umberto Grano and Joosen right behind them in joint sixth place.

So it was that the CSL coupés carried off the European Touring Car Championship for the sixth and final time. The car's FIA homologation ran out at the end of the season, and there could be no more front-line appearances for 1980. It had unquestionably been the most successful touring-car racer of its generation. Dominating European events for so long was an astounding achievement, marred only slightly by the declining quality of the opposition in its final years.

94

THE CSL AND THE RACING COUPÉS

CHASSIS NUMBERS FOR CSL MODELS

BMW cognoscenti usually recognize four distinct groups of roadgoing CSL models, plus an entirely separate group of competition cars.

First-series production cars (1971–1972)
These cars were essentially modified 3.0 CS models with lightweight panels but the standard drivetrain with its carburettor engine. Their serial numbers were contained within the standard 3.0 CS sequences, and there were 169 of them in all. Their numbers are prefixed by 221 and they fall into the standard sequence running from 221 0001 to 221 4006. Some of them became competition machines; one example is 221 1365, supplied to Alpina for completion as a Group 2 racer but not eventually completed until 1977 as that company's Gösser Beer-sponsored car.

Second-series production cars (1972–1973)
These were the 1973-model cars with 3003cc fuel-injected engines. There were 429 of them with left-hand drive and a further 500 with right-hand drive – a total of 929 in all. Their identification numbers were 227 5001 to 227 5429 (LHD) and 228 5001 to 228 5500 (RHD).

Third-series production cars (1973–1974)
These were the 1974-model cars with 3153cc engines. There were just 110 of them, all with left-hand drive, and all with the 'Batmobile' aerodynamic addenda. Their identification numbers were 227 5430 to 227 5539.

Fourth-series production cars (1974-1975)
These were the 1975-model cars and were essentially the same as the 1974 models. There were just 57 of them, and they had their own series of identification numbers: 435 5001 to 435 5057

Competition cars
The cars designated by BMW as competition machines were picked from the standard production sequences in the beginning, but from 1973 onwards were numbered in a special sequence. It is not currently possible to identify every one of these cars, of which there were supposedly 21 in all. As with all competition cars, rebuilds and replacements confuse the issue, and records are the last thing on the mind of those who build and prepare the cars. The sequence used for these late competition cars appears to have followed on from that for the third-series production sequence (1974), ending with 227 6000.

This is the VIN plate of a 2800 CS. The car in fact went on to become a Group 2 3.0 CSL racer with 3.5-litre engine, but retained its original number.

The chassis plate of a CSL. The car is shown as a 3.0 CS but only the serial number proves that it was built as a CSL – and one of the very last.

95

CHAPTER FIVE

DEVELOPING A SUCCESSOR

By the end of the 1960s, BMW had a four-tier model range. Oldest, and therefore first in line for replacement, were the Neue Klasse four-door saloons, which dated from 1961. The big coupés of the E9 series were next in line, as they dated in essence from 1964 and the E120, even though their six-cylinder incarnations were much newer and had been introduced only in 1968. Introduced in 1966 were the strong-selling two-door derivatives of the Neue Klasse, the 02 or E14 range. At the top of the range were the big E3 saloons, related mechanically to the E9s and introduced at the same time, in 1968.

Even though the 1960s had been very successful for BMW, it was still a relatively small company and had to husband its engineering resources carefully. Over-rapid expansion had put paid to its Bavarian rivals at Glas, a fact which the BMW Board knew only too well after picking up the pieces of that company in the middle of the decade. So the product replacement policy that was established by about 1970 was quite cautious, even if it was outwardly ambitious.

First, the engine line-up would be expanded. The existing four-cylinders would remain in production but would be supplemented by a new range of small six-cylinders, with swept volumes of between 2.0 and 2.5 litres. Then above them would be further developments of the existing six-cylinders, which would cater for all sizes anticipated above 2.5 litres.

At the bottom end of the range, the two-door cars would then be replaced by a new range of small saloons; these attracted the code of E21 and the marketing name of 3 Series. For BMW, these would be very important, as the existing 02 models gave the company a strong seller in a market sector where Mercedes-Benz was not represented. The initial range of two-door models was slated for summer 1975 introduction.

The big coupés would be next in line for replacement. As low-volume models, they could not benefit from the same dedicated level of investment as either the two-door or the four-door saloons. However, they could piggy-back on the new engineering that would be developed for the four-door models, which, as the more up-market of the two ranges, would have more in common with these prestigious cars. The project to develop them was given the code number of E24, and the marketing name chosen was 6 Series. The target date for their introduction was spring 1976. Finally, the big E3 saloons would be replaced in 1977 by a new range known as the E23 or 7 Series, with which BMW hoped to present a fully credible competitor for the Mercedes-Benz S-Class range. These cars would share some of their engineering with the 6 Series coupés, and the two ranges could be further developed in parallel.

This product policy was further complicated by BMW's wish to expand sales in the USA. The marque had become firmly established in that very large market in the later 1960s, largely thanks to the 02 two-door saloons, and the BMW Board saw ample scope for expansion there. However, from 1968 the Federal Government had begun to introduce legislation to improve crash survivability and to reduce noxious exhaust emissions. The plan was for such legislation to get tighter every year and nobody in the car industry knew quite where it was likely to end. This introduced a huge element of uncertainty into the future plans of every manufacturer that wanted to sell cars in the USA. Wisely, BMW decided to bite the bullet and develop its cars with the current and future legislation in mind. One result was that there would often be major differences between the cars sold in the USA and those sold in other countries during the 1970s and 1980s.

DEVELOPING A SUCCESSOR

TOP AND ABOVE: *Italian coachbuilder Bertone was keen for BMW to take an interest in his designs. Ideally, they would buy one and pay him a royalty on every car built, however, the clever Spicup, built on a 2800 saloon platform in 1968, remained a one-off. It was more roadster than coupé.*

97

■ DEVELOPING A SUCCESSOR

Pictured here with the striking Turbo coupé that marked the start of his tenure at BMW, Paul Bracq was the man with overall responsibility for its look.

BELOW: *The Turbo coupé was a real show-stopper – and deliberately so – yet its ideas did not remain unused, and the later BMW M1 showed strong traces of its influence.*

98

DEVELOPING A SUCCESSOR

Developing the E24

As far as the new big coupés were concerned, therefore, everything had to wait until the basics of the new E12 5 Series range had been settled. It was 1973 before serious work on the E24 programme began. In the mean time, BMW had lost no time in doing some preliminary research, and as part of this they had asked an outside styling consultancy to propose ideas for the shape of the new coupé.

That outside consultancy seems to have been Giugiaro's Italdesign company, established in 1968 after the designer had left Bertone. Bertone had of course been responsible for the 3200 CS coupé of 1962, and the company was still submitting designs for BMW's consideration in the late 1960s. Among those were the 1969 Spicup, a futuristic two-door sports model on the 2800 platform, and the 1970 Garmisch two-door saloon, originally sketched in 1969. No doubt the Bertone connection had brought Giugiaro to BMW's attention, although it is not clear which side made an approach to the other about a new coupé design.

One way or the other, the Giugiaro coupé proposal did not sit well with BMW's new Sales Director Bob Lutz, who had joined BMW at the start of 1972 after long-serving Paul Hahnemann left as the result of a clash with the company's Chairman, Eberhard von Kuenheim. Lutz later wrote a book about his experiences in the motor industry (*Guts – 8 Laws of Business from One of the Most Innovative Business leaders of Our Time*), and he remembered it like this:

> I arrived in Munich just as the company was preparing the replacement for the beautiful 3.0 CS coupé. One of the problems that the company hoped to rectify in the new car was the relative difficulty of getting in and out of it.…The company's answer was a taller, rather stodgy design, ordered up at an outside styling consultant. I

Central to BMW's model policy for the 1970s was a new medium saloon, which entered production as the first 5 Series. Known internally as the E12 type, it shared much of its engineering with the new big coupés.

DEVELOPING A SUCCESSOR

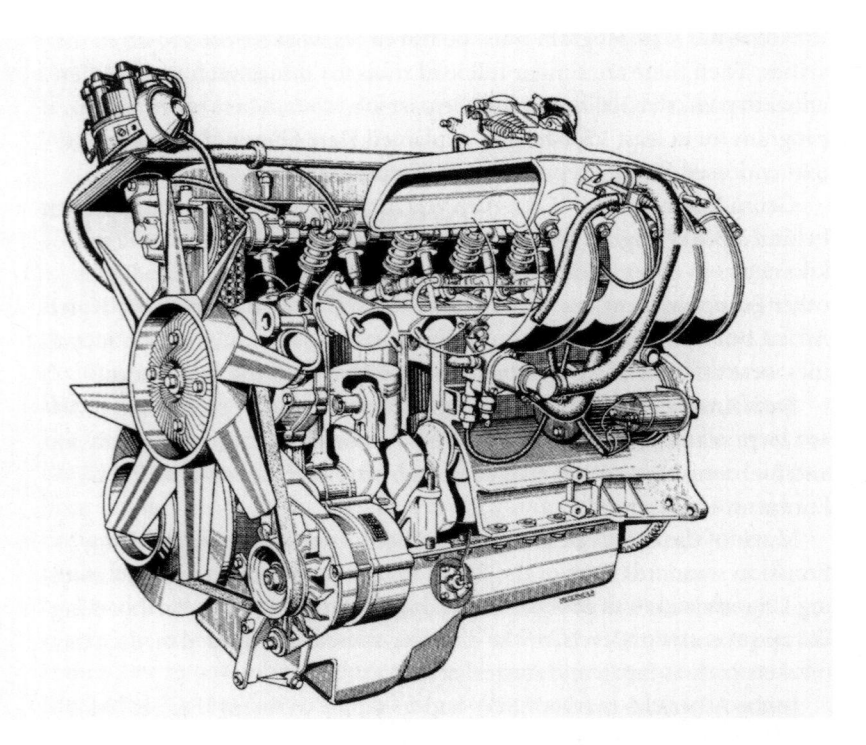

The big-block six-cylinder engine had proved itself in the E9 coupés, and was earmarked for use in their replacements as well. This cutaway publicity drawing shows a fuel-injected version from 1976, the year when the new E24 models became available.

rebelled, and sketched out another, lower design on a piece of notebook paper – which, after passing through BMW's styling department, eventually became the 6 Series coupé.

By this stage, the BMW styling department was in the hands of Paul Bracq, a talented Frenchman who had spent much of the 1960s in a similar position at Mercedes-Benz and who had been recruited by BMW in 1970. Here, he had replaced the hugely respected Wilhelm Hofmeister, who retired in January that year. On the engineering side, meanwhile, product development was firmly under the control of Berhnard Osswald, who had been in the job since 1965 and still had a few years to go before he, too, would retire. Reporting to him, and with specific responsibility for the E24 range, was chassis development engineer Walter Stork, another recent recruit to BMW, who had joined in 1970. Certainly, the E24 6 Series was developed at an interesting time for BMW, when some of the old hands who had overseen its revival during the 1960s were still in place and some of the new talent that would take it through the next decade had begun to have an influence.

The critical engineering component around which the E24 would be designed was the 'platform' that was drawn up for the E12 5 Series. The new saloon was intended to be slightly larger than the Neue Klasse type it replaced, in line with a planned move up-market, and the wheelbase dimension chosen for it was 2625mm. This was longer than the 2550mm of the Neue Klasse, and it can hardly have been a coincidence that it was exactly the same as the wheelbase of the E9 coupés. In practice, the production E24 would have a wheelbase of 2626mm, after an extra millimetre had crept into the design during the development process.

That new platform was also drawn up around the engines it was planned to carry. The plan was for the new saloon to have both four-cylinders drawn from the existing M10 range and six-cylinders drawn from the M30 range. The M30 range was also to provide the engines for the new big coupé, just as it had done for the E9 coupés, so the synergy was perfect. As for suspension, the MacPherson strut front and semi-trailing-arm rear designs that had served BMW so well during the 1960s could be developed further. The front struts were angled rearwards and wheel travel was increased to deliver more ride comfort than before. At the rear, the springs and dampers were arranged so that they both acted on the hub carriers; on earlier BMWs, they had been mounted separately. The front-disc, rear-drum braking system

DEVELOPING A SUCCESSOR

Ideas pioneered on the Turbo coupé also found their way into the early stages of the E24 design programme, as the low, streamlined nose in this 1972 proposal demonstrates. A major preoccupation at the time was how to meet US crash-safety regulations without compromising the car's looks, and the inset sketches here suggest a way of doing that.

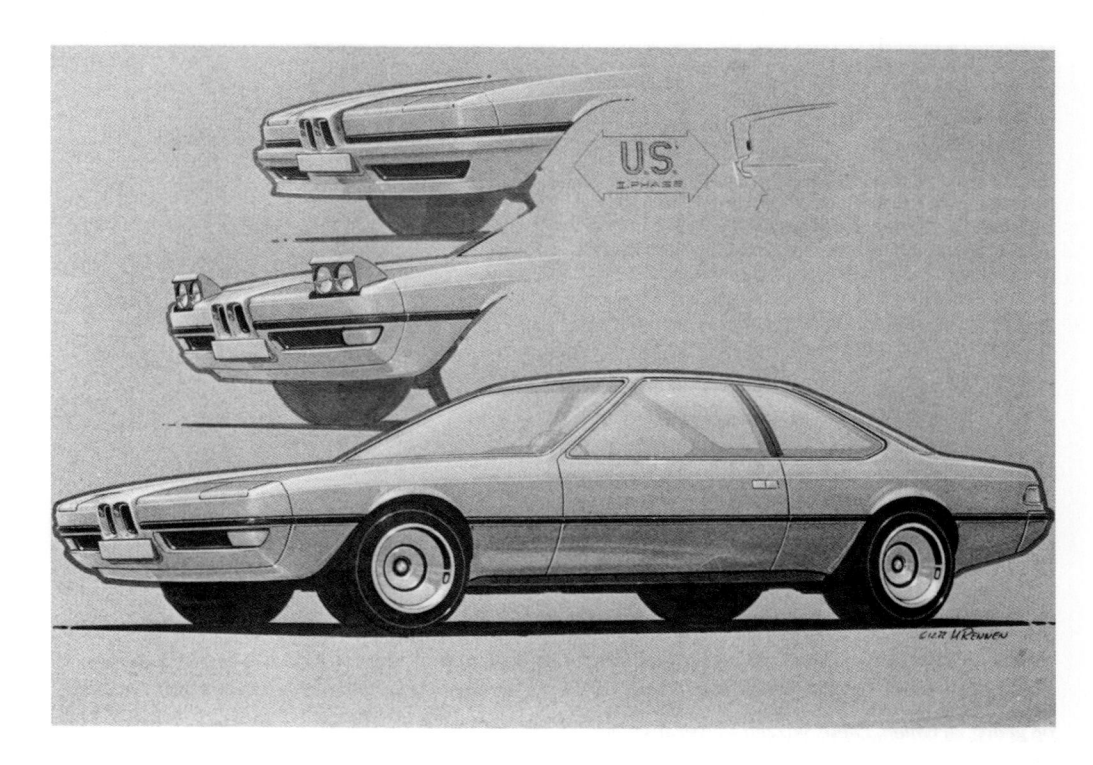

was good enough for the lower-powered versions of the saloon, but the E24 coupés would have an all-disc installation that was also planned for the bigger-engined versions of the saloon.

A key difference between the 5 Series saloon and the 6 Series coupé, however, would be the driving position. It would be set lower and further back in the coupé and would have an impact on the space available in the cabin for rear-seat passengers. Offering less cabin space in the 6 Series than in the considerably less expensive 5 Series saloons was never going to be a problem, though. Coupés – even those with four seats – are not bought by those who regularly carry four people.

This driving position had to be established before Paul Bracq and his team could begin work on the shape of the new coupé. A further important consideration that affected their work was US safety legislation. New crashworthiness tests devised by the Federal authorities made clear that the elegant, pillarless design of the E9 coupés would no longer be viable because it offered too little strength in the roof. One of the planned new tests involved dropping a car on its roof to see how well it protected its occupants from being crushed, so the roof of the new coupé would have to be reinforced in some way. BMW's solution was to incorporate a rollover bar in the centre, between the B pillars. Bracq successfully concealed it by having the upper sections of those pillars painted matt black to blend visually with the windows on either side of them. Using Parsol Bronze tinted glass helped in this process – and the choice was very deliberate because the bronze glass was only 60 per cent as effective as the alternative green type.

The body engineers also had their say in other areas of the car, where they had to work in tandem with the styling team to get the desired result. The rollover bar was supplemented by some localized reinforcement around the windscreen and rear window, while the passenger cabin was protected at the front by a sturdy cross-member ahead of the instrument panel and at the rear by reinforcement in the area of the parcels shelf. BMW publicity material would later refer to 'rigid longitudinal supports', and the front of the car was designed to crumple progressively in an impact and so dissipate the forces as much as possible before they reached the passenger compartment. This crumple zone was later claimed to be 23 per cent stronger than its equivalent on the E9 coupés, while the body was said to have 60 per cent greater torsional strength.

All of this strengthening added extra weight to the new coupé, and by the time it reached production the 6 Series

DEVELOPING A SUCCESSOR

was between 90 and 115 kg (roughly 200–250 lb) heavier, model for model, than the E9 it replaced. In fact, BMW had over-engineered the body to some degree; when the E24 was revised at the start of the 1980s for the 1983 model-year, a second look at the structural design made it possible to take quite a lot of weight out of the bodyshell without sacrificing any of its crashworthiness.

Working within such constraints, the design that Paul Bracq and his team achieved was remarkably elegant. It looked heavier than the E9s, but that was inevitable; it was longer, lower and wider, too. One key achievement was an increase in the glass area of 7 per cent, which gave it much of the airy, spacious appearance (and feel from the inside) that had been so successful on the older cars.

Bracq was keen on concealed headlights that were raised from the bodywork electrically when needed, and he showed these in the BMW Turbo concept car that occupied much of his time before its introduction in 1972. Some of the early sketches his team did for the E24 also incorporated pop-up headlamps, but in the end there seems to have been a corporate decision that the front end of all the new designs for the 1970s should have a family resemblance. That meant a 'shark-nose' design (as on the E9s), which was raked backwards from its upper edge, with four circular headlamps in a blacked-out horizontal grille and BMW's trademark twin-kidney grilles picked out in bright metal in the centre. True, it was a little conservative, but it was the right decision for BMW, who needed to create a strong family identity for their products. Putting pop-up headlamps on to just one range of cars would have detracted from that.

The shape of the E24 could not progress independently. It had to retain a family resemblance to the other new BMWs under development at the start of the 1970s, and at the same time it had to be readily recognizable as a relative of the E9 coupé it was destined to replace. A further important consideration was that it had to look like a bigger and more expensive car than the E12 5 Series on whose platform it was based, and Bracq achieved this partly by giving it longer front and rear overhangs. An extra 135mm (5.3in) overall made an important difference without unbalancing the styling, and also enabled the team to give the car a larger boot than their E9 predecessors. With 14.6 cu ft by the time production began, it was nearly 25 per cent larger than the 11.8 cu ft boot of the older design.

The forward-leaning 'shark-nose' design may have been distinctive, but at a time when aerodynamics were becoming increasingly important in car design, it did seem like a retrogressive feature. There was, of course, a very good reason why its continued use did not cause concern at BMW headquarters in Munich: BMW did not yet have their own wind tunnel. When they wanted to use one – as they had when designing the aerodynamic addenda for the 'Batmobile' racing coupés in 1973 – the only realistic option was to hire the tunnel that belonged to Mercedes-Benz in Stuttgart. BMW was hardly going to take the prototypes of any new car designed to steal sales from Mercedes models into a Mercedes-owned facility, so none of the new designs of the 1970s were tested in a wind tunnel. It is said that their high drag coefficients came as a nasty shock to BMW executives when some were eventually tested, many years later.

Even though Paul Bracq had been discouraged from using the concealed headlamps of his 1972 Turbo show car in production designs, he did manage to incorporate one of its distinctive features in the shape of the E24. In fact, it was liked so much that he was asked to use it on all the new BMWs of the 1970s. This feature was a raised 'flute' in the centre of the bonnet, which not only added definition to that panel but also linked with the twin-kidney grilles on the nose. The E21 3 Series and E23 7 Series had it as well as the E24 6 Series. The E12 5 Series, signed off for production before Bracq had really had time to make his mark at BMW, lost its original flat bonnet in August 1976 to take on the new 'house' style.

One particularly tricky styling problem arose from the US Federal safety regulations. Those regulations demanded that cars on sale in the USA after the start of 1974 should have bumpers that prevented damage to the main lights in a low-speed parking collision. Existing production BMWs had bumpers mounted on damper struts that helped to absorb low-speed impacts. Unfortunately, these looked simply hideous, adding odd protrusions front and rear that unbalanced the styling, and BMW's guess that they would be a major deterrent to sales in countries where they were not required by law must surely have been right.

Between them, Bracq's team and the BMW engineers were unable to come up with a better solution by the time the E24 models had to be signed off for production, which was probably in late 1974 or early 1975. So the E24 models destined for the USA were given special extended bumpers. Everybody at BMW knew they were ungainly, but they treated them as the necessary evil that they were. Other countries had a much more elegant design, and it was not until many years later that BMW came up with a bumper design that would both meet US requirements and look attractive. On the E24s, it reached production on the 1988 models – and by then the cars were less than two years from the end of their production run.

Interior of the E24

The cabin design of a high-performance coupé such as the E24 has to combine function with a form that reflects the car's sporty nature. At the same time it must remind the owner (and any other occupants) that this car was an expensive purchase made by a person with discerning tastes. In the case of the E24, it also had to have a clear family resemblance to the interior of other contemporary models from BMW.

As in the E9 coupés, the rear seat was designed as two individual 'armchairs'. On top of that, the latest US safety regulations were insisting on head restraints for the front seats and there was every reason to assume that rear head restraints might become mandatory at some point in the future. As a result, the rear seats and parcels shelf were designed to accommodate head restraints if these became necessary, or to work visually without them if they did not.

The front seats were designed with bolsters to provide the expected support and sporty feel, and of course they incorporated adjustable head restraints as well. Their structures could not be shared with any others in the BMW range, because only in the E24 would they be required to tilt forwards to give access to the rear seats; although the seats in the two-door E21 3 Series had to do the same, the seats were physically smaller and unsuitable for the E24. For those customers who wanted less comfort and more support, it would be possible to specify Recaro racing-style seats. Upholstery in a car of this class was always going to include leather, and in fact this was made standard for production. Even the alternative velour facings came with leather bolsters when the E24 was launched.

Then there was the dashboard. On both the E12 5 Series and E21 3 Series, it had an angled centre section that gave the driver a better view of instruments and controls than was available with a conventional 'flat' dashboard. The E24 design followed a similar theme, with the angled section helping to give the feel of a wrap-around 'cockpit' such as might be found in a com-

The interior design came together in a full-size wooden buck, pictured here during 1973. The idea of having two separately shaped rear seats was already in place.

■ DEVELOPING A SUCCESSOR

Meeting safety requirements was often a problem for the stylists, but this versatile solution for the rear head restraints was a masterpiece. A speaker for the ICE system was fitted into the horizontal surface of the housing. Ironically, many cars for the safety-conscious USA would be built without rear head restraints!

petition car. The design of the four-spoke steering wheel was also shared with the E12 and E21 models, although the wheel always looked a little too big and chunky for a sporting coupé. Nevertheless, a telescopic steering column was a practical refinement that was much appreciated by customers once the cars had gone on sale.

Of course, a flagship car deserves the latest technology, and BMW decided to launch the E24 with a brand-new system that they called Active Check Control. This was a pioneering electronic showcase for BMW in the mid-1970s. It consisted of a panel on the dashboard, outboard of the driver, that incorporated seven green warning lights. These covered engine oil level, engine coolant level, brake fluid level, brake pad wear, windscreen washer fluid level, brake lights and tail-lights.

The lights came on as a check when a 'Test' button was pressed. However, the oil light did not operate when the engine was running, and the bulb warning lights only worked when the car's lights were on. 'It is less complicated than it sounds,' explained the UK magazine *Autocar* when testing its first 6 Series in October 1976. 'Before moving off, switch on side lamps, put a foot on the pedal and touch the button; if seven tell-tales come on, you know all is well.' Even so, some early customers had trouble with it, and word began to circulate that it was little more than a gimmick. The basic idea was sound enough, though, and it was not long before other manufacturers were copying the basic principles of the system for their own cars.

DEVELOPING A SUCCESSOR

The Final Stages of the E24

As development progressed, so the engineering of the E24 range was refined. Although comfort was a high priority, the engineers decided to use shorter springs and stiffer dampers than those on the parent E12 5 Series platform, in order to give more sporty handling. For similar reasons, they ensured that the worm-and-roller steering – otherwise the same as on the E9 coupés – had faster response. From top management came approval to equip the new BMW flagship with the latest steering development, which was a variable-ratio power-assistance system that provided enough assistance to make low-speed manoeuvring easy but reduced assistance progressively as speed rose so that there was still plenty of steering 'feel' at speed. Another engineering novelty, in this case planned for use on the E23 7 Series that was under development, was an engine-driven hydraulic pump that supplied pressure for both the steering and the brakes. As for the brakes, all-round discs were not enough. The team decided to fit ventilated discs on all four wheels, perhaps as much for their showroom appeal as for their undeniably improved stopping power. The front pair were to have twin hydraulic circuits as standard for all markets.

The engines had always been planned as members of the six-cylinder M30 family, and for initial introduction the latest version of the 3.0-litre would power the core model of the range. A long-stroke 3.2-litre version was under development for the forthcoming 7 Series and also for the final long-wheelbase E3 saloons, and its extra size would partially compensate for the power losses that were inevitable on emissions-controlled engines for the USA. It could also be used to create a top-of-the-range model for Europe. Finally, the question arose of whether there should be a stripped-out entry-level E24 to replace the 2500 CS version of the E9 coupé. A 625 CS model with the 2.5-litre M30 engine was certainly planned but, as engine development man Georg Ederer told Jeremy Walton (BMW 6 Series Enthusiast's Companion), weight counted against it and it was cancelled at the last minute.

As for gearboxes, the E24 range would need both manual and automatic types. The gearbox chosen as standard

The overall dimensions of the E24 were of course dictated by a number of factors, not least the length of the big six-cylinder engine. This cutaway drawing, released when the cars were new, shows how everything had been carefully packaged into the design.

■ DEVELOPING A SUCCESSOR

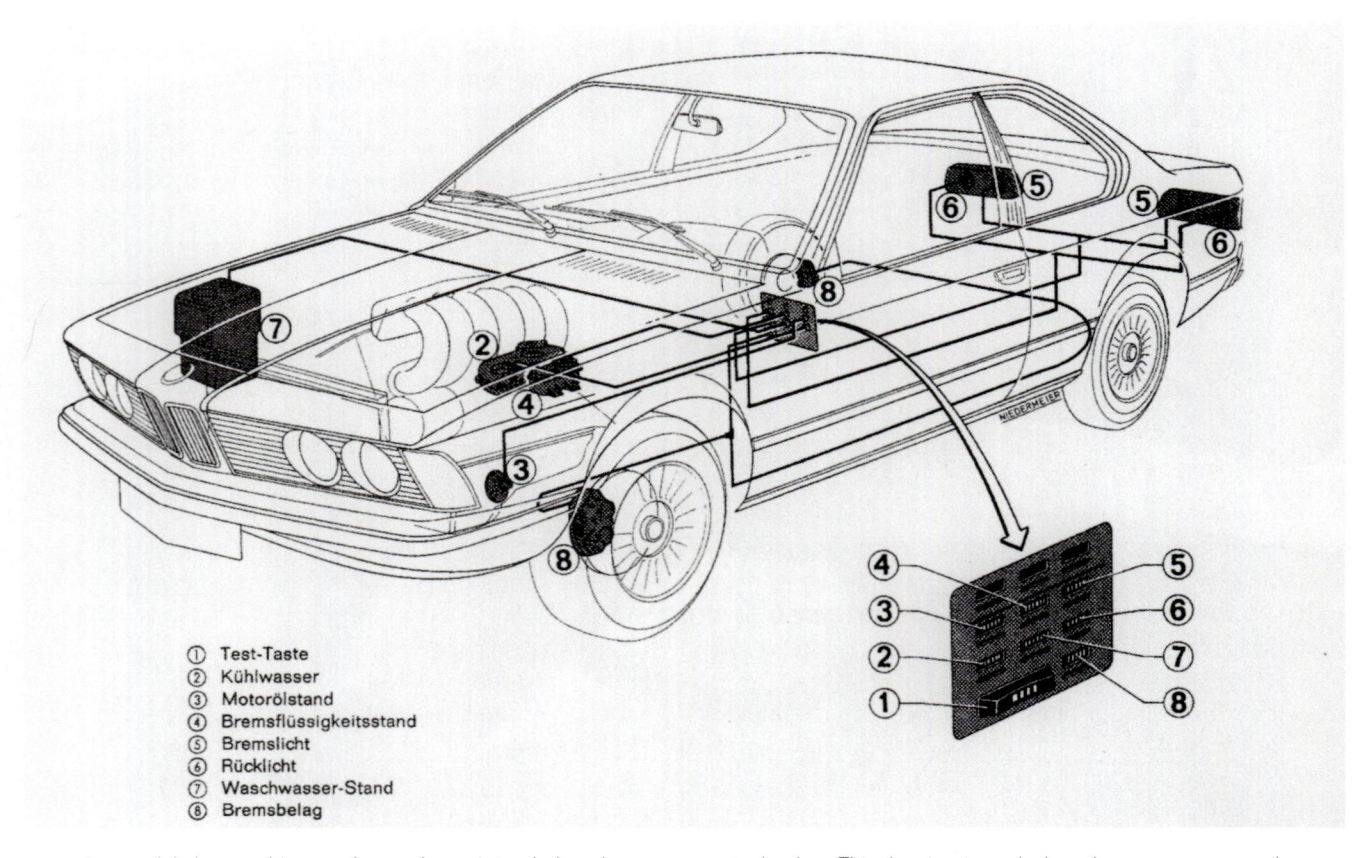

① Test-Taste
② Kühlwasser
③ Motorölstand
④ Bremsflüssigkeitsstand
⑤ Bremslicht
⑥ Rücklicht
⑦ Waschwasser-Stand
⑧ Bremsbelag

As a prestige model, the new big coupé was always intended to showcase new technology. This drawing, issued when the cars were new, shows the layout of the Check Control system, with its dashboard panel: (1) test button; (2) coolant; (3) oil level; (4) brake-fluid level; (5) brake lights; (6) tail lights; (7) washer-fluid level; and (8) brake-pad wear indicator.

BMW's new big saloon for the mid-1970s was the E23, the first 7 Series. It was a formidable statement of intent, although early examples became notorious for minor problems. The car shared much of its engineering with the E24 coupés.

106

DEVELOPING A SUCCESSOR

This sketch by Paul Bracq himself reflects both some of the lines of the production E24 and some ideas for the front end. By the time it was prepared in March 1976, the car had already entered production with a more prosaic design, so this sketch must have represented ideas for an eventual facelift.

equipment was a four-speed manual made by Getrag in Germany as their 262/9 type; although five-speed types were available, car buyers in the early 1970s generally showed little interest in them. For the optional automatic alternative BMW turned to ZF, who were already supplying automatics for other models in the range. At this stage, the best gearbox they had available was the three-speed 3 HP 22 type, introduced in 1973, which could handle torque inputs up to 320Nm (235lb ft) – and that seemed likely to be enough for the foreseeable future.

Assembly arrangements for the new coupé also presented no problem. The cars would directly replace the E9 coupés that were being assembled by Karmann in Osnabrück, who also had the contract to manufacture their bodyshells. Neither BMW nor Karmann could see any reason to change a wholly effective working relationship, and the decision that E24 assembly should be handled in the same way was probably taken quite early on. So, as with the E9s, the cost of shipping major components from Munich to Osnabrück, and of shipping the completed cars back to Munich by rail, was not a deterrent. The E24s were, after all, to be expensive machines, and that cost could be absorbed into their showroom prices.

CHAPTER SIX

THE FIRST GENERATION E24s, 1976–1982

There were two major phases in the production of the E24 models. The first one lasted from the beginning until mid-1982. At that stage, extensively re-engineered (although cosmetically nearly identical) versions of the car were introduced, and these represented the second phase of production. They remained available until the E24s were withdrawn in 1989.

As far as the European buying public was concerned, the first phase began at the Geneva Motor Show in March 1976, when the E24s were announced. Assembly had actually begun at the Karmann plant in Osnabrück in November 1975, in order to build up a stock of cars to act as media and dealer demonstrators, and to ensure that showroom examples of the new models would become available as early as possible.

The press ride-and-drive exercise was held in Marbella during April 1976, but only left-hand-drive European examples of the car were available, even though the UK and US press were invited along to gain some first impressions. Cars for sale in the USA would have a number of major differences from the European examples (see later in this chapter), and none were available until the end of

This early 630 CS shows off its well-resolved lines. The nose followed the latest BMW corporate style, and the big windows linked the design back to that of the E9 models that the new coupés replaced. Despite the best efforts of the styling team, however, there was an undeniable suggestion of heaviness about the car's appearance.

THE FIRST GENERATION E24s, 1976–1982

This is the gold publicity car also pictured on the opposite page. The setting – presumably in the south of France – was once again intended to suggest the car's appeal to wealthy customers. This was a very early European-specification car, and was probably built at the end of 1975.

the year. As for the UK, no right-hand-drive models would be made until October that year.

The European line-up consisted of two models, each available with a choice of manual or extra-cost automatic transmission. These models were badged as the 630 CS and 633 CSi. The 630 CS came with a carburettor-fed 3.0-litre engine that delivered 185PS, 0–100km/h (62mph) in 9.0 seconds and a top speed of 210km/h (130mph). The more expensive 633 CSi had the long-stroke 3.2-litre engine with Bosch L-Jetronic injection, electronic ignition and 197PS, and could hit 100km/h (62mph) in 8.5 seconds before going on to a 215km/h (133.5mph) top speed. These were very healthy performance figures for a full four-seater coupé in the mid-1970s.

Specifications inevitably differed from one country to the next to suit buyer tastes, which was one reason why the UK never received the carburetted model at all. Nevertheless, the UK was one of the markets to take cars with headlamp washers as standard; they were optional in many countries, and in Scandinavian countries were replaced by the headlamp wash-wipe system demanded by local regulations. Electric windows and electric door mirrors were standard everywhere (although in some countries the passenger's mirror cost extra). The standard European upholstery had velour wearing surfaces with leather bolsters; all-leather was another extra-cost option. Most markets had head restraints for all four seats, and in one of the two lidded stowage boxes behind them was a first-aid kit. Inertia-reel front seat belts were standard.

Further extra-cost options included metallic paint and an electric slide-and-tilt sunroof, sports suspension (gas dampers, thicker anti-roll bars and stiffer springs) and multi-spoke BBS-Mahle alloy wheels. A limited-slip differential made by ZF was available; although it was advertised as standard on UK cars in the beginning, it was in practice an extra-cost option. Buyers could spend more on Recaro front seats and on a three-spoke steering wheel that suited the car's GT nature far better than the standard stodgy four-spoke item. An uprated 65-amp alternator could also be had, and of course air conditioning was also an extra-cost option. In the UK, Alpina multi-spoke alloy wheels were made part of the standard specification from the beginning.

'It is a very impressive car indeed,' concluded the UK weekly *Autocar* after road-testing a manual-gearbox 633 CSi for its issue dated 16 October 1976. The magazine pointed out that the car was aimed at 'the sort of market

■ THE FIRST GENERATION E24s, 1976–1982

A tilt-and-slide sunroof with electric operation became an extra-cost option.

RIGHT: *The tail badges on these early cars were mounted on a black plinth. These were the two European launch models; there was also an emissions-controlled 630 CSi for North America.*

An early publicity picture for the car, showing a 630 CS cornering hard. Handling was excellent, despite the weight. There was no door mirror for the passenger's side of the car unless the buyer ordered one.

110

THE FIRST GENERATION E24s, 1976–1982

THE TWR HALLMARK EDITION

Tom Walkinshaw Racing was set up in 1976 to design and build both road and racing cars, and to manage racing activity as well. During 1977, the company developed a specification for the 633 CSi that it called the 'Hallmark'. The name came from the hallmarked solid-silver ashtray, and the uprated car was approved by BMW in the UK and in Germany, although the cars were available only in the UK. The typical cost of one of these uprated cars was around £21,000 at a time when a standard 633 CSi cost less than £15,000. Few were built, and the precise number is not known.

The Hallmark specification included a blueprinted engine. Springs and dampers were uprated, and the road wheels were changed to Alpina multi-spoke types with 7-inch front rims and 8-inch rears, running on the latest Pirelli P7 low-profile tyres. The cars were given a special apron front spoiler and could be supplied with hand-painted coachlines as well. Interior changes included a Motorsport steering wheel and 'Hallmark' emblems on the head restraints.

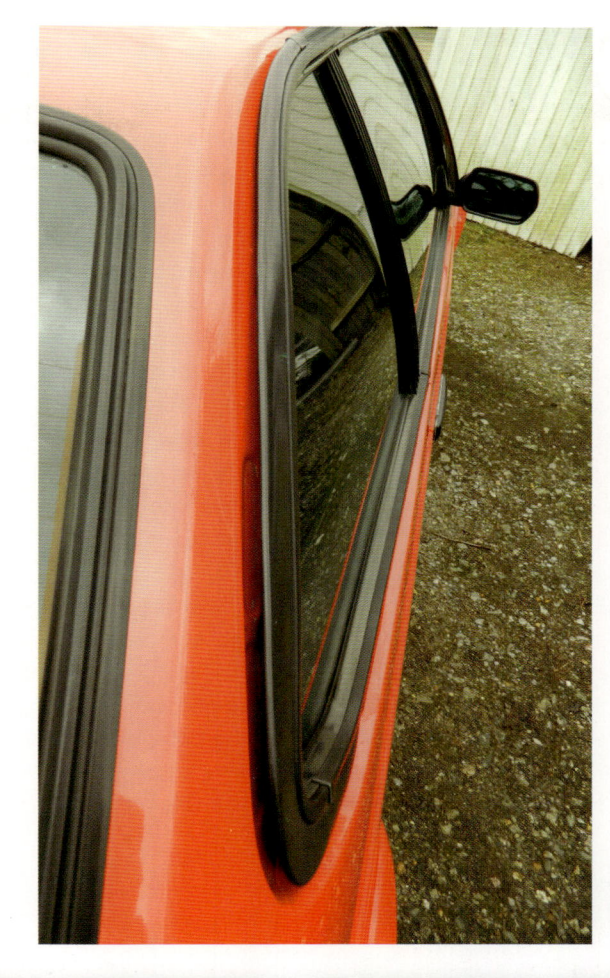

ABOVE RIGHT: BMW were always good at concealing the air outlets for the passenger cabin. On the E9 coupés, it had been behind the BMW emblem on the rear pillar; on the E24, it was behind the rain guttering. This is actually a later E24 model, with the all-black Shadowline exterior trim option.

RIGHT: Seen in a more dignified setting, this is that same early car, registered in Munich as M-ED 2449. This picture was intended to demonstrate that the car looked perfectly at home in elegant surroundings.

111

THE FIRST GENERATION E24s, 1976–1982

where buyers will justifiably expect great things. We can only say on conclusion of a test we have thoroughly enjoyed, that owners are not likely to be disappointed.'

Autocar found the 633 CSi to be quicker than the old 3.0 CSi, although not as quick as a lightweight 3.0 CSL. Fuel consumption, an important issue in the UK after the 1973–1974 Oil Crisis, was very reasonable, and the test spoke of the car's 'ability to better 20mpg while regularly putting more than 90 miles in every hour in motorway travel…. With moderate use of the performance, owners should quite readily stretch the economy to 25mpg.' Fit and finish were also of a very high standard (although a window had to be adjusted to reduce wind noise): 'the superb engine and responsiveness of the 633… will delight the owner once he has bought the car [but] the impressive interior finish and layout… will sell it to him in the first place.'

Less satisfactory was the ventilation, a common BMW failing of the time, and of course the price of just over £14,000 on the road did give rise to some comment. 'A fine car, but a formidable price,' said *Autocar*. However, it looked as though BMW had judged the car well for its intended market: of the 8000 that the company hoped to build each year, no fewer than 500 were expected to come to the UK, which was expected to be the second-largest export market for the E24 range after the USA. When *Motor Sport* tried an example for its August 1977 issue, Bill Boddy described the 633 CSi as 'near perfection'.

Enter the 635 CSi

'Near perfection' may have been an accurate description of the 633 CSi press demonstrator that *Motor Sport* borrowed, but some customers were not so lucky. The wind noise that *Autocar* experienced with their demonstrator car never could be eliminated entirely, and it seems that a number of customers had similar problems. Some cars appeared to leak through their door and window seals, too, and there were some reports of trim that either did not fit properly or rattled and squeaked.

This would never do in a car of the 6 Series' pretensions, and BMW moved swiftly to put things right. From August 1977, assembly was moved to their own factory at Dingolfing, where they were able to keep a closer eye on any problems that arose and to put them right more quickly. Karmann retained the contract to manufacture and paint the bodyshells, but that was all. They had built 9800 E24s since the autumn of 1975.

The dashboard of the E24 had an angled centre section, which gave a cockpit-like feel to the driving position. The instruments were beautifully clear, but the four-spoke wheel looked a bit heavy-handed.

THE FIRST GENERATION E24s, 1976–1982

The Active Check Control system had its own panel, just outboard of the steering column. It was intended to simplify the business of regular checks on the car's systems, but at the time was sometimes thought to be an unwelcome complication or even just a gimmick.

Introduced in 1978, the 635 CSi became the new top model. Stripes and spoilers are the obvious distinguishing features on this early publicity car, together with the optional cross-spoke wheels.

THE FIRST GENERATION E24s, 1976–1982

Meanwhile, BMW had supplemented the range with a third engine option, this time a 3.5-litre size that came in a model called the 635 CSi. For a time, this would be available alongside the original 630 CS and 633 CSi models, although it would not made available for the USA until many years later. For European markets that took left-hand drive, it was introduced in July 1977 as a 1978 model. Although nobody could know it at this stage, the 635 CSi would go on to become far and away the best-selling version of the E24 range.

The genesis of the new 3.5-litre engine was a complex one and, as time would tell, its evolution was not over yet. Its origins lay in the 3498cc Siamese-bore Motorsport engine (coded M49) that Paul Rosche had developed during 1973 for the CSL 'Batmobile' racers. That engine had been further developed, not least with four-valve cylinder heads for racing, and by the mid-1970s BMW was working on a version with a slightly shorter stroke that gave a swept volume of 3453cc. In four-valve form, that made the M88/1 DOHC engine that went into the M1 coupé of 1978. In two-valve SOHC form with the M30 cylinder head, tuned for the road rather than the track and with conventional wet-sump lubrication instead of the dry-sump type of the racing and M88 engines, it became the M90 engine that powered the 635 CSi.

In production trim, the M90 developed 218PS at 5200rpm and 304Nm (224lb ft) of torque at 4000rpm. Those figures show that both maximum power and maximum torque came lower down the rev range than on either the 3.0-litre or 3.2-litre E24 engines. Most important, though, was the increased flexibility of the 3.5-litre engine, which delivered 259Nm (191lb ft) of torque all the way from 2000rpm to 5900rpm. This was more than the old 3.0-litre carburettor engine could muster at its 3500rpm torque peak. A bigger-bore exhaust than on the other E24 models of the time also gave the engine its own, deeper note when extended.

Also new, at least on a standard production E24, was a five-speed close-ratio Getrag gearbox, with direct top gear and dog's-leg gate pattern. It was a 265/5-70 type, and came with a clutch whose springs had been uprated to handle the additional torque from the engine. There was no automatic option. Suspension was stiffened with thicker anti-roll bars, and there were rubber bump stops in the front springs. All versions – including the right-hand-drive cars for the UK that became available in mid-1978 – came

The overall layout of the 635 CSi was of course the same as that of the smaller-engined cars. However, as this cutaway drawing from 1978 makes clear, the engine's inlet manifold was quite different. Also visible is the boot-lid spoiler, which was unique to the model. Note that the drawing shows a car without the rear head restraints.

THE ERNST FUCHS ART CAR

Austrian artist Ernst Fuchs was invited to create the fifth BMW Art Car from a 635 CSi during 1982. It was the first Art Car to be created from a series production model rather than a racer and the first Art Car to be entrusted to a European artist.

Fuchs has explained that his design for the car was partly inspired by a dream he had as a child. 'When painting this car I was able to express a wide range of experiences, fears, desires and invocations, as well as aesthetic, artistic freedom. I call this car "Firefox on a rabbit hunt". A rabbit can be seen running across the motorway at night and leaping over a burning car – a primal fear and a daring dream of defeating the dimensions within which we live. It tells me which colours to choose. I read its lines, its shape and I can hear its call to speed. I see this beautiful rabbit jump through the flames of love – defeating fear itself.'

The Ernst Fuchs Art Car was certainly colourful. It was based on a black 635 CSi in 1982. MICHAM6/WIKIMEDIA

THE FIRST GENERATION E24s, 1976–1982

with BBS-Mahle alloy wheels with rims half an inch wider than those optional on the 633 CSi. Tyres were now 195/70 VR 14 low-profile types, and the original equipment from the factory was Michelin XDX radials.

BMW distinguished the 635 CSi from the less expensive E34 coupés by a deep apron front spoiler that was moulded from GRP and contained four horizontal air intakes. At the rear, they added to the boot lid a black lip spoiler made of deformable plastic; the BMW roundel that it displaced was mounted in the centre of the spoiler's vertical face. Although their primary function was undeniably to mark out the top model of the range, these spoilers also had a real function at high speeds – the front one reduced lift by 50 per cent on the front wheels and the rear one reduced rear-wheel lift by 15 per cent.

All this brought extra performance to the E24 models without reducing refinement. Nevertheless, it did not make them the fastest models in the BMW range: as *Autocar* magazine pointed out, a 323i saloon was quicker to 100mph than a 635 CSi. Above that speed, the big coupé asserted its advantage, peaking at 140mph. That dog's-leg gearchange also proved controversial; it may have added a degree of sporting credibility to the car but it could be less than co-operative.

In the UK, the car's arrival in autumn 1978 led to a range realignment. Manual versions of the 633 CSi ceased to be available, and only the automatic version of that car remained on sale, priced at £15,379. The 635 CSi, invariably with the five-speed manual gearbox, became the flagship model, with a price of £16,499. A year later, the 633 CSi disappeared from UK showrooms altogether, leaving only the 635 CSi on sale in that market.

Autocar magazine tested one for its issue of 6 January 1979, and was very impressed. Nevertheless, it believed that the rival Jaguar XJ-S with its 5.3-litre V12 engine represented better value and trumped the BMW in all respects except fuel economy and looks: 'The BMW will find favour with the man who ranks style as important as performance, and who prefers a vestige of sporting sound to total refinement.' Wind noise, this time from around the door mirrors and sunroof, was still a problem, in spite of quality improvements made at Dingolfing. The old-fashioned water-valve heater, too, was a disappointment at a time when even volume-car makers were switching to more efficient air-blending types.

Overall, *Autocar* found the car to be 'a delight to drive fast as well as slowly'. 'Ultimate cornering... is slightly let down by the usual BMW trailing-arm readiness to break away quite abruptly if the driver decelerates in the bend', but the engine was superb, 'the epitome of BMW zestfulness – that glorious smooth eagerness of a BMW six which is such a hallmark of the breed.'

The special 635 CSi models sold in Sweden and some other countries make an interesting footnote to this part of the E24 story. Although badged as 635 CSi models and having all the additional spoilers and equipment associated with these cars, they actually had the 3.2-litre engine from the 633 CSi. This state of affairs continued right through the first phase of E24 coupé production and on into 1984, when proper 3.5-litre 635 CSi cars became available.

> **PAINT AND TRIM OPTIONS**
>
> Colour names are given in the original German, with the BMW colour code in brackets. Note that these lists are taken from BMW publications and have not been checked against build records. Some colours may not have been available in some countries, and some colours may have survived into the beginning of the following model-year before being phased out.

The 1980 Model-Year Changes

There were further changes in the pipeline, this time at the bottom end of the E24 range, and 1979 proved to be the last model-year for the 3.0-litre cars. The last 630 CS models were built in August 1979, and a month later BMW's European showrooms began to take deliveries of a new entry-level model called the 628 CSi. Assembly had actually begun in June.

June 1979 also brought a number of changes that affected the 1980 model-year 633 CSi and 635 CSi production models that generally became available in the autumn. Multi-point central locking became standard (the earlier version operated only from the driver's door) and all-velour trim became the default option, although some markets, such as the UK, made it a no-cost alternative to the leather that now became part of their standard spec-

THE FIRST GENERATION E24s, 1976–1982

ification. An LED digital clock replaced the original analogue type, fitting into the same dashboard space and still surrounded by a control for the heater blower. A 12-function On Board Computer was also added to the options list, allowing rapid calculation of such things as fuel consumption, time to destination, and so on.

There were further-reaching engineering changes, too. Most important was the availability of a Bosch ABS system as a cost option, but the arrival of a new Bosch DME (Digital Motor Electronics) system was also a big step forward. BMW were first into the market with this new system, which was introduced on the 7 Series saloons at the same time. With a 256-point mapping memory, it allowed far finer control of engine fuelling and ignition, which was of enormous help in the battle to improve efficiency and reduce exhaust emissions.

The 633 CSi models now took on a new twin-pipe exhaust system with stainless-steel elements and larger intermediate silencers. The 635 CSi models, meanwhile, gained a redesigned tail spoiler. Now made of rubber, it was shallower than the type it replaced, and allowed the BMW roundel to be relocated in its original place on the boot lid.

As its name implied, the new 628 CSi had a 2.8-litre engine. It was a small-bore version of the 3.0-litre M30 that had already made a name for itself in the latest 528i saloons, but it was barely less powerful than the previous version, with 184PS instead of 185PS at the same 5800rpm. The torque output certainly was lower – 235Nm (173lb ft) at 4200rpm rather than 255Nm (188lb ft) at 3500rpm – and the torque delivery below 3500rpm in the 628 CSi was rather disappointing. The compensations came in better fuel economy and less temperamental behaviour. This engine completed the transition to fuel injection within the E24 range, coming with a Bosch L-Jetronic system and transistorized electronic ignition. It did not yet share the DME of the two larger engines in the E24s, however.

The 628 CSi could be had with a choice of four gearboxes. Standard for most markets was the four-speed manual, and the three-speed automatic was an expected

The underbonnet view of a 628 CSi. BMW engines used common components wherever possible to save manufacturing costs, and the inlet manifold of this engine was marked to show that it suited the 2.5-litre engines as well as the 2.8-litre types.

117

THE FIRST GENERATION E24s, 1976–1982

extra-cost alternative. However, it was also possible to order the car with the five-speed 'dog's-leg' Sports gearbox used in the 635 CSi, or with a new Getrag five-speed overdrive gearbox, which had the fifth gear out on a spur alongside the standard H-pattern shift gate. BMW expected this option to appeal to those who were buying the smaller-engined E24 to get its fuel economy, which was better than in either the 633 CSi or 635 CSi.

Not every one of BMW's markets took the 628 CSi in the beginning. The model never would go to the USA, and the UK and other right-hand-drive countries had to wait until autumn 1980 and the start of the 1981 model-year before production of cars to suit their requirements began. In the UK, the car expanded the E24 range back up to two models (the other being the 635 CSi) and was seen very much as a response to increased concerns about fuel economy prompted by the second Oil Crisis of 1979–1980. For BMW GB, it was also seen as a response to the new Mercedes-Benz 280 SLC model, itself introduced mainly for reasons of fuel economy.

The UK cars were priced at £16,635 at the end of 1980, which was nearly £1000 cheaper than the automatic-only Mercedes. They came with the five-speed overdrive gearbox as standard, and without many of the items standard on the 635 CSi or formerly standard on the old 633 CSi models. There was no front apron spoiler, and the rear brakes had solid discs instead of the ventilated types used on other E24s, while the front brakes were smaller 272mm (10.7in) ventilated discs. ABS was not even on the options list. Metallic paint cost extra, as did a sunroof, headlamp washers, air conditioning, cruise control, a limited-slip differential and a radio-cassette unit. The wheels were the multi-spoke Alpina alloys already familiar in the UK market, with the 6-inch rims of the discontinued 633 CSi models.

Motor magazine tested one for its issue of 27 December 1980. They expected that 23mpg would be possible with the five-speed overdrive gearbox, but they were unimpressed by the car's performance: 'Its fourth and fifth gear pick-up can only be described as poor … [and] outright performance for a car with sporting pretensions can only be judged as fair, with its shortage of low-speed torque being the main shortcoming.' Overall, the 628 CSi was 'aimed more at the well-heeled executive than [the] sporting enthusiast'.

The 1981 and 1982 Models

The next round of changes came in autumn 1980. All the European 628 CSi, 633 CSi and 635 CSi models took on redesigned rear bumpers with long side extensions that now reached the wheel arches. The idea was similar to that already tried on the US models with their extended bumpers, but was different in execution.

There were wheel changes too. All models for the 1981 model-year now took on BBS-Mahle alloy wheels with a new design. A 6.5-inch rim width became standard across the range, along with wider 205/70 VR low-profile tyres. A brand-new option was multi-spoke alloy wheels with metric dimensions and the latest Michelin TRX tyres in a 220/50 VR 390 size (see opposite). These wheels and tyres represented advanced technology at the time and that of course was the appeal that BMW expected them to have for E24 customers. However, the later discontinuation of TRX tyres and their non-standard sizes would cause headaches for owners further down the line.

The 1981 model-year was the last one for the 633 CSi models in Europe, although versions of the car would remain available for the USA and for Japan for a further three seasons. The 628 CSi and 635 CSi were left as the major models, but there were no major specification changes for them at the start of the 1982 model-year in autumn 1981.

The US-Model 630 CSi

While European markets received the two-level E24 range of 630 CS and 633 CSi at the beginning of E24 production, the North American range was limited to a single model called the 630 CSi. This entered production in June 1976 and the first examples were sold as 1977 models towards the end of the year. By this stage, BMW had full control over its North American operations, having ended its agreement with long-term importer Max Hoffmann during 1975 and established a new subsidiary called BMW North America.

The main reason for launching the 630 CSi as the US car (the variant was never available in any other markets) was that the injected 3.0-litre version of the M30 engine had already been homologated with the Federal authorities and was already available in the 530i saloon in the USA. It used a Bosch L-Jetronic injection system for fuel

THE FIRST GENERATION E24s, 1976–1982

MICHELIN TRX WHEELS AND TYRES

Tyre manufacturer Michelin introduced its TRX tyre-and-wheel system in 1975, the designation picking up the 'X' of the pioneering Michelin radial tyre and 'TR' for *tension répartie* ('shared stress').

This was the first time a tyre and wheel had been designed specifically to work together, and its development had been driven by Michelin's search for better roadholding through a lower sidewall height but without a corresponding loss of ride comfort. In order to achieve what they wanted, Michelin designed tyre and wheel together. A redesigned wheel rim and tyre bead gave a very strong bond between tyre and wheel and also gave better stress distribution within the tyre.

The special tyre rim and bead were not compatible with those of conventional wheels and tyres, and so Michelin decided to avoid confusion among users by giving the TRX wheels and tyres metric dimensions instead of the conventional Imperial sizes. Somewhat inevitably, the non-standard dimensions caused problems in the tyre aftermarket and, equally inevitably, rival tyre manufacturers soon developed low-profile tyres with similar advantages. These were not only cheaper but also fitted on rims with conventional dimensions.

The TRX tyre was no longer fitted as original equipment after a few years, but at the time of writing Michelin continued to make batches of tyres to suit cars that had TRX wheels from new.

delivery and had a low 8.0:1 compression ratio to suit the low-octane unleaded fuel that was by this time the only type available through US filling stations. Power output was quoted as 176bhp to North American SAE nett standards, which probably meant it was rather less powerful by German DIN standards. Although torque was not too far behind the European 630 CS, with a peak of 187lb ft, the spread of that torque was altogether less satisfying and made the 630 CSi a much less flexible car than its European counterpart.

None of this was helped by the fact that the 630 CSi weighed some 320 lb more than a European 630 CS. The main reasons for this were the heavier bumpers, the additional emissions control gear, and of course the high level of standard equipment. Air conditioning (using a new system jointly developed by Behr and BMW) was fitted to every car sold in the USA, and rear head restraints were a standard fit on the 630 CSi.

For BMW, the cars must have been something of a headache to accommodate on the assembly lines, because there were no fewer than four different base versions. There were '49-State' models for sale in most parts of the USA, and then there were Californian-specification models for sale only in that state, which required additional emissions control gear in the shape of a catalytic converter that robbed the engine of even more power and torque. Each of these versions could be had with either a manual or an automatic gearbox. On the face of it, preparing special versions for California was something that BMW could have managed without, but sales figures told a different story: over the year when the 630 CSi was the only E24 available in the USA, nearly as many cars were sold in California alone as were sold in all the other 49 states put together. The production figures were 932 for the 49 states and 862 for California – a difference of just 12 per cent or so.

It is often said that the 630 CSi was very much less of a sports coupé than its European equivalents. Performance figures recorded by leading US magazines varied widely, which rather suggests that the actual performance available from the cars did the same. *Road & Track* recorded 9.7 seconds for the 0–60mph sprint in June 1977; *Road Test* produced a miserable 10.6-second figure in July; *Car and Driver* managed a much more respectable 8.4 seconds in December 1977. All the cars were four-speed manual examples rather than automatics, and all appear to have been '49-State' cars and not the Californian-specification models, which were further stifled.

Both *Road & Track* and *Road Test* thought the cost of the car was excessive, but neither acknowledged that the massive complication on the assembly lines and the relatively small sales volumes must have been two major reasons for this. Another reason was that it had to be pitched at or around the level of rival cars – when a Mercedes-Benz 450 SLC coupé cost $27,000 and a Jaguar XJ-S cost $20,000, the $24,000 cost of a 630 CSi did not seem at all unreasonable.

What really upset reviewers, however, was the fact that the 630 CSi cost nearly twice as much as a BMW 530i

119

■ THE FIRST GENERATION E24s, 1976–1982

saloon, which was priced at around $13,000. The 630 CSi was heavier, slower, and had a smaller passenger cabin, which made the $11,000 difference very noticeable. 'If you're after twenty-five grand worth of automotive pleasure,' said *Road Test*, 'there are better ways to spend your money…. [The 630 CSi] has to be judged on status and status alone.' Yet there were compensations. *Road & Track* described the car as 'one of the world's best roadgoing GTs', with 'the most sophisticated production inline six in the world'. The balance between comfort and dynamics was right, too: 'the ride is not only soft but well controlled and is accompanied by superb handling.'

Assembly of the 630 CSi lasted just 16 months, from June 1976 until September 1977. All 1794 examples were built at the Karmann plant in Osnabrück, but they would be the only US-specification E24s that were. The replacement 633 CSi models would be assembled at BMW's Dingolfing plant in Bavaria.

The US-Model 633 CSi

BMW took heed of the criticisms levelled at the original 630 CSi in the USA, and for 1978 replaced it with a new model, this time a Federalized version of the 633 CSi. This had almost certainly been planned from the start: the delay occurred in getting the larger engine homologated for the USA. It was the 633 CSi that saw BMW's North American customers right through to the summer of 1985; European buyers, meanwhile, had been offered the bigger-engined 635 CSi since mid-1978.

The biggest problem with the 630 CSi had been its lack of acceleration, and the larger engine addressed this by delivering a welcome dose of extra torque. Power barely changed, going to 177bhp (SAE nett) from the 630 CSi's 176bhp, but the torque improved to 196lb ft at 4000rpm from the old car's 185lb ft at 4500rpm in 49-State form. The 633 CSi was 'still not the answer',

An early US-model 633 CSi demonstrating its stability under hard cornering. The bumpers have sliding inserts to absorb low-speed collisions, and there are side-marker lights in their front and rear wraparound sections.

THE FIRST GENERATION E24s, 1976–1982

The extended bumpers had quite an effect on the car's side profile but they represented a brave attempt to deal with a real problem. Note that US cars were always pictured with door mirrors on both sides.

according to *Car and Driver* in its November 1978 issue, 'but a step in the right direction.' The test figure of 8.3 seconds for the 0–60mph standing-start in a manual-gearbox car was quite impressive, but as it was only a tenth of a second faster than the figure that *Car and Driver* had obtained from its 630 CSi (an unusually rapid example, as noted earlier), the reviewer was rather disappointed. *Road & Track* recorded a figure of 8.4 seconds, and was less disappointed.

The 633 CSi had addressed other criticisms, too. Now included in the base price ($25,495 on the east coast and $25,595 on the west coast) were metallic paint, BBS-Mahle alloy wheels on VR-rated tyres, an electric sunroof and an AM/FM stereo radio-cassette. There had been complaints that the rear headrests blocked the view out of the back of the car, and so the 633 CSI had none – and never would have any in its US guise. The 633 CSi also had restyled rear bumpers with a wraparound that reached as far as the trailing edge of the wheel arch; these helped to reduce the impression that the big rear bumper was an afterthought. The only major option was the ZF limited-slip differential.

■ THE FIRST GENERATION E24s, 1976–1982

PAINT AND TRIM OPTIONS

For most model-years, there was a choice of around 20 paint colours; the bias was towards solid types for 1977, but by the 1979 model-year there were more metallic than solid choices.

For the 1977 and 1978 model-years, upholstery was available in leather or velour-and-leather. For the 1979–1982 model-years, the choice was between leather and velour.

E24 COUPÉ PRODUCTION FIGURES

Note: figures are for calendar year.

	628	630	633	635	Total
1975					17
1976					4916
1977		2518		3263	5781
1978		924	3387	1286	5597
1979	286	249	2439	3755	6729
1980	1018		2043	3567	6628
1981	785		1781	3086	5652
1982	1112		2326	4153	7601
1983	972		3325	3673	7970
1984	741		2007	5510	8258
1985	593			9033	9626
1986	367			6660	7027
1987	77			5615	5692
1988				3666	3666
1989				1064	1064
Grand total					**86,216**

'The increased torque is the key to what makes the 633 CSi a more pleasant car to drive,' said *Road & Track*. However, the major magazines in the USA were still rather lukewarm about some aspects of the revised car. 'Don't ask for horsepower and g forces,' said *Car and Driver*. 'They're not the point. The point is elegant, silent, comfortable, enjoyable touring, and that's what you'll get.' Two years later, *Sports Car Graphic* for November 1980 still had concerns: 'The 633's acceleration is not terribly impressive, but it is adequate. ...As a GT car, the 633 CSi falls

By 1982, when this publicity picture was taken, the USA still had only a single model of E24, the 633 CSi. The 635 CSi had not yet been prepared for US conditions, although a few were imported by individuals, who then had to have them expensively modified to meet local regulations.

122

THE FIRST GENERATION E24s, 1976–1982

E24 PRODUCTION FIGURES BY CALENDAR YEAR, 1976–1982

The 1975 'pilot-production' figures are added into those for 1976. he figures for 1982 include the first of the re-engineered '1983' E24/1 models (see Chapter 7).

	1976	1977	1978	1979	1980	1981	1982
628 CSi				202	691	410	613
628 CSi Auto				84	249	182	266
628 CSi RHD					17	47	53
628 CSi RHD Auto					61	146	179
630 CS	1158	666	610	166			
630 CS Auto	507	468	314	83			
630 CSi USA	214	714					
630 CSi USA Auto	196	670					
633 CSi	2125	1862	1039	277	167	74	
633 CSi Auto	542	803	610	452	182	62	
633 CSi RHD	112	157	82				
633 CSi RHD Auto	79	409	423	434			
633 CSi USA			467	487	676	913	1102
633 CSi USA Auto			546	488	652	626	933
633 CSi Japan			247	301	366	106	299
635 CSi			1193	3030	2094	1605	2400
635 CSi Auto			319	822	727	1009	
635 CSi RHD			98	267	212	238	165
635 CSi RHD Auto				139	439	515	574
Year total	**4933**	**5749**	**5629**	**6729**	**6628**	**5652**	**7593**

short of the mark, but as a luxury coupé with no affectations, it sets a standard.' From the *Road & Track* test nevertheless came the summary that the 633 CSi was 'a wonderful high-speed road machine that's eager to work in concert with the driver for exhilarating and entertaining motoring'.

Just like the 630 CSi, the 633 CSi was initially produced in four different versions for the North American market. The three-speed automatic gearbox remained an extra-cost alternative to the standard four-speed manual, and there were versions of both to 49-State and Californian specification. The separate Californian specification lasted in production only until March 1979, which was a blessing because the thermal reactor that was part of the specification proved to be a troublesome device.

For the 1980 model-year, a three-way catalytic converter with oxygen sensor became standard on all US models. This finally did away with the need for BMW to produce four different types of 633 CSi in four different chassis number sequences for the USA. From now on, there were just two types, one with the four-speed manual gearbox and the other with the three-speed automatic. The 1980–1982 models also had special speedometers that read only to 85mph, as required by Federal law.

Around 6000 examples of the 633 CSi were built for North America between 1978 and 1982, when the re-engineered cars entered production. The manual cars proved more popular overall, although automatics had a slight edge in the model's first year.

123

■ THE FIRST GENERATION E24s, 1976–1982

TECHNICAL SPECIFICATIONS, E24 6 SERIES MODELS 1976–1982

Engines:
628 CSi
Type M30 B28 six-cylinder petrol, installed with a 30-degree tilt to the right
2788cc (86mm x 80mm)
Single overhead camshaft, driven by Duplex chain
Seven-bearing crankshaft
Compression ratio 9.3:1
Bosch L-Jetronic fuel injection
184PS at 5800rpm
235Nm (173lb ft) at 4200rpm
630 CS
As above, except:
Type M30 B30
2985cc (89mm x 80mm)
Compression ratio 9.0:1
Single Pierburg 4A1 downdraught carburettor
185PS at 5800rpm
255Nm (188lb ft) at 3500rpm
630 CSi
As above, except:
Compression ratio 8.0:1
Bosch L-Jetronic fuel injection
176bhp (SAE) at 5500rpm
187lb ft at 4500rpm
633 CSi
As above, except:
Type M30 B32
3210cc (89mm x 86mm)
Compression ratio 9.3:1 (8.0:1 for USA)
Bosch L-Jetronic fuel injection
197PS at 5500rpm
283Nm (209lb ft) at 4300rpm
In US 49-State tune:
  177bhp (SAE) at 5500rpm
  196lb ft at 4000rpm
635 CSi (1978–1981)
As above, except:
Type M90
3453cc (93.4mm x 84mm)
Compression ratio 9.3:1
218PS at 5200rpm
304Nm (224lb ft) at 4000rpm
635 CSi (1982)
As above, except:
Type M30 B34
3430cc (92mm x 86mm)
Bosch Motronic fuel injection
218PS at 5200rpm (185PS with optional catalytic converter)
Exhaust system with catalytic converter available as an option from September 1985

Gearboxes:
Four-speed Getrag 262 manual gearbox standard for 630 CS, 633 CSi to 1979, 628 CSi
  Ratios 3.855:1, 2.203:1, 1.402:1, 1.000:1, reverse 4.29:1
Five-speed manual gearbox optional on 628 CSi and standard on 633 CSi from 1979
  Ratios 3.82:1, 2.20:1, 1.40:1, 1.00:1, 0.81:1, reverse 3.70:1
Five-speed manual gearbox standard on 635 CSi
  Ratios 3.822:1, 2.202:1, 1.398:1, 1.000:1, 0.813:1, reverse 3.45:1
Five-speed Sports manual gearbox standard on 635 CSi
  Ratios 3.717:1, 2.403:1, 1,766:1, 1.263:1, 1.000:1, reverse 3.70:1
Three-speed ZF 3 HP 22 automatic gearbox optional on 630 CS, 628 CSi and 635 CSi from 1982
  Ratios 2.48:1, 1.48:1, 1,00:1, reverse 2.09:1

Axle ratios:
628 CSi	3.45:1
630 CS	3.45:1
633 CSi	3.25:1
635 CSi (to 1981)	3.07:1

Suspension, steering and brakes:
Front suspension with McPherson struts, coil springs and anti-roll bar
Rear suspension with semi-trailing arms, struts, coil springs and anti-roll bar; self-levelling on 635 CSi from 1987

Worm-and-roller steering with 16.9:1 ratio and variable power assistance as standard

Disc brakes all round, with 280mm diameter on front wheels and 272mm on rear wheels; twin hydraulic circuits and hydraulic servo assistance standard; ABS standard on 635 CSi, optional on 628 CSi from 1982

Dimensions:
Overall length: 4755mm (187.2in)
Overall width: 1725mm (67.9in)
Overall height: 1365mm (53.7in)
Wheelbase: 2626mm (103.4in)
Front track: 1422mm (56in)
Rear track: 1487mm (58.5in)

Wheels and tyres:
6J x 14 alloy wheels standard on 628 CSi (to 1982), 630 CS and 633 CSi
6.50J x 14 alloy wheels for 635 CSi
195/70 VR 14 tyres for 628 CSi (to 1982), 630 CS, 633 CSi and 635 CSi (to 1981)
205/70 VR 14 tyres for 628 CSi and all 635 CSi (from 1982)
202/55 VR 390 TRX optional for 635 CSi (1982-1987)

Unladen weights:

628 CSi	1475kg (3252lb) to 1982
	1450kg (3197lb) from 1982
628 CSi automatic	1495kg (3296lb) to 1982
	1470kg (3241lb) from 1982
630 CS	1475kg (3252lb)
630 CS automatic	1495kg (3296lb)
633 CSi	1495kg (3296lb)
635 CSi	1520kg (3351lb) to 1981
	1470kg (3241lb), 1982–1987
635 CSi automatic	1490kg (3285lb)

PERFORMANCE FIGURES FOR E24 6 SERIES MODELS

628 CSi	0–100km/h	9.0–9.5 sec
	Maximum	210–215km/h
		(130–133.5mph)
630 CS	0–100km/h	9 sec
	Maximum	210km/h (130mph)
633 CSi	0–100km/h	8.5 sec
	Maximum	215km/h (133.5mph)
635 CSi	0–100km/h	8 sec
(to 1981)	Maximum	222km/h (138mph)
635 CSi	0–100km/h	8.5 sec
(1982 on)	Maximum	225km/h (140mph)

CHAPTER SEVEN

THE SECOND GENERATION E24s, 1982–1989

BMW seized the opportunity to update the 6 Series for the 1983 model-year, combining some major chassis revisions with an extensively re-engineered bodyshell. Although the new 1983 E24 was, as *Autosport* magazine noted on 9 September 1982, 'outwardly barely distinguishable from its predecessors, it [was] a very different beast under the skin'. BMW even knew it by a different product code; it was no longer an E24, but an E24/1.

Changes to the E24

The original E24 had been based on the platform of the E12 5 Series saloons, and from 1981 these gave way to completely re-engineered E28 models. The new suspension developed for the E28s was ultimately an evolution of that designed for the E23 7 Series cars, and it was an obvious choice for the mid-life re-work of the E24s as well.

Engineering developed in the later 1970s delivered the E28 saloons to replace the E12 5 Series cars. The new models in turn shared many features – particularly the revised suspension – with the second-generation E24 models.

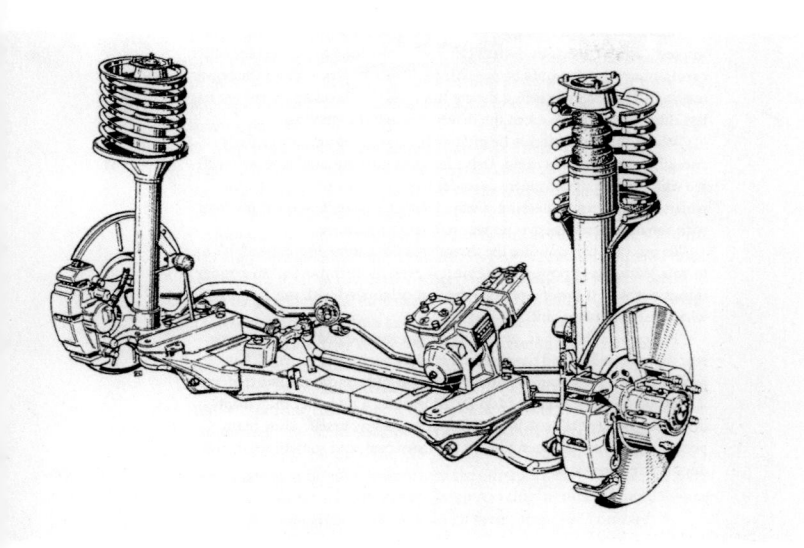

THE SECOND GENERATION E24s, 1982–1989

The revised front suspension brought better steering feel than before.

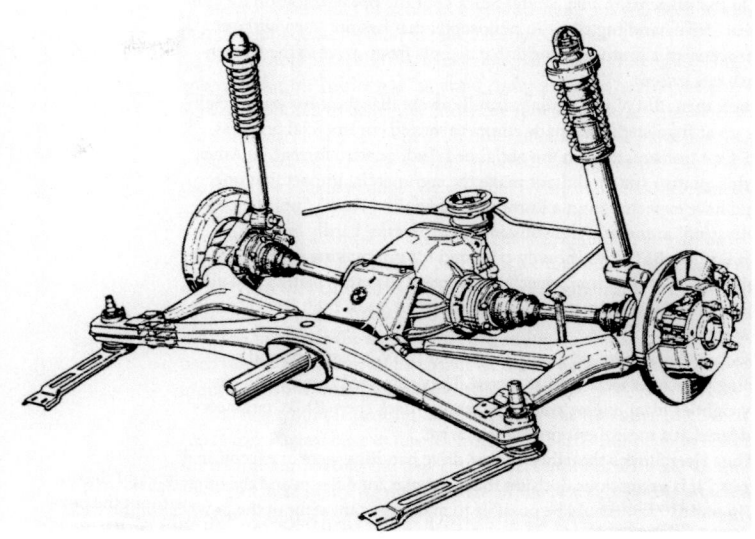

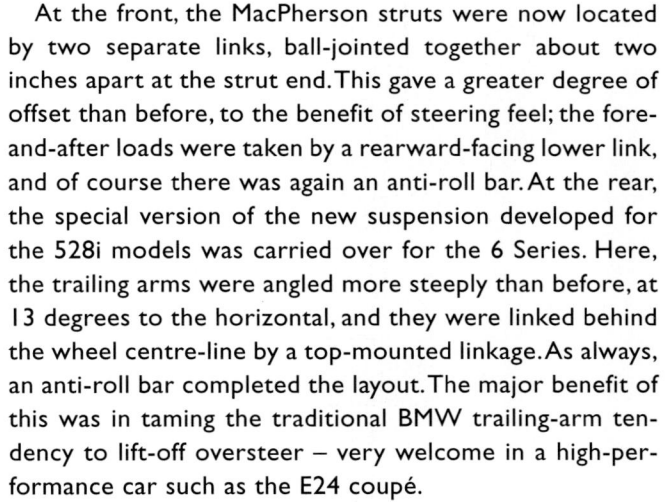

The new rear suspension came from the 528i, top model of the latest 5 Series range. Its principal benefit was in reducing the lift-off oversteer that had affected first-generation E24s.

At the front, the MacPherson struts were now located by two separate links, ball-jointed together about two inches apart at the strut end. This gave a greater degree of offset than before, to the benefit of steering feel; the fore-and-after loads were taken by a rearward-facing lower link, and of course there was again an anti-roll bar. At the rear, the special version of the new suspension developed for the 528i models was carried over for the 6 Series. Here, the trailing arms were angled more steeply than before, at 13 degrees to the horizontal, and they were linked behind the wheel centre-line by a top-mounted linkage. As always, an anti-roll bar completed the layout. The major benefit of this was in taming the traditional BMW trailing-arm tendency to lift-off oversteer – very welcome in a high-performance car such as the E24 coupé.

All this was mounted to a lightened, stiffened bodyshell. BMW had taken a second look at the way they had originally designed the 6 Series body, and had realized they could both shed weight and make the shell stronger by careful re-shaping in critical areas of the inner structure and by using the latest steel technology. As a result, although the 1983 models had the same levels of torsional stiffness and crash resistance as their predecessors, they were also an average of 60kg (132lb) lighter across the model range.

There were no visible signs of these modifications on the outside, although the 1983 E24s that entered production in June 1982 were readily recognizable due to other changes. Both 628 CSi and 633 CSi had a new front spoiler, which was shallower than the one on the 635 CSi and came with a pair of neatly integrated fog lamps. The 635 CSi, meanwhile, kept its deep GRP spoiler with four horizontal air intakes, and its standard fog lamps were still hung below the front bumper. It still had its black boot-lid lip spoiler, too.

A careful look would reveal the more widely flared front wheel arches that covered the greater wheel offset associated with the new suspension. Much less obvious – except to those in the know – was the change in the mounting of the radio aerial, which was now on the right-hand rear wing instead of the left-hand front as before. And only a really close look would reveal one other change: the arrival of high-intensity fog guard lamps within the rear light clusters. All models also took on new headlights with two-stage reflectors that gave a better spread of light; these were recognizable from close up by the visible 'step' in the reflector.

The 635 CSi also boasted a new engine. Out went the old 3453cc engine with its Siamesed bores, and in came a

THE SECOND GENERATION E24s, 1982–1989

The second-generation cars were easily distinguishable by their extended bumper wraparounds. As this 635 CSi also makes clear, the boot-lid model badges were now mounted directly to the panel.

The rechargeable torch was a thoughtful feature, kept in its own compartment alongside the glove-box.

The tail-lights of the second-generation E24s incorporated fog guard lamps.

THE SECOND GENERATION E24s, 1982–1989

The redesigned front apron of the second-generation cars is clear on this 628 CSi. A discreet black chin spoiler improved the aerodynamics as well.

new 3430cc size. There are two theories about why the change was made: one says that there had been service problems with the older engine, the other that it came about because of production rationalization. This rationalization enabled BMW to use the same 86mm stroke (and therefore the crankshaft, pistons and conrods) in the new 3.4-litre engine, the existing 3.2-litre type, and the smaller-bore 2.7-litre 'eta' economy variant used in the new 525e model.

There were three interesting consequences. First, the engine was always called a 3.5-litre despite its new 3.4-litre capacity, because BMW marketing did not want a change. Second, the new inlet manifold, which was shared with the 3.2-litre engine that was still available in US-market and Japanese cars, now carried the numbers '3.2/3.5' cast into it. Third, the engine now became a member of the M30 family once again, specifically an M30 B34 type.

The 635 CSi version of the engine was tuned to deliver exactly the same power and torque outputs as the old 3.5-litre M90. This was made simpler by its use of the latest Bosch Motronic digital control system, a second-generation DME. A further Motronic advantage related to fuel economy, with a new 'map' for the cold-start warm-up phase optimizing fuel usage, and the engine being able to idle 50rpm lower than before despite its higher compression ratio of 10:1. There was an over-run fuel shut-off, too. In tandem with the five-speed overdrive gearbox, this helped reduce fuel consumption by around 15 per cent as compared with earlier versions of the 635 CSi.

The 635 CSi was of course just one of three models in the range for 1983, the other two being the 628 CSi and 633 CSi. All three could be had with either manual or automatic gearboxes, and the standard manual gearbox was now an overdrive five-speed, in pursuit of better fuel economy. The 'sports' five-speed with its close ratios and direct top was still available to order and, although the 633 CSi kept its three-speed automatic, the 628 CSi and 635 CSi both switched to a new four-speed type. Once again made by ZF, this new automatic incorporated an overdrive top gear to improve fuel economy. In the UK, the three types of transmission were interchangeable options on the 635 CSi, with no extra-cost penalty.

129

THE SECOND GENERATION E24s, 1982–1989

Velour upholstery and a three-spoke steering wheel characterize the interior of this UK-market 628 CSi, which has an automatic gearbox.

The 628 CSi and 635 CSi were available in both left- and right-hand-drive forms, and both were sold in the UK. The 633 CSi was not sold in the UK, but it was the sole model at this stage to be sold in the USA. There was also a special version of the 633 CSi for Japan, broadly similar to the emissions-controlled North American cars and with left-hand drive – a prestige feature in right-hand-drive Japan.

On the inside, there were further changes across the range. Although the layout of the main instrument dials remained unchanged, the dials themselves had a new style and the speedometer incorporated a fuel-economy gauge. This, with typical BMW attention to detail, was operated electrically and was therefore rather more accurate than the vacuum types favoured by other manufacturers. There was a new layout for the Active Check Control panel, and a Service Interval Indicator warned the driver when a service was due. A new 10-function On Board Computer also became standard on 635 CSi models, although it did cost extra on the 628 CSi. There were revised heater controls, too, now with sliders as well as rotary dials. A three-spoke steering wheel also became standard: more square-rigged than the optional Motorsport three-spoke wheel, it was still much better-looking than the old four-spoke type.

The second-generation cars had a new Check Control panel, which monitored a different set of functions.

130

THE SECOND GENERATION E24s, 1982–1989

The 1984 Mainstream Models

The changes introduced for the 1983 models were only the beginning of a revitalized 6 Series range, and in autumn 1983 there were further changes across the range. Most important of these was the arrival of a new flagship model called the M635 CSi. It was announced in September 1983, but it did not actually go on sale until early 1984, and then only in left-hand-drive form and not for the USA.

The existing model range of 628 CSi, 633 CSi and 635 CSi remained unchanged, but the automatic gearbox option of the 635 CSi now came with a brand-new electro-hydraulic control system. This gave the driver a number of options that had not been available before, and they were reflected inside the car by a rotary control next to the selector lever. The first setting, 'Sport', gave maximum acceleration in all gears and a rapid kick-down when required. The second setting, 'Economy', allowed the gearbox to change up at lower engine revs, to the detriment of acceleration but obviously to the benefit of fuel economy. The third setting, '3-2-1', allowed gears to be held for such purposes as maximum engine braking on downhill sections or on uphill hairpins.

There were several other changes for the 1984 models. The 635 CSi took on a redesigned front apron; still deeper than on the other cars, it now incorporated the fog lamps, which tidied up an untidy feature of earlier 635 CSi models. Less visible, and available on all models, was driver-controllable headlamp levelling. It cost extra, but was useful for those who regularly carried heavy loads in the boot because it altered the angle of the dipped beam to compensate for a tail-down, nose-up attitude. ABS now became standard on the 635 CSi and optional on the 628 CSi. A new extra-cost interior option was soft Buffalo leather upholstery, and the latest On Board Computer now came with eight functions. This was standard for the more expensive models in most countries, but was probably universally an extra-cost option for the 628 CSi.

The M635 CSi

By the end of the 1970s, BMW had begun to widen the scope of its Motorsport division, and during the first half of the following decade its plans became clearer. It was the M635 CSi that became the first of the new M models, which were intended as the ultimate in roadgoing high-performance machinery.

This was the three-position rotary control for the switchable automatic gearbox. The 'chrome' on the lettering of the control panel tended to wear off with use.

Less than a year after it went on sale, it would be joined by the M5, the high-performance flagship of the E28 5 Series saloon range and a car that, incidentally, used the same engine as the M635 CSi. Then in 1986 came the M3, a high-performance derivative of the E30 3 Series cars that was at least partially developed with competition in mind. The only disappointment was that the idea of using the 'M' with the series number (as in M3 and M5) did not occur to BMW's marketing people until after the Motorsport derivative of the E24 range had gone on sale with the rather cumbersome name of M635 CSi.

It looks as if BMW resisted the temptation to develop their big coupé beyond the 635 CSi until the lightened cars with their improved roadholding were ready for the 1983 season. Once those had been signed off for production, the Motorsport division got to work.

Central to the concept of a Motorsport roadgoing car was a specially developed engine, and in the case of the M635 CSi, this used the old 3453cc swept volume and not the 3430cc size of the latest M30 engine in the 635 CSi. The reason was simple: it was developed before that new size had become available. Work began as early as 1980, and was overseen by the Motorsport division's Georg Thiele, reporting to Horst Rech as overall programme manager for the high-performance coupé.

■ THE SECOND GENERATION E24s, 1982–1989

Appropriately painted red, this was an early M635 CSi model. There is no cheapskate omission of a passenger's door mirror here. The headlamps have their own wipers, the Motorsport badge sits discreetly on the grille (see detail, below left), and just visible are the TRX alloy wheels.

Body-coloured door mirrors were another distinguishing feature of the M635 CSi.

132

THE SECOND GENERATION E24s, 1982–1989

Another early publicity car shows the rear view of the M635 CSi. Note the black tail spoiler and the simple 'M' badge on the right of the boot lid.

Besides, the Motorsport division had a decided affinity with the 3453cc block, having developed it originally for the racing CSL 'Batmobiles' in the 1970s and then refined it as the powerplant of the very special, limited-production M1 coupé of 1978–1981. In M1 guise, it was known as an M88/1 engine, but it could not be used unmodified in the E24 bodyshell. That car, like all the others in the BMW range at the time, always had its engine mounted with a 30-degree slant to the right, in order to allow for lower bonnet lines.

The Motorsport division re-engineered the four-valve cylinder head to suit that 30-degree slant, making changes to the water passages and the inlet tracts. The M1 engine had been dry-sumped, but for the new Motorsport 6 Series, the 3453cc block was given the wet sump of the M90 engine used in the early 635 CSi models. The M88's 264-degree camshaft and big 37mm inlet and 32mm exhaust valves were retained, but the compression ratio was raised to 10.5:1 from the original 9:1. This change was made possible by the accurate fuel-metering and timing control now available from the latest Bosch ML-Jetronic injection and Motronic engine-management systems. The new engine was known as an M88/3, and boasted 286bhp at 6500rpm and 250lb ft at 4500rpm, outputs which were simply astonishing for the mid-1980s.

When Jeremy Walton interviewed Georg Thiele (in *BMW 6 Series Enthusiast's Companion*), he learned that a great deal of development effort had gone into the design of a six-into-one exhaust manifold that would allow the exhaust gases to flow as freely as possible. For the camshaft drive, a single-row chain was considered adequate, although the higher-revving M1 engine had used a twin-row chain. A new and larger radiator was also needed, to keep engine temperatures under control.

There was no automatic gearbox option. Instead, the close-ratio five-speed Getrag manual type was made standard, with its direct top and dog's-leg shift gate, but with different intermediate ratios from those seen on the early 635 CSi. To handle the torque of the Motorsport engine, the 635's clutch was uprated with stronger springs, while the final drive had an increased oil capacity. In fact, it was borrowed from the E23 7 Series cars and, as it was physically larger than the type used in other E24s, the E24 floorpan had to be modified to fit round it. A special 3.73:1 gearset was developed for the M635 CSi, and would later be used for the M5 saloons as well.

133

THE SECOND GENERATION E24s, 1982–1989

In order to achieve better weight distribution, the Motorsport division moved the battery from the standard E24 position under the bonnet to a new one in the boot. That reduced the boot capacity from 413 litres to 335 litres. Modifications to the suspension and brakes became necessary, in order to handle this much power and torque safely. The Motorsport division lowered the M635 CSi by 10mm as compared with the 635 CSi, fitting springs that were 15 per cent stiffer and adding specially developed Bilstein gas dampers together with thicker anti-roll bars, the rear one being progressive. For the front brakes, they specified 300mm cross-ventilated discs with ATE four-piston calipers, while the rear brakes retained their 272mm solid discs but had calipers whose pistons were 2mm larger in diameter. As was only to be expected, ABS came as part of the standard package. Perhaps less expected was the fact that the standard BMW towbar could not be used with the M635 CSi.

The M88 engine of the M635 CSi was related to the type that had been designed for the M1 mid-engined supercar. Like the rest of the car, it was discreet but purposeful in appearance. It is seen here in a UK-market car with right-hand drive.

THE SECOND GENERATION E24s, 1982–1989

The battery was moved to the boot on the M635 CSi, mainly to improve weight distribution. It was concealed under a neat cover, which carried a folding warning triangle in its top.

135

■ THE SECOND GENERATION E24s, 1982–1989

The side view of an M635 CSi shows how the additional spoilers helped to elongate the car and reduced the heavy appearance of the first-generation E24 models.

Wheel-arch extensions covered the wider wheels and tyres of the M635 CSi.

Twin tailpipes were a distinguishing feature of the M635 CSi – discreet, as always.

THE SECOND GENERATION E24s, 1982–1989

These modifications were reflected in a dressing up of the styling, but it was surprisingly discreet. Most obvious was a decal that framed the waistline and the feature line along the flanks. The M635 CSi had a more aggressive front apron spoiler with a ribbed matt black extension and inset fog lamps, but it also had the same lip spoiler on its boot lid as the 635 CSi. There were 'M' badges on the grille and the boot lid, and the glass was tinted green rather than the bronze used on other E24 models. Mirror bodies were painted to match the bodywork.

A careful look would reveal that the wheel-arch flares had been made thinner, to accommodate larger tyres. These came on Michelin 165 TR 390 alloy wheels, and standard wear were 220/55 VR 390 tyres. As an option, buyers could order BBS three-piece alloys in a TRX size. This was 210 TR 415, and with these wheels came 240/45 VR 415 tyres.

The finishing touches inside the cabin included Recaro front seats with all-cloth Highland upholstery that featured check-pattern centre panels and plain outer panels. Overmats seem to have been part of the standard specification, and four inertia-reel seat belts were standard, too. Every M635 CSi also came with an 'M'-branded three-spoke steering wheel, a 280km/h (170mph) speedometer, and a rev counter that carried the Motorsport division's 'M' branding.

Early testing of the M635 CSi prototypes was carried out at Germany's Nürburgring, a favourite BMW circuit of the time. In those days, the track was open to the public, who could pay at the gate and take their vehicles on to the circuit, even when testing was under way. One story entrenched in BMW lore involves local motorcycle enthusiasts, who heard that the new high-performance coupé was being tested at the circuit and turned out in force to pit their machines against it. The official version of the story has it that the M635 CSi outpaced all of them, but that BMW eventually abandoned the test because there were simply too many motorcyclists on the track.

On another occasion during 1983, BMW's Paul Rosche had invited the reigning Formula 1 world champion, Nelson Piquet, to put an M635 CSi through its high-speed paces on the famous Nordschleife. Unfortunately, the enthusiastic Piquet entered a bend rather too fast after just a couple of kilometres and the car was wrecked after leaving the track.

Endorsement from on high.... Formula 1 World Champion Nelson Piquet took delivery of an M635 CSi for his personal transport.

■ THE SECOND GENERATION E24s, 1982–1989

UK-market M635 CSi models had side repeater indicators.

Whether any changes were made to the specification as a result is something that BMW have not disclosed, but Piquet himself was undeterred by the experience. He later bought a black M635 CSi for his own use as a road car.

By the autumn of 1983, the cars were ready for journalists to try. *Autosport* magazine was able to drive a left-hand-drive car in Germany in time for its issue of 17 November 1983. The M635 CSi was, according to reporter Marcus Pye, 'a car which handle[d] like a dream, beautifully responsive and balanced'. The free-revving engine was docile in traffic but 'once the needle swings past 3000rpm it feels like a jet aircraft as its brakes are released under full power to commence take-off'.

Autocar tried one during the same November 1983 ride-and-drive exercise for the media, but did not reveal the results until its 28 April 1984 issue, just as the cars were going on sale in Germany. Again, the test car was a left-hand-drive model and the magazine's reporter was impressed:

ABOVE AND OPPOSITE: On the move or standing still, the M635 CSi had a remarkably discreet appearance for a car of its performance. The shape worked well with both light and dark colours, as these two UK-market cars demonstrate. CRAIG PUSEY

THE SECOND GENERATION E24s, 1982–1989

[The engine is] exhilarating... with obviously more go from 4000rpm onwards, but it performs pretty well from as low as 2500, and the progression from the good to the spectacular is comparatively subtle. ...The M635 CSi seems... to have the right compromise in engine noise, pleasingly muted at low to medium speed, and only becoming anything like loud as one goes faster – but the sound is that particularly lovely one to a red-blooded driver, of a lusty straight six.

He was slightly more equivocal about the ride:

The stiffer springing is very obvious at lower speeds, with a distinctly joggly ride that contrasts noticeably with the comfort of the standard car. ...But, given the sort of car it is, the ride deterioration is not unacceptable.

Wind noise was disappointingly high – a not uncommon problem with E24s – while fuel consumption dropped to 13.9mpg when the car was being pressed, although 22mpg was possible in 'more normal if still typically fast driving'.

139

■ THE SECOND GENERATION E24s, 1982–1989

The 1985 Models: A 635 for the USA

Any additions to the E24 range were bound to be an anticlimax after the M635 CSi, but there were a few changes in September 1984 for the 1985 model-year. Notably, ABS became standard across the range, while the 635 CSi now had a second-generation On-Board Computer as standard equipment. Highland cloth upholstery also became available as the main alternative to leather.

Production of the 633 CSi had ended in the summer, and in the USA the model was replaced by a version of the 635 CSi. The range now consisted of three models: 628 CSi, 635 CSi and low-volume M635 CSi. Of these, the USA was receiving only 635 CSi models and the UK had only the 628 CSi and the 635 CSi, at least until February 1985.

Sales of the 635 CSi models in the USA had been made possible by adding a catalytic converter to the exhaust of the 3.5-litre engine. The installation certainly robbed the engine of a great deal of power, and with an 8.0:1 compression ratio the US-style 635 engine developed just 182bhp at 5400rpm – a miserable 1bhp more than the final version of the 3.2-litre engine of the 633 CSi it replaced. Torque was certainly improved, but

North America finally got its 635 CSi. The side-marker lights are illuminated in this publicity picture; once again, rear head restraints were not fitted. The wheels are standard 14-inch alloys, and not the TRX type favoured in Europe.

140

THE SECOND GENERATION E24s, 1982–1989

214lb ft at 4000rpm was not a huge improvement over the 633 CSi's 196lb ft at 4250rpm. Fortunately, the 95 lb of extra weight that the 635 CSi carried over its predecessor was offset by a lower 3.45:1 final drive to keep acceleration up to scratch. As a result, although the 635 CSi had made it to the USA at last, it was barely any better than the car it replaced, thanks to the restrictions demanded of its larger engine. Unsurprisingly, several specialist companies did good business for a while, bringing in European-specification cars as 'personal imports'.

When *Car and Driver* magazine tested one for its February 1985 issue, it was somewhat lukewarm in its praise. 'A quick car, if not blinding in acceleration' was the verdict, and the car needed 8.2 seconds to reach 60mph and peaked at 132mph. *Road & Track* magazine managed a maximum of 131mph. The old 633 CSi had needed 8.4 seconds to reach 60mph from rest, and had boasted a top speed of 120mph. These cars had standard speedometers, as the US law requiring 85mph types had been repealed for the 1983 model-year. Unspoken, although waiting to catch out buyers at the showrooms, was the 'Gas Guzzler Tax' imposed by the US Government on cars that it considered to be too wasteful of fuel. The 635 CSi, unfortunately, was a classic example.

Nevertheless, worthwhile specification improvements helped distinguish the latest US-model E24 from its predecessor. This was the first E24 to reach the USA with an ABS braking system as standard, and of course it had the front spoiler of its European equivalent, which was a new feature for the USA. However, the lip spoiler was noticeably absent from the boot lid, perhaps because it looked wrong (or had no effect) with the US-specification extended rear bumper that was still fitted.

Leather upholstery was standard, and US cars probably all managed without the rear headrests available in Europe. Upholstery was universally in leather, with a leather-rimmed three-spoke steering wheel and electrically adjustable front seats. The wheels were new to the USA, being the latest TRX type with 165 x 390 dimensions, and a limited-slip differential was an extra-cost option. The good news, as far as *Car and Driver* was concerned, was that this was 'the best-handling BMW since the M1'.

Other Countries

The end of 633 CSi production and the availability of a 635 CSi with catalytic converter had an impact on the availability of E24s in other countries, too. Sweden was one beneficiary of the new arrangements, and the 633 CSi it had been receiving for many years with 635 CSi badges gave way for the 1985 model-year to a real 635 CSi. Even so, it was still not the car that other countries were getting. Perhaps because of delays in homologating the new catalyst-equipped cars for Sweden, the replacement for the 635 CSi-badged 633 CSi was a 635 CSi with yet another variation of the 3.4-litre engine. This had 204PS at 5500rpm and 229lb ft at 4000rpm, a specification that seems to have been agreed with the Swedish authorities for both 635 CSi and 735i deliveries in the 1985 model-year.

The loss of the 633 CSi also meant that Japan now switched to a catalyst-equipped 635 CSi with right-hand drive. In Australia, meanwhile, where no E24 models had been available since spring 1981 (when the options had been limited to the 633 CSi), the E24 made a comeback for 1985 as a 635 CSi to what was more or less the Japanese specification.

AN AIRBAG FOR THE E24

February 1985 was a key date for BMW, with the introduction of the first airbag for an E24. Airbags were still new and expensive technology, and engineering them into the passenger's side of a car not originally intended to take them was hugely costly. Adding an airbag into the steering wheel was considerably easier, and that was what BMW did as an option for the E24s. Their first attempt at an airbag steering wheel was not attractive, and the one introduced in February 1985 was a very plain-looking four-spoke type. Its appearance can hardly have helped sales, although those who valued safety above all else would not have been deterred by its unimaginative design.

■ THE SECOND GENERATION E24s, 1982–1989

February 1985 saw the introduction of right-hand-drive M635 CSi models and the UK was one of those markets that welcomed its first M635 CSi cars. These came with a formidable price tag of £33,750, and had the wider TRX tyres on three-part BBS wheels as standard. These first cars had no side-turn signal repeaters; these would be introduced on the 1986-model cars in September 1985. They did come as standard with a sunroof, and with what BMW called 'sports seats'; the Recaros that were standard in Germany could be had to order at extra cost. They also had five-speed overdrive gearboxes instead of the close-ratio dog's-leg type, and it appears that this more conventional gearbox had now become standard M635 CSi wear for all markets.

The 1986 Models: More KATs

BMW's domestic market was not far behind the USA in requiring catalytic converters. The West German Government in Bonn had originally wanted to enforce the use of catalytic converters on all new cars from January 1986, but during 1984 it postponed the deadline until 1 January 1989 after protests from the German motor industry and from other EEC countries. However, cars with engines of 2 litres or larger had to comply from 1 January 1988 – and that group, of course, included all variants of the E24 range sold in Germany.

Bonn advised German car makers to offer catalytic converters from as early as July 1985, and from that date increased tax on leaded fuel while decreasing that on the unleaded type necessary for catalyst-equipped engines by a corresponding amount. This was one incentive to buyers. A second and more powerful one was the legislation that excused cars equipped with catalytic converters from road tax up to 31 December 1988 (or 31 December 1987 for those with engines of 2 litres or larger). There was also an increase in road tax for cars without catalytic converters from 1 January 1986.

With the catalytic-converter version of the 635 CSi already developed for the USA, BMW was in a good position to meet its own government's requirements. Howev-

LEFT AND OPPOSITE: Seats on the M635 CSi were upholstered in leather – available in cream as well as black – and carried the coveted 'Motorsport' tag on their backrests. The front pair were unique to the model.

THE SECOND GENERATION E24s, 1982–1989

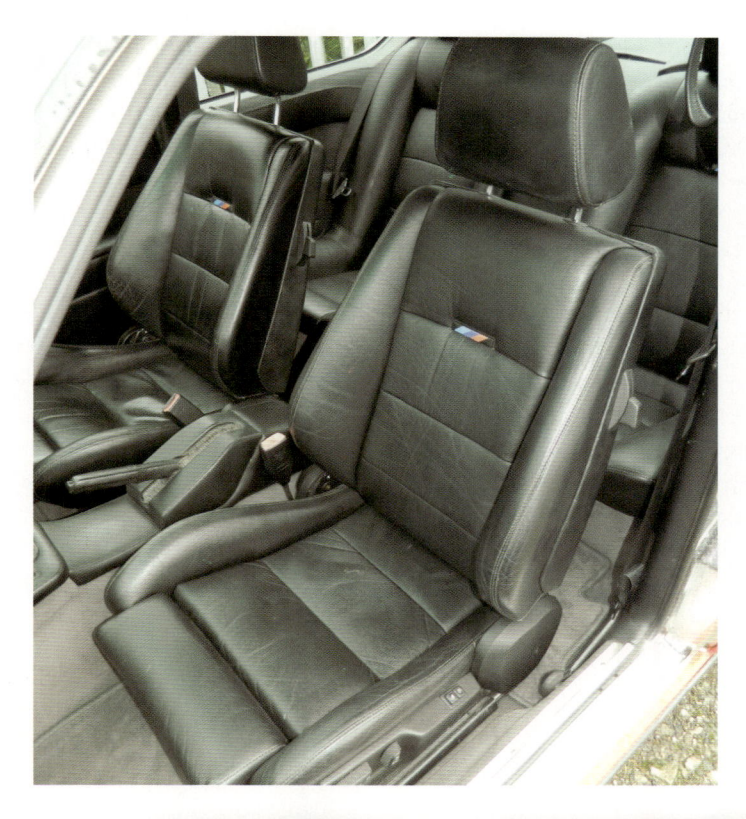

THE SECOND GENERATION E24s, 1982–1989

er, the company knew very well that there would be considerable customer backlash if its 635 CSi suddenly dropped from 218PS to the 185PS (182bhp) tune of the US-model cars. Worse, it was quite clear that rivals Mercedes-Benz were working on catalyst-equipped engines whose power outputs were expected to be very close to those of the non-catalyst variants.

BMW decided to introduce its new engines in stages. From September 1985 for the 1986 model-year, a 635 CSi with catalyst-equipped exhaust became available as an option on the German market. It was in the same 185PS tune as the US cars, and BMW probably did not expect many takers: after all, those who bought an expensive car like the E24 were unlikely to be swayed in their choice by the relatively paltry savings offered under the government scheme. The point, though, was to show willing.

The right-hand-drive M635 CSi would become available in Australia a year later, where *Sports Car World* magazine jumped the gun by reporting on a UK-market example in its August 1985 issue. Impressed by the car's performance, the magazine none the less complained about its lack of refinement:

> BMW's portrayal of the car as a luxury coupé is stretching the truth. Unlike the smooth and quiet engine in the standard 635, the 24-valve version always makes its presence felt. Floor the throttle and a rumble at idle turns into a deep, satisfying growl and finally a full blooded roar as the engine nears peak revs. [However,] the pleasing thing is that while engine noise is always audible, it never becomes harsh.

For most countries where the E24s were sold, the 1986 model-year saw headlamp wipers become part of the standard specification. They had, of course, already been standard on cars sold in the Scandinavian countries. The 635 CSi and M635 CSi switched to a new design of tail spoiler, this time without the side 'arms' of its predecessor and known as a M Technic type. There were some new additions to the options list, too. Cars could be ordered

Check cloth upholstery was specified on this late UK-market car, which also has the rear head restraints.

THE SECOND GENERATION E24s, 1982–1989

THE ROBERT RAUSCHENBERG ART CAR

The sixth in the series of BMW Art Cars was created by American artist Robert Rauschenberg from a US-specification 635 CSi in 1986. The work was notable as the first in which the artist used photographic methods to transfer images on to the car's bodywork. Some of these images were taken from well-known classical paintings.

The Rauschenberg Art Car was the second E24 to be given an artist's treatment.

145

■ THE SECOND GENERATION E24s, 1982–1989

This late UK-market car has the two-colour side stripes – and some very noticeable rust in the front wing.

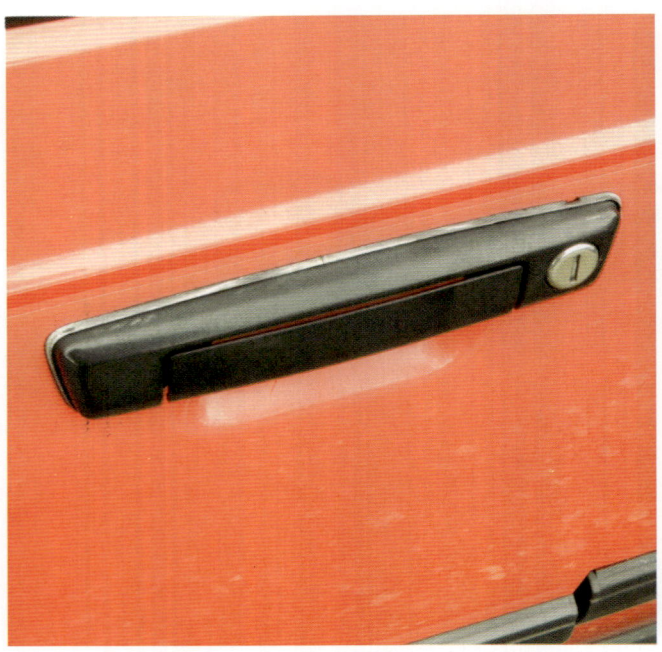

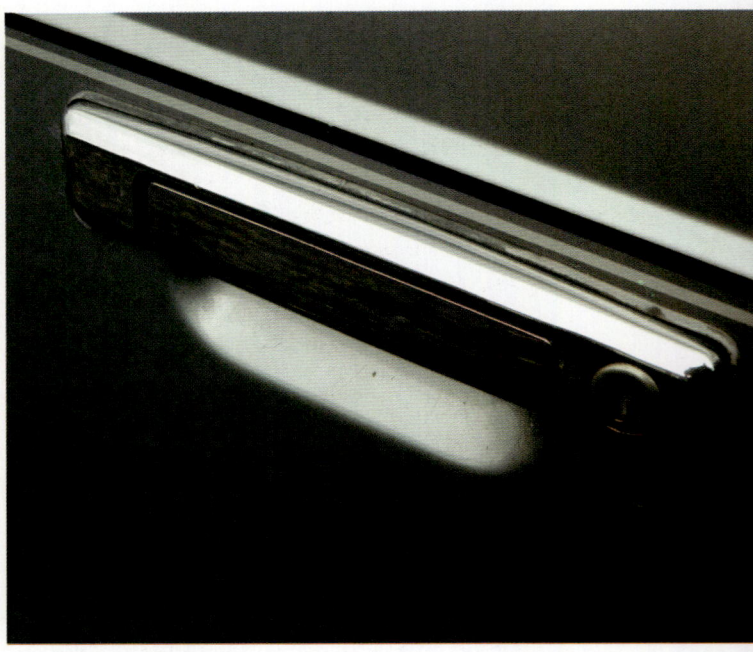

Door handles were normally in bright metal, but were blacked out as part of the Shadowline trim option.

THE SECOND GENERATION E24s, 1982–1989

The Shadowline option brought blacked-out exterior trim around the windows.

with what BMW astutely called Shadowline trim, which meant matt black trim around windows and elsewhere in place of the standard bright-metal finish. On the inside, a rear-seat air-conditioning unit became available. Mounted in a fully-trimmed console that sat between the two individual rear seats, it was useful only to those who regularly carried rear-seat passengers, and it certainly did restrict the already rather tight space in the back of the cabin.

The 1987 Models: DME III

It had been clear for some time that the salvation for high-performance cars in the face of the stifling effects of catalytic converters lay in the use of computer-controlled engine-management and fuelling systems. In Germany, Bosch already had a clear lead in this area, and for the 1987 model-year their third-generation Digital Motor Electronics (DME III) became available on BMW's big six-cylinder engines. Both the new 735i saloons of the E32 range and the 635 CSi coupés had it, and it made an enormous difference.

Catalyst-equipped 3.5-litre engines for 1987 delivered 211PS at 5700rpm and 225lb ft at 4000rpm, up from the 185PS at 5400rpm and 214lb ft at 4000rpm of the earlier KAT 3.5-litre engines. The power figure was not so far adrift of the 218PS at 5200rpm in the non-KAT 635 CSi, even if it was achieved at a higher engine speed, and the torque was comparable. This made the KAT version of the car a much more attractive proposition, and this was particularly important in Germany, where BMW was still jockeying for position in the big coupé market with Mercedes-Benz.

DME III also played an important role in keeping the M635 CSi saleable. It was an integral element of the KAT version of the car that entered production in December 1986. This engine now took on a new name as well. The earlier non-KAT engine had been an M88/3, but the Motorsport division had now decided to use special type-codes for its engines, even though they might be develop-

147

THE SECOND GENERATION E24s, 1982–1989

The late-pattern bumpers and the final design of boot-lid spoiler on the UK-market M635 CSi models.

ments of mainstream production types. As a result, the KAT version of the 24-valve engine became an S38 B35.

With 260PS at 6500rpm and 242lb ft of torque at 4500rpm on a 9.8:1 compression ratio, the engine was respectably close to the non-KAT version with 286PS and 250lb ft at the same engine speeds. Allied to a lower 3.91:1 final drive (borrowed from the 7 Series), the KAT version of the M635 CSi lost only about 5km/h (3mph) off the maximum speed and about half a second from the 0–60mph sprint time, and therefore still turned in figures that made it a worthy flagship of the E24 range.

However, even the latest Motronic engine-management system with DME III could not save the 628 CSi. BMW decided against modifying its engine to take a catalytic converter and withdrew it from production in May 1987. The reason was not that the power losses would have been unacceptable; the fact was that the car was not selling well. Sales had begun to slip badly in 1985 and over the nine years of its production just 5950 cars had been built, giving an average of 661 cars a year.

The 1987 models generally incorporated no other significant changes, but one that made a real difference was the addition of a pop-up wind deflector for the electric sunroof. Wind buffeting and noise with the roof open had been a source of criticism since the E24's early days, and at last BMW was able to cure the problem. There was also a change to the optional wheels of the M635 CSi. The original three-piece BBS cross-spoke alloy wheel gave way to a single-piece wheel with the same design because the earlier wheels had proved susceptible to early corrosion.

A new extra-cost interior option was also introduced for European M635 CSi models in early 1987, although it

THE SECOND GENERATION E24s, 1982–1989

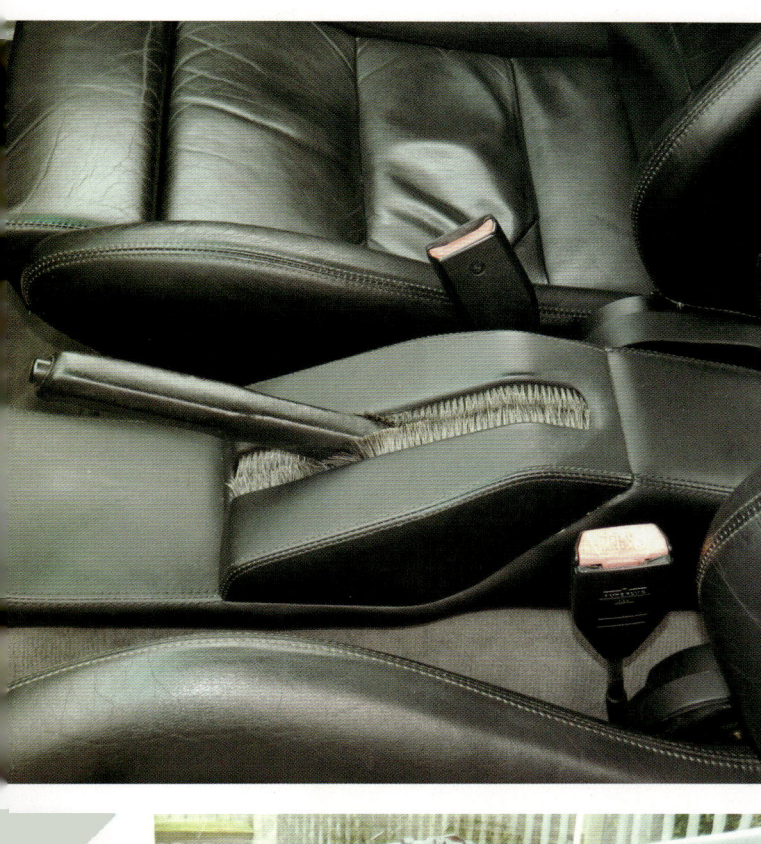

Leather trim on the centre console – part of the 'all-leather' interior – tidied up one of the few cheaper-looking areas of the E24's interior. The trip computer is clear next to the ICE head unit. The dashboard benefited from the all-leather treatment, too, although there were problems with it in the USA.

remained rare in the beginning. This was known as the 'full leather' type. It featured soft Nappa leather for the seats and added leather to the door trims and rear side panels, the A and B pillars and the grab-handles, the headlining and sun visors, the centre console and transmission tunnel, the instrument panel, the glove box and driver's stowage box, and the knee panel under the dashboard.

149

■ THE SECOND GENERATION E24s, 1982–1989

THE M6 FOR JAPAN

A special M6-badged car was built for Japan between November 1986 and March 1988. Essentially similar to the European-specification M635 CSi KAT, it had left-hand drive, which gave it a special cachet in Japan's right-hand-drive market. The headlights were of course right-hand-drive types.

The Japanese M6 was the only E24 ever exported to Japan with a manual gearbox, and always had a high level of equipment. Standard wear were the larger BBS alloy wheels, and the car came with an electric sunroof and a radio compatible with Japanese stations. The front seats were electrically adjustable, the rear air conditioning was standard, and there was a manually operated rear sunblind. Later cars had heated front seats and a position memory for the driver's seat. Shadowline exterior trim was an extra-cost option, but all cars seem to have had the black exhaust tips that were a feature of the E28 M5 at the time.

There were 164 Japanese M6 cars in all, including two pre-production examples built in July 1986. Only 48 cars were built with the pre-facelift specification; the other 116 were 1988-specification cars. The full range of paint colours was available, and interiors were in Highland cloth as standard or in Buffalo leather, which was in Anthracite on early cars and Siam Grey on later examples.

A 1986 Japanese-specification E24 M6.

1988: Greater Euro-US Commonization

By the middle of the 1980s, European car manufacturers had reached a far better understanding of how they could cope with the variations of specification needed between domestic and US versions of their products. The real key was electronic engine management, and BMW had been among the pioneers of the latest Bosch Motronic system. Catalytic converters, which were becoming the internationally accepted method of exhaust-emissions control, no longer needed to strangle engines in the way that they first had. Motronic (and comparable systems made elsewhere) reduced the power and torque losses to far more acceptable levels.

Careful design of combustion chambers helped, too. All these benefits came together in new versions of the 3430cc six-cylinder engine that were announced in June 1987 for both the 1988 model-year 635 CSi and 735i. These latest versions of the 3430cc 'six' had a new cylinder head that gave a 9.2:1 compression ratio in European trim, and had of course been designed to run on the unleaded fuel that was needed for use with catalytic converters. The non-KAT version of the engine came with 220PS at 5700rpm and 232lb ft at 4000rpm, which compared very favourably with the figures for the earlier non-KAT engine (218PS at 5200rpm and 224lb ft at 4000rpm). In KAT trim and for the USA, power was down to 208PS, slightly below the 1987 model-year figure.

This was far from the only change for the 1988 E24 range, however. The most obvious one was the arrival of new bumpers which further commonized the European- and US-specification cars. Both types shared plastic side sections painted to match the bodywork (the US ones incorporating marker lights, of course). The European cars had a fixed bumper 'insert' while that on the US cars was mounted on damper struts; under low-speed impact, it could move back into the housing created by those side sections.

Front airdams on all models were also slightly modified, and for 1988 incorporated fog lamps with rounded corners instead of the rectangular type on earlier cars. European cars took on a new self-levelling rear suspension, again as standard, and all now came with the BBS alloy wheels and 240/45 VR 415 TRX tyres. Headlamps were uprated yet again with a new ellipsoid design that was

THE SECOND GENERATION E24s, 1982–1989

The bumper wraparounds on late cars had a black stripe that lent additional character.

The bumpers were fixed on European-specification cars, but it is easy to see how the sliding section fitted on US-market models.

■ THE SECOND GENERATION E24s, 1982–1989

Driving lamps were set into the apron spoiler on the M635 CSi.

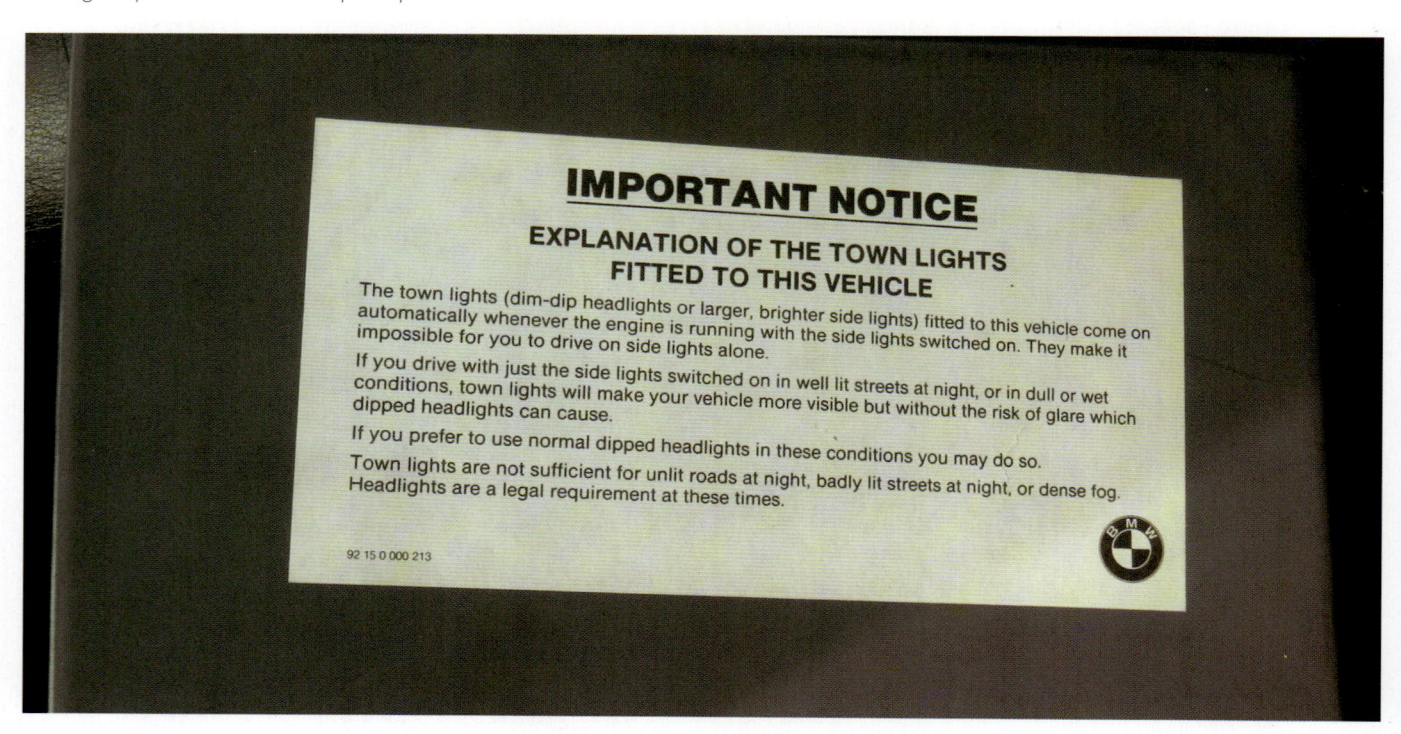

For a brief period in the late 1980s, UK regulations required a 'dim-dip' lighting system, which made it impossible to drive on side lights alone. An instruction sticker was added to the owner's literature pack on cars equipped in this way.

THE SECOND GENERATION E24s, 1982–1989

shared with the fog lamps – and with the latest 7 Series saloons. In the UK, the 'full-leather' option introduced at the start of the 1987 calendar-year in Europe became available with the marketing name of Highline, and it included the power-adjustable front seats with their three-position memory.

The M635 CSi meanwhile had its own changes. It lost its unique apron spoiler and for 1988 shared the spoiler of the 635 CSi. The gearshift grip was changed to the supposedly more ergonomic type introduced for the 1987-model 7 Series cars. In the UK, the new Highline leather interior was also made standard.

All European cars now came with green tinted glass instead of the earlier bronze-tinted type, no doubt because its greater heat-absorbing efficiency was necessary for correct functioning of the new automatic air-conditioning system that became standard on European models. Instead of juggling separate heater and air-conditioning controls, the driver simply had to set a target interior temperature and leave the system to achieve it.

The M6 and L6 for the USA

The arrival of a KAT version of the M635 CSi during the 1987 model-year was an obvious prelude to the next stage: introducing the Motorsport coupé to the US market. There were further changes to be made before it was quite ready, but the first examples reached the USA in July 1987 as 1988 models after a February 1987 announcement. The new car was given a new name, too – the M6 – which tied it in more closely with the other Motorsport cars, the M3 and the M5. In Europe, the M635 CSi had established itself so well with that name that BMW probably thought there was no point in re-badging it as an M6.

Like every other E24 sold in the USA as a 1988 model, the M6 came with a driver's side airbag as standard. It now had a redesigned steering wheel that was much more attractive than the earlier type. Every example also had a sunroof, air conditioning and a limited-slip differential. The wheels were BBS three-piece alloys with the 210 TR 415 size. It had leather upholstery rather than the fabric type of the European models, and the front seats had electric

BMW's US arm introduced the L6 (Luxury Six) coupé to run alongside the M6 (Motorsport Six) coupé, but it was not a great success.

153

■ THE SECOND GENERATION E24s, 1982–1989

adjustment with a three-position memory. Also standard was an AM/FM stereo ICE system with no fewer than eight speakers.

The only option on the US-model M6 was heated front seats, which were standard on the Canadian derivative. The 'full-leather' interior was also available at extra cost, and was marketed with the same Highline name as in the UK. Unfortunately, the leather dash top did not take kindly to the hot sun in some US states. A number were damaged, so the Highline option gave way to a modified version of Highline leather with a standard plastic dashboard, familiarly known as 'Halfline'.

BMW North America believed that they would be able to sell more 635 CSi models on the back of showroom interest in the new M6, and to that end they introduced a third E24 model that was never made available anywhere else. Known and badged as an L6 – the name supposedly standing for 'Luxury Six-cylinder' – the car was essentially a 635 CSi automatic with the 'full-leather' interior and a collection of other E24 options that included the rear air-conditioning package.

Final trim and preparation of these cars, including the application of their L6 badges, was carried out by BMW North America. The showroom price was close to $50,000, which was still less than the $58,200 (inclusive of 'Gas Guzzler Tax') demanded for an M6 on the West Coast of the USA. On this occasion, however, BMW's US arm got it wrong: the L6 proved to be a slow seller and was withdrawn from the catalogues at the end of the 1988 model-year. According to legend, some of these cars remained unsold up to four years later.

The Last E24s

The 1989 season was to be the last one for the E24 range, and in the autumn of 1989 it became clear why there had been so many equipment upgrades in the car's final years. BMW did not replace it with a new 6 Series but rather with an even more expensive luxury GT called the 8 Series. The upgrades, and the higher prices that came with them, had been preparing the market for the new model.

The final M635 CSi models had the dual side-stripe treatment.

THE SECOND GENERATION E24s, 1982–1989

E24 PRODUCTION FIGURES BY CALENDAR-YEAR, 1983–1989

Note that manufacture of cars for these seven model-years was actually spread over eight calendar years because it began in mid-1982. To the figures shown below should therefore be added a proportion of those shown in Chapter 6 for the 1982 calendar-year.

	1983	1984	1985	1986	1987	1988	1989
628 CSi	524	401	304	186	45		
628 CSi Auto	255	191	160	89	15		
628 CSi RHD	31	35	16	16	6		
628 CSi RHD Auto	162	114	113	76	11		
633 CSi USA	1659	1173					
633 CSi USA Auto	1155	776					
633 CSi Japan	511	58					
635 CSi	1904	1365	1061	539	173	48	2
635 CSi Auto	1257	962	892	413	106	21	2
635 CSi RHD	84	72	66	33	28	20	9
635 CSi RHD Auto	423	475	566	537	594	352	295
635 CSi KAT			255	170	242	250	32
635 CSi Auto KAT			203	181	250	280	26
635 CSi RHD KAT				57	1		
635CSi Auto RHD KAT				218	1	49	2
635 CSi USA		695	1457	1037	278	185	61
635 CSi USA Auto		532	2268	2265	1998	1643	583
635 CSi Auto Japan		2	502	506	457	381	
M635 CSi		1404	1477	302	72	28	
M635 CSi RHD		8	286	102	45	31	52
M635 CSi KAT				5	69	43	
M6 USA				255	1193	319	
M6 Japan				40	108	16	
Year total	7965	8263	9626	8386	5692	3666	1064

Note: of 1767 M6 models numbered as built to US specification, 135 were actually built to Canadian specification with items such as km/h speedometers. This means that only 1632 cars were built for the USA. There were 60 cars for Canada in the 1987 model-year, 73 in the 1988 model-year and just two in the 1989 model-year.

■ THE SECOND GENERATION E24s, 1982–1989

For the 1989 model-year, the European M635 CSi gained the latest style of bumper at the rear, together with a colour-coded tail spoiler. It came with the electrically adjustable front seats and their three-position memory, now with the controls relocated to the seat base from their earlier position on the centre console. In the UK, BMW GB created its own Motorsport Edition of 20 cars, all of which had left the Dingolfing assembly lines between October 1988 and January 1989. These had Shadowline exterior trim and tri-colour M logos on labels attached to all four seats. They came with three special colour and trim combinations: ten had Misano Red paint with Black Nappa Highline leather, five had Nogaro Silver metallic paint with Black Nappa Highline leather, and five more had Macao Blue metallic paint with Lotus White Nappa Highline leather. There were also unproven rumours that these engines had special manifolding and management systems to deliver 292bhp.

The last Motorsport E24s were built in February 1989, and the end of production was not long in coming for the only other model still left in the E24 range. The last of 86,216 cars, a 635 CSi, left the assembly lines in Dingolfing on 4 April 1989, and the E24's reign as one of Europe's leading luxury coupés was over.

PAINT AND TRIM OPTIONS

For most model-years, there was a choice of around 20 paint colours, the majority being metallic types.

Upholstery was available in velour up to 1988. Leather was available throughout this period, with a 'full-leather' option from mid-1987. Highland cloth arrived on the M635 CSi for the 1984 model-year and replaced velour as the alternative to leather in some countries from autumn 1985.

TECHNICAL SPECIFICATIONS, E24 6 SERIES MODELS 1983–1989

Engines:

628 CSi
Type M30 B28 six-cylinder petrol, installed with a 30-degree tilt to the right
2788cc (86mm x 80mm)
Single overhead camshaft, driven by Duplex chain
Seven-bearing crankshaft
Compression ratio 9.3:1
Bosch L-Jetronic fuel injection
184PS at 5800rpm
235Nm (173lb ft) at 4200rpm

633 CSi
As above, except:
Type M30 B32
3210cc (89mm x 86mm)
Compression ratio 9.3:1 (8.0:1 for USA)
197PS at 5500rpm
283Nm (209lb ft) at 4300rpm
In US 49-State tune:
    177bhp (SAE) at 5500rpm
    196lb ft at 4000rpm

635 CSi (1982–1987)
Type M30 B34
3430cc (92mm x 86mm)
Compression ratio 10.0:1
Bosch Motronic fuel injection
218PS at 5200rpm
304Nm (224lb ft) at 4000rpm

635 CSi with catalytic converter (1984–1987)
As above, except:
Type M30 B34 KAT
185PS at 5400rpm
290Nm (214lb ft) at 4000rpm

635 CSi (1987–1989)
As for 1982-1987 635 CSi, except:
220PS at 5700rpm
232lb ft at 4000rpm

635 CSi KAT (1987–1989)
As above, except:
208PS at 5700rpm
220lb ft at 4000rpm

156

THE SECOND GENERATION E24s, 1982–1989

M635 CSi (without catalytic converter)
Type M88/3 six-cylinder petrol, installed with a 30-degree tilt to the right
3453cc (93.4mm x 84mm)
Compression ratio 10.5:1
286PS at 6500rpm
333Nm (245lb ft) at 4500rpm

M635 CSi KAT and M6
As above, except:
Type S38 B35
Compression ratio 9.8:1
260PS at 6500rpm
328Nm (242lb ft) at 4500rpm

Gearboxes:
Five-speed Getrag 265 manual gearbox optional on 628 CSi and standard on 633 CSi
  Ratios 3.82:1, 2.20:1, 1.40:1, 1.00:1, 0.81:1, reverse 3.70:1.
Five-speed Getrag 260 manual gearbox standard on 635 CSi
  Ratios 3.822:1, 2.202:1, 1.398:1, 1.000:1, 0.813:1, reverse 3.45:1
Five-speed Sports manual gearbox optional on 628 CSi, 635 CSi 1982–1987, and early M635 CSi
  Ratios 3.717:1, 2.403:1, 1,766:1, 1.263:1, 1.000:1, reverse 3.70:1
Five-speed Getrag 280/5 manual gearbox standard on M635 CSi from 1985
  Ratios 3.51:1, 2.08:1, 1.35:1, 1.00:1, 0,81:1, reverse 3.70:1
Three-speed ZF 3 HP 22 automatic gearbox optional on 633 CSi
  Ratios 2.48:1, 1.48:1, 1,00:1, reverse 2.09:1
Four-speed ZF 4 HP 22 automatic gearbox optional on 628 CSi and 635 CSi from 1982; 635 CSi with type 4 HP 22 EH from 1983
  Ratios 2.48:1, 1.48:1, 1,00:1, 0.73:1, reverse 2.09:1

Axle ratios:

628 CSi	3.45:1
633 CSi	3.25:1
635 CSi	3.07:1
635 CSi (USA)	3.45:1
635 CSi KAT	3.64:1
M635 CSi	3.73:1
M635 CSi KAT	3.91:1
M6	3.91:1

Suspension, steering and brakes:
Front suspension with McPherson struts, coil springs and anti-roll bar
Rear suspension with semi-trailing arms, struts, coil springs and anti-roll bar; self-levelling on 635 CSi from 1987
Worm-and-roller steering with 16.9:1 ratio and power assistance as standard
Disc brakes all round, with 280mm diameter on front wheels (300mm ventilated discs on M635 CSi and M6) and 272mm on rear wheels; twin hydraulic circuits and hydraulic servo assistance standard; ABS standard on all 635 CSi and M635CSi, optional on 628 CSi and then standard from September 1984

Dimensions:
Overall length: 4755mm (187.2in); US models 4920mm (193.7in)
Overall width: 1725mm (67.9in)
Overall height: 1365mm (53.7in) all models except M635 CSi
1354mm (53.3in) for M635 CSi and M6
Wheelbase: 2626mm (103.4in)
Front track: 1422mm (56in)
Rear track: 1487mm (58.5in)

Wheels and tyres:
6J x 14 alloy wheels on 633 CSi
6.50J x 14 alloy wheels for 628 CSi and 635 CSi
165 TR 390 or 210 TR 455 alloy wheels for M635 CSi and M6
195/70 VR 14 tyres for 633 CSi
205/70 VR 14 tyres for 628 CSi and 635 CSi
220/55 VR 390 TRX optional for 635 CSi (standard in some markets)
220/55 VR 390 or 240/45 VR 415 for M635 CSi and M6

Unladen weights:

628 CSi	1450kg (3197lb)
628 CSi automatic	1470kg (3241lb)
633 CSi	1495kg (3296lb)
635 CSi	1470kg (3241lb)
635 CSi automatic	1490kg (3285lb)
635 CSi KAT	1475kg (3252lb)
635 CSi KAT auto	1495kg (3296lb)
M635 CSi	1510kg (3329lb)

THE SECOND GENERATION E24s, 1982–1989

PERFORMANCE FIGURES FOR E24 6 SERIES MODELS

628 CSi	0–100km/h	9.0–9.5 sec
	Maximum	210–215km/h (130–133.5mph)
633 CSi	0–100km/h	8.5 sec
	Maximum	215km/h (133.5mph)
635 CSi	0–100km/h	8.5 sec
	Maximum	225km/h (140mph) or 217km/h (135mph) with catalytic converter
635 CSi KAT	0–100km/h	8.5 sec
	Maximum	225km/h (140mph)
M635 CSi	0–100km/h	6.5–7.0 sec
	Maximum	250–255km/h (155–158mph)
M635 CSi KAT and M6	0–100km/h	6.5–7.0 sec
	Maximum	240–245km/h (149–152mph)

IDENTIFICATION NUMBERS FOR E24 MODELS, 1976–1989

For clarity, identification numbers are shown here with a gap between the first three figures of the number and the last four. This gap is not present on the cars' identification plates.

628 CSi
European models

557 0001 to 557 1349	LHD manual	model 5131	
	Total	1349	
557 5001 to 557 5539	LHD automatic	5141	539
559 5001 to 559 5066	RHD manual, UK	5132	66
559 7001 to 559 7210	RHD automatic, UK	5142	210
815 0000 to 815 2027	LHD manual	5171	2027
815 5000 to 815 5154	RHD manual	5172	154
816 0000 to 816 0951	LHD automatic	5181	951
816 5000 to 816 5651	RHD automatic	5182	651
		Total	5947

630 CS
European models

436 0001 to 436 1725	LHD manual	5111	1725
436 2001 to 436 2875	LHD manual	5111	875
436 5001 to 436 5897	LHD automatic	5121	897
436 6001 to 436 6475	LHD automatic	5121	475
		Total	3972

630 CSi
US models

550 0001 to 550 0432	LHD manual, California	5133	432
550 5001 to 550 5496	LHD manual, 49-State	5134	496
551 0001 to 551 0430	LHD automatic, California	5143	430
551 5001 to 551 5436	LHD automatic, 49-State	5144	436
		Total	1794

633 CSi
European models

437 5001 to 437 8713	LHD manual	5231	3713
437 9001 to 438 0000	LHD manual	5231	1000
438 0001 to 438 0218	RHD manual, UK	5232	218
438 1001 to 438 1133	RHD manual, UK	5232	133
438 5001 to 438 6202	LHD automatic	5241	1202
438 7001 to 438 8449	LHD automatic	5241	1449
439 0001 to 439 0251	RHD automatic, UK	5242	251
439 1001 to 439 2094	RHD automatic, UK	5242	94
556 5001 to 556 5831	LHD manual	5231	831
		Total	8891

158

THE SECOND GENERATION E24s, 1982–1989

Japanese models

439 5001 to 439 5523	LHD automatic	5249	523
554 0001 to 554 0468	LHD automatic	5209	468
819 5000 to 819 5265	LHD automatic	5207	265
819 7000 to 819 7630	LHD automatic	5289	630
		Total	1886

US models

552 0001 to 552 0237	LHD manual, California	5233	237
552 5001 to 552 5450	LHD manual, 49-State	5234	450
553 0001 to 553 0269	LHD automatic, California	5243	269
553 5001 to 553 5507	LHD automatic, 49-State	5244	507
555 5001 to 555 6248	LHD manual, 49-State	5235	1248
556 0001 to 556 1113	LHD automatic	5245	1113
672 5001 to 672 8592	LHD manual	5274	592
699 5000 to 699 7531	LHD automatic	5284	2531
750 5000 to 750 5949	LHD manual	5236	949
751 0000 to 751 0754	LHD automatic	5246	754
		Total	8650

635 CSi

European models

127 5001 to 127 5949	LHD manual, KAT	5351	949
128 0001 to 128 0940	LHD automatic, KAT	5361	940
188 6001 to 188 6058	RHD manual, KAT	5352	58
188 7001 to 188 7270	RHD automatic, KAT	5362	270
554 5001 to 555 0000	LHD manual	5331	5000
555 0001 to 555 0825	RHD manual	5332	825
558 0001 to 558 1958	LHD automatic	5341	1958
558 5001 to 558 6143	RHD automatic	5342	1143
559 0001 to 559 3072	LHD manual	5331	3072
817 0000 to 817 4999	LHD manual	5371	4999
817 5000 to 817 5466	RHD manual, UK	5372	466
818 0000 to 818 4572	LHD automatic	5381	4572
818 5000 to 818 8766	RHD automatic, UK	5382	3766
940 2000 to 940 4342	LHD manual	5371	2342
		Total	30,360

Japanese models

076 5001 to 076 6848	LHD automatic	5389	1848
		Total	1848

US models

060 5001 to 060 8713	LHD manual	5374	3713
061 0001 to 061 5000	LHD automatic	5384	5000
326 5001 to 326 9289	LHD automatic	5384	4289
		Total	13,002

M635 CSi

European models

076 0001 to 076 0524	RHD manual, UK	5532	524
105 0001 to 105 3283	LHD manual	5531	3283
228 5001 to 228 5117	LHD manual, KAT	5511	117
		Total	3924

M6

Japanese models

256 3001 to 256 3164	LHD manual	5519	164
		Total	164

US models

256 0001 to 256 1767	LHD manual	5514	1767
		Total	1767

■ THE SECOND GENERATION E24s, 1982–1989

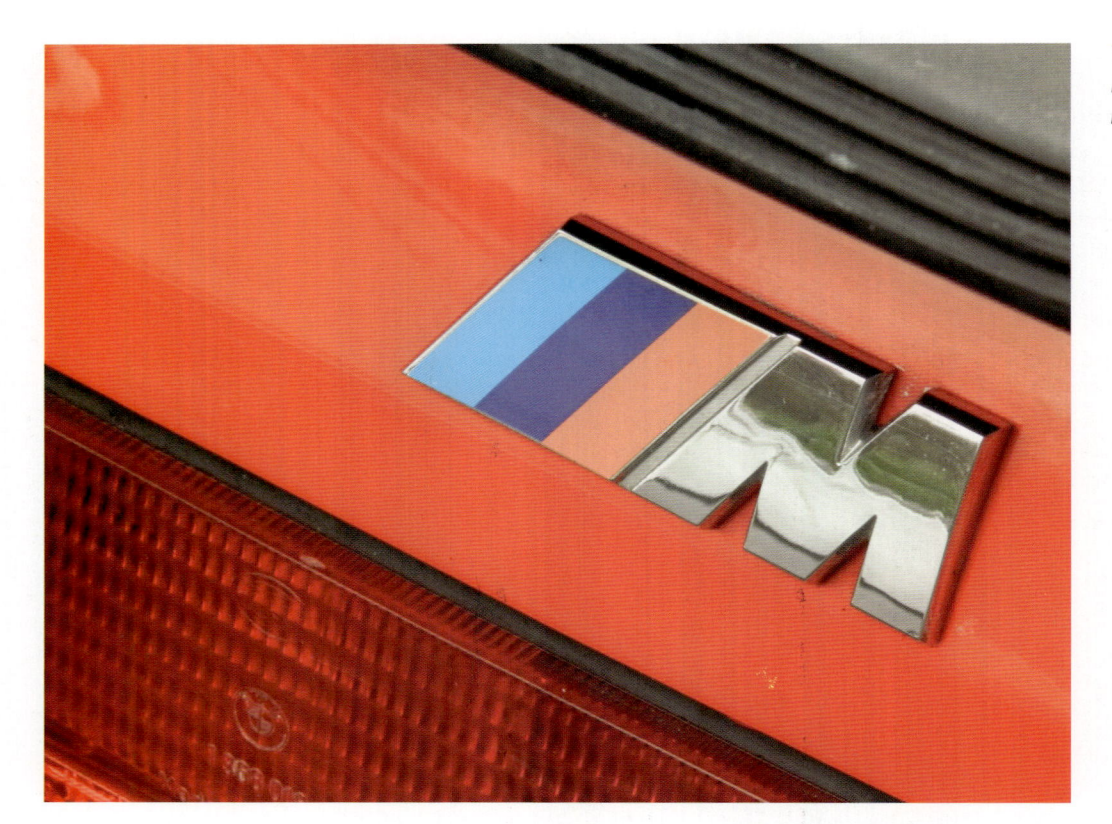

The distinctive and coveted BMW Motorsport logo on the rear of an M6.

The identification labels on a late UK-market M635 CSi – in fact, one of the 20 special Motorsport editions, as identified by the paint colour label.

160

THE SECOND GENERATION E24s, 1982–1989

Two views of a couple of US-specification M635 CSis, one featuring the BMW Motorsport badge and stripes (above), the other in more understated guise in distinguished black paintwork (below).

161

CHAPTER EIGHT

THE E24 IN COMPETITION

Racing was never an element in the early planning for the E24 coupés. These cars were always intended as luxury coupés – luxury coupés with high performance, certainly, but BMW simply saw no need in the beginning to prepare them for competition work. The homologation for the CSL coupés would allow them to race until 1979, by which time the new E24s would have been on the market for three years, and there were plenty of other models in the BMW stable that could be turned into highly competitive racers if the need arose.

However, BMW had not counted on the enthusiasm of its racing customers...

The BMW coupés were a major presence on the tracks in the first half of the 1980s; every car in this picture is an E24.

THE E24 IN COMPETITION

The wider rear tyres of the racing coupé are in evidence here as Dieter Quester gets down to business in a Schnitzer-prepared car.

Dieter Quester in another Schnitzer-prepared car.

■ THE E24 IN COMPETITION

1980

The Austrian team that called itself Racing Corporation Vienna had been racing BMWs since the middle of the 1970s, and between 1977 and 1979 had campaigned a 3.0 CS coupé to some effect. Once the 3.0 CS was no longer eligible under FIA rules, it was natural that the team should turn to BMW for a car to replace it, and the obvious choice was the latest 635 CSi coupé.

Group 2 regulations for 1980 required a relatively small production run of just 1000 cars a year, and the 635 CSi easily qualified – during 1979, more than 3500 examples of the car had been manufactured for world markets. With homologation papers in place, Racing Corporation Vienna set about preparing a car to compete in that year's European Touring Car Championship.

There could be no question of picking up where the CSL racers had left off and taking the cars on to the logical next stage. The Group 2 regulations expressly forbade such things as 24-valve cylinder heads and the special gearboxes that had been used on the later racing E9 coupés. However, old-fashioned tuning methods could still produce worthwhile results, and the green Racing Corporation Vienna 635 CSi hit the tracks with 367bhp. That was very nearly 70 per cent more power than a showroom-standard car of the period.

Drivers Harald Neger and Heribert Werginz brought to the party their experience with the team's old 3.0 CS car. The third member of the team for 1980 was Umberto Grano, who had done so well at the wheel of the Luigi Racing CSL. With the main sponsorship coming from consumer electronics maker Grundig and from BMW Italy (who had earlier supported Luigi Racing), the car made an excellent debut during March at the Monza round of the European Touring Car Championship with a win at the four-hour race. Interestingly, they were not alone. Finishing further down the rankings in ninth place was a second BMW 635 CSi, driven by the privateer team of Dieter Schmid and Karl Hurler. Clearly, there was already wider racing interest in the E24 models.

At Vallelunga in April, the Racing Team Vienna 635 CSi repeated the trick: Harald Neger claimed pole position and went on to set the fastest lap and to win the race. Although the car did not finish at the Brno GP in June, when it was put out of commission after an accident, it was back on form again for the RAC Tourist Trophy in September when it claimed another victory under Negel-Holz sponsorship. Here, it was joined by a second 635 CSi, entered by BMW Italy. This car had Maurer sponsorship and was driven by Dieter Schmid and Eddy Joosen, but did not finish after the head gasket failed.

1981–1982

Despite this very promising start, the 635 CSi seemed to fail to build on its success during 1981. BMW Italy continued to provide support, this time to a car run by the Swiss Eggenberger Racing team and further sponsored by leather-goods maker Enny. Umberto Grano and Helmut Kelleners were engaged to drive it for the Brno GP in June, and they duly won the event. However, things then went very quiet for a time. One reason may have been the fact that BMW were busily working on a lightened E24 – not for racing but in order to improve road performance (see Chapter 7). With such a car in the offing, racing teams would have chosen to wait rather than spend their money on trying to make the existing car go faster. Another reason must have been that the FIA regulations were about to change. Group 2 would cease to exist after 1981, and in its place would come a new category called Group A.

Group A was initially intended to encourage privateers and was described as being for 'modified touring cars'. It called for competition machines based on production cars, and set limits on power, weight, overall cost and the technology permitted. As far as the basic production cars were concerned, it required an annual production of 5000 examples, a figure which at that stage was way beyond the sales of the 635 CSi.

So for 1982 the E24 disappeared from the tracks, and the BMW 'works' support went to the lower-powered 528i saloons that were being built in adequate numbers. It soon became clear, however, that if BMW were to stand any chance in this new competition category, they were going to need a bigger and more powerful engine. The 528i was simply not up to the Motul-sponsored TWR Jaguar XJ-S racers with their 5.3-litre V12 engines. The only option was going to be the 635 CSi once again.

1983

BMW let it be known that they intended to homologate the big coupé for Group A racing, and before long there was a queue of willing customers. So it was that the 635 CSi, by now with lightened bodyshell and 3430cc engine, gained its homologation papers on 1 March 1983. Since then, many enthusiasts have wondered why the company did not wait

THE E24 IN COMPETITION

Watch manufacturer Eterna sponsored the E24 coupés in the 1983 season.

a few months and then homologate the much more powerful M635 CSi with its 24-valve Motorsport engine. The answer is in fact very simple. BMW were realistic enough about the Motorsport car's sales prospects to know that it would never achieve the 5000 cars a year needed for Group 2 homologation. They were right, too: production of the car never even reached 2000 copies a year.

In fact, even the 635 CSi encountered a little homologation trouble in the beginning, because the FIA was unhappy about the use of rubber for the rear spoiler and plastic for the front spoiler and rain gutters. All these were genuine production features, however, and so they were added to the coupé's Group A homologation in due course.

Jeremy Walton records that there were 25 takers for Group A coupés in 1983, and that it was Schnitzer Motorsport who prepared most of them. Hartge also prepared cars for its own use. As things were to turn out, the 1983 season would be the best one for the 635 CSi, although the car would continue to make its mark right through its brief international racing career.

BMW support was put behind the Schnitzer-prepared cars, which also had sponsorship from Swiss luxury watch manufacturer Eterna and ran as Team Schnitzer-Eterna. Top driver was Dieter Quester, who had long been asso-

Dieter Quester was one of the most successful E24 drivers on the tracks in the 1980s.

165

■ THE E24 IN COMPETITION

THE GROUP A 635 CSi

The Group A cars were always going to be very different from the standard showroom models, even if they looked very much like them, and the FIA regulations allowed a good number of modifications. One thing that had counted against the E24s as competition cars before was their great weight, but in fact BMW need not have worried on this score. In racing trim, a Group A 635 CSi with aluminium rollover bar in place of the standard steel type weighed 1161kg (2554 lb), which was 245kg (540 lb) less than the production car. In fact, in order to meet the minimum 1185kg (2607 lb) weight stipulated for their class, they had to carry 24kg (53 lb) of ballast!

Over the four years from 1983 to 1986, BMW supplied more than 50 racing 635 CSi cars to teams around the world. These cars did not start life as standard production models, but were specially built and had 'chassis' or identification numbers outside the standard production sequences. For example, the three cars used by the Schnitzer team in 1983 were numbered RA1/007, RA1/013 and RA1/31.

Most of the racing 635 CSi cars had left-hand drive,

If the shape of the dashboard was familiar, there was a great deal about the cockpit of this 1983 Group A car that was special. The three-spoke wheel afforded the driver a clear view of the multi-dial instrument panel.

THE E24 IN COMPETITION

although two right-hand-drive cars were built for teams supported by BMW Great Britain during 1984. Essentially, BMW supplied the basic car: preparation and detail finish were then down to the teams themselves. On the tallest of the axle ratios available, BMW claimed a Group A racer was capable of 155mph, although more typical was a top speed of about 150mph. When the German magazine *auto, motor und sport* tested a Group A car, it recorded a 0–62mph time of 6.9 seconds – it was quick, but very similar to the performance available from the M635 CSi road car.

These special racing coupés all came with bodyshells that had been strengthened by additional seam-welding, and of course they also had an internal roll cage. As for wheels, the most commonly used type were centre-lock multi-piece 16-inch alloys made by BBS, with 11-inch rims. The choice of tyres was always down to the individual team, but the 635 CSi racers generally ran on Dunlops in the beginning, switching to Pirellis during 1984.

At the heart of every racing car is a specially developed engine, but the Group A regulations were always very restrictive of permitted development. Even so, the outputs attained in 1983 (typically 285PS at 6000rpm and 349Nm/257 lb ft at 5000rpm) were significantly bettered in later racing seasons. The Schnitzer cars racing in 1986 were claimed to have 334PS at 7100rpm.

Right from the start, the engines that BMW supplied to those teams racing a 635 CSi were very different from the standard production type, which had a 92mm bore. Under the regulations, a manufacturing tolerance of 0.6mm was permitted; the engines that came from the Motorsport division made use of that tolerance, which gave a swept volume of just over 3475cc.

The engines were allowed to run racing pistons, too, and BMW had theirs made by Mahle, ensuring that the pistons also raised the compression ratio to 11.1:1. The inlet ports and manifolding were carefully re-worked to minimize airflow restrictions, and the cars ran a 324-degree camshaft with 46mm inlet and 38mm exhaust valves. Although the Motronic engine-management system could be reprogrammed, the exhaust manifold had to remain standard.

Power was transmitted to the rear axle by a five-speed gearbox with dog's-leg shift gate that was essentially similar to the 'sports' gearbox available for the 635 CSi. Its ratios differed, though, being 2.330:1, 1.680:1, 1.353:1, 1.146:1 and 1.000:1. The three optional final-drive ratios spanned a range from 3.07:1 to 3.91:1, and all gearsets were usually accompanied by a 75 per cent limited-slip differential. On the options list were stronger bushes for the differential.

Suspension components could be modified, and BMW made available some of the components that had been used earlier in the CSL coupés that had raced in Group 2 and IMSA events. There was a selection of Bilstein springs and dampers to suit different circuits, and it was possible to order solid suspension joints, different lower front suspension arms, and special rear trailing arms. Steering lacked the standard power assistance, and quicker-than-standard ratios were available.

The racing brakes had bigger discs than the production type, and four-piston calipers, too. The components originated with either ATE in Germany or AP Racing in Britain. The racers had neither ABS nor – usually – hydraulic power assistance for the brakes, although this was reinstated for some long-distance racing events. The race cars always had a balance control in the cabin, allowing the driver to alter the front-to-rear brake balance to suit the characteristics of different circuits.

Tiff Needell tried Frank Sytner's 635 CSi for the 17 November 1983 issue of *Autosport* magazine:

> *The 635 BMW provides a very civilized way to enter international motorsport. The basics are provided by Munich, but there is plenty of room for... anyone... to tune and improve their individual steeds. Although a very smooth and forgiving car to drive, I feel there is very much to come yet from the BeeEms for that very reason.*

■ THE E24 IN COMPETITION

ABOVE AND BELOW: The 1983 Cheylesmore Motorsport car is still campaigned in historic racing events for Group A cars. It is pictured here with Jody Halse at the wheel, although the car still carries the name of its original driver, Hans Stuck, on the door. CRAIG PUSEY

168

THE E24 IN COMPETITION

ciated with BMWs, and in particular with the CSL racing coupés. For 1983, he would win the driver's title in the European Touring Car Championship, although the manufacturer's title that year went to Alfa Romeo. The competition was hotting up: alongside the formidable TWR-prepared Jaguars, there were now Rover Vitesses and turbocharged Volvos to beat.

Quester quickly settled into a good season, winning the ETCC's opening round at Monza in a 635 CSi co-driven by Carlo Rossi. In May, an Eggenberger 635 CSi sponsored by BMW Italy and driven by Helmut Kelleners and Umberto Grano won at Mugello. Quester then finished second with co-driver Hans Heyer at the Brno GP in June, behind an XJ-S. A few weeks later at the Nürburgring, the winning car was the 635 CSi of Quester and Winkelhock.

Meanwhile, 635 CSi racers had begun to proliferate on the tracks. At the Spa 24-hour event in July, the field included no fewer than 17 of them, and 11 not only stayed the course but were among the top 20 finishers. The overall result could hardly have been better for BMW. First place went to a 635 CSi prepared by the Belgian Juma team and driven by Thierry Tassin with Armin Hahne and Hans Heyer. Right behind in second place was the Schnitzer car, driven by Dieter Quester with Carlo Rossi and Manfred Winkelhock.

At Silverstone in September, Quester managed a strong fifth place in the Canon RAC Tourist Trophy event with Hans Heyer as co-driver, after the car he was originally allocated lost a wheel. Two weeks later at Zolder, he was less fortunate: an accident in practice put Quester's car out of contention, but the event was a huge triumph for BMW. The first seven places all went to their big coupés, with Kelleners and Grano claiming first in the Eggenberger Motorsport car after a last-minute fuel problem relegated Marc Duez in the Hartge Motorsport car to second place.

Even though British cars, in the shape of the Jaguar XJ-S and the Rover Vitesse, were fighting for top honours during the 1983 season, two British teams also chose to campaign BMW coupés. One was the Grace International Racing Partnership, whose lead driver was Frank Sytner, BMW dealer and, in 1982, a Rover driver for the TWR team. The other team was Cheylesmore Motorsport, who had Hans Stuck as their lead driver.

The Cheylesmore car with Stuck partnered by Jonathan Palmer fought some formidable duels with Steve Soper's TWR-prepared Rover Vitesse, but was never quite in contention for podium places. More successful was the Alpina-engined Sytner car. This made its debut in May at Donington, an event which qualified as a round of the European Championship, but was put out of action after losing a wheel on the twelfth lap. Six weeks later, it came third in another round of the British Touring Car Championship, then second at another Donington event, and finally fourth at the British GP, although results after that were disappointing.

1984

Team Schnitzer again took the lead in European racing with the 635 CSi for the 1984 season, this time with sponsorship from BMW Originalteile (the factory's spare parts organization). There were other strong teams fielding the BMW coupés, notably Hartge Motorsport, the Bastos-sponsored Juma team, and Eggenberger, who were supported by BMW Italy. Yet, despite the proliferation of BMWs on the tracks, the going was considerably tougher

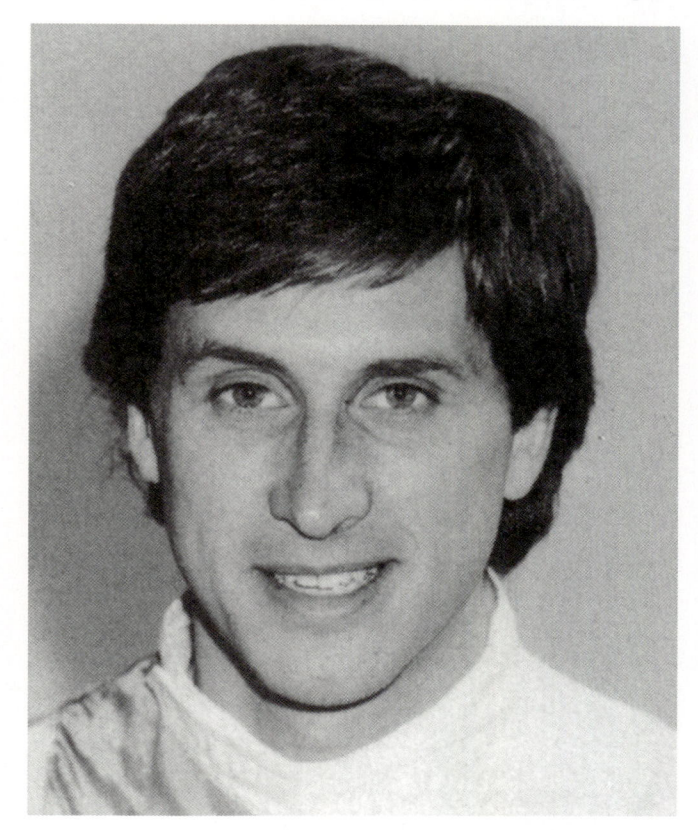

Roberto Ravaglia drove a big coupé for the Schnitzer team during 1984. He would go on to become a major driver with the BMW M3.

169

■ THE E24 IN COMPETITION

Harald Grohs piloting the Vogelsang coupé at Hockenheim in 1984.

this season. The V12 Jaguars were dominant, and both the turbocharged Volvos and the Rover Vitesses regularly finished high in the rankings.

It was the Eggenberger car that had most success. Crewed by Helmut Kelleners and Gianfranco Brancatelli, it won at the Nürburgring and at Silverstone, took third place at the Zeltweg and in Salzburg, a fourth at Enna in Sicily and fifth in Brno. The Bastos Juma car won at Vallelunga, and a Schnitzer car with Roberto Ravaglia at the wheel won at the closing event of Mugello in October. Yet the BMW coupés were constantly among the front runners throughout the season, claiming at least half of the top ten places in each of the 12 events except for Enna, Salzburg (four places at each) and Zolder (just two, of which one was Hans Stuck's second place).

The 1984 season was also the first one for a new series of events, the Deutsche Tourenwagen Meisterschaft (DTM, or German Touring Car Championship). Designed for Group A cars and featuring a well-thought-out handicap system, the 12 rounds of the first series attracted some strong entries. Among them was the Gubin Sport 635 CSi of Volker Strycek who, although not winning a single round, demonstrated enough consistency to take the title.

1985

Team Schnitzer looked into the possibility of building an 'evolution' 635 CSi for the 1985 season, and a power output of 365PS was suggested. The regulations would have permitted such a car to race as long as 500 were built for sale in Europe, but the plan failed to gain traction. So Team Schnitzer again ran two cars, with one of them being carried over from the 1984 season. The sponsorship this year came from BMW Belgium, and the sponsorship stickers read 'M Technic'.

A number of factors were new for 1985. Not least of these was the withdrawal of Jaguar from the competition, reasoning that they had nothing left to prove. The success-

170

THE E24 IN COMPETITION

Hans Stuck at the wheel of a Schnitzer-prepared coupé in 1985. Right behind is one of the Eggenberger cars, wearing the colours of sponsor BMW Italia.

ful Eggenberger team were poached by Volvo. The arrival of the new DTM series had also put a rather different perspective on things, and the Schnitzer plan was to contest events in this series as well as the ETCC. It was clear from the beginning, though, that their main focus was on the domestic title. Meanwhile, in Australia, Frank Gardner's John Player Special-sponsored team contested the Australian Touring Car Championship with a 635 CSi; Jim Richards took the title for them.

It ended up being a Volvo year. To drive their two cars, Schnitzer assembled a strong team consisting of Roberto Ravaglia, Gerhard Berger, Johnny Cecotto and Dieter Quester; their efforts were rewarded with just a single win in the ETCC. But what a win that was: car number 5 took first place at the Spa 24-hour event in July, crewed by Ravaglia, Berger and Marc Surer, and car number 3 came in second for its crew of Quester, Cecotto and Markus Oestreich.

■ THE E24 IN COMPETITION

Spa, 1985: Roberto Ravaglia pilots a Schnitzer-prepared coupé, with another E24 right behind him.

1986

By 1986, it was clear that BMW were pinning their future competition hopes on the new M3 saloon, but the car had not yet been homologated and Schnitzer once again gamely fielded a team of two 635 CSi cars. BMW Belgium provided the sponsorship and the logos on the cars now read 'BMW Technic'. As things were to turn out, this would be another excellent season for the big coupés, although it would also be their last at the forefront of European motorsport.

The undoubted star of the season was Roberto Ravaglia. Teamed with a variety of co-drivers, he took four wins (at Misano, the Nürburgring, Nogaro and Jarama) and four second places (at Donington, Hockenheim, Silverstone and Zolder), plus a third at Spa. These placings earned him second place in the ETCC drivers' championship, a single point behind Rover driver Win Percy until the FIA reassessed the position and awarded the title to Ravaglia. Dieter Quester, lead driver in the second Schnitzer car, also turned in some excellent results. He finished first at Spa and also took a pair of third places, at Monza and Zeltweg.

THE E24 IN COMPETITION

In the left-hand car, Dieter Quester acknowledges the crowd after winning at Spa in 1986. Both his car and the third-placed car of Roberto Ravaglia alongside have sustained damage during the event.

Finishing the ETCC manufacturers' championship in third place with the big coupés (Group A, Division 3) and in second place with their smaller saloons (Group A, Division 2), BMW were greatly encouraged. The 635 CSi was clearly not dead yet, and there was talk of fielding them again for the 1987 season alongside the new M3s. However, the M3s proved so much faster during testing that the plan was abandoned, and all the competition effort was put behind the new saloons. This time around, there was to be no glorious swan song like the one there had been for the CSL coupés.

173

CHAPTER NINE

TUNED AND MODIFIED COUPÉS

The 1960s saw the beginnings of a new breed of performance tuner in Germany. Typified by Alpina, which went on to become the best known, these tuners brought a more organized and business-like attitude to an activity that had traditionally been carried out in back-street garages by talented but unsung specialists. BMW regularly encouraged their efforts, which were often advertised through racing programmes. Again, Alpina was the outstanding example, but there were eventually many others.

Most importantly, these new tuners focused not only on producing high-performance but temperamental racing machinery, but also on developing cars (or accessories) that were suitable for road use. Customers in Germany, where the Autobahn was largely free of speed restrictions, responded with enthusiasm, and so the market expanded. Before long, there were calls for cosmetic alterations, too, and this market grew very rapidly in the later 1970s and 1980s as the specialists found new and wealthy customers in the Middle East.

All this expansion coincided with the availability of the big BMW coupés. With the exception of the BMW-Glas 3000 V8, every one of the big coupés attracted its own coterie of what the Germans call 'tuners', using the term to refer to bodywork modifiers as well as performance tuners in the strictest sense of the term.

The Alpina E120s

The only one of the major tuners in business when the E120 coupés reached the market in 1965 was Alpina. Established by Burkard Bovensiepen at Kaufbeuren at the start of the year, Alpina took its name from the typewriter manufacturing company owned by the Bovensiepen family. It took its inspiration from the latest BMW M10 engine, for which Bovensiepen had developed a twin-carburettor conversion in 1963. Customers had been impressed by the additional performance this brought to the original 1500 version of the engine. BMW had been impressed too: during 1964 Sales Director Paul Hahnemann made sure that that the company would honour the standard warranty on any 1500 fitted with the Bovensiepen conversion.

Many customers who came to Bovensiepen for this engine upgrade enquired about other performance and handling enhancements, and Bovensiepen realized that he had found a waiting market. He developed suspension modifications to improve the handling of the BMW 1500, and he also began to modify cylinder heads. To provide a more complete service, he sought out aftermarket accessories such as seats and steering wheels that would complement his own tuning kits. By late 1964 he was able to offer a whole series of worthwhile upgrades for the BMW saloon.

BMW's cautious expansion in the early 1960s meant that there would be no new engines for several years, and nor would there be any new car platforms; even the 2000 C and 2000 CS were based on the platform of the 1500 saloon. This commonality of components suited Alpina perfectly, because a modification or accessory that worked on one model would often work just as well on another. As a result, when the E120 coupés reached the market, in June 1965, Bovensiepen was able to offer a ready-made range of performance and other enhancements.

Even so, the 2000 C and 2000 CS did not attract performance enthusiasts in the way that the basic saloons or the later two-door models did in their time. They were too expensive for the everyday enthusiast, and tended to attract buyers who wanted luxury and exclusivity rather than outright speed or sharp handling. Yet there were a few customers who turned to Alpina to provide those elements that the factory-built cars lacked.

In the beginning, the Alpina system was not to provide complete conversions but to offer a menu of options from which customers could choose. It was then up to the customer to have those parts fitted. Before long, it became

TUNED AND MODIFIED COUPÉS

Alpina always liked to make it quite clear that a car incorporated their work. This CSL has the Alpina name neatly incorporated into the standard side stripes.

apparent that many customers wanted a one-stop service, allowing them to order items from Alpina and then have them fitted at the point of purchase. So it was probably at some time during 1966 that fully converted 2000 CS coupés became available from the Alpina works, which by this time had re-located to Buchloe.

The cost of a fully converted Alpina 2000 CS was 23,900 DM – a premium of 6900 DM over the 1965 showroom price for the standard car. For this, customers got a car with performance and handling that actually matched the big coupé's pretensions. The 0–100km/h time dropped to 10 seconds from the standard car's 14 seconds, and the top speed went up to 201km/h (125mph) from the standard 185km/h (115mph).

These huge improvements were achieved through what Alpina called their '2000 Spezial' engine conversion. This brought 145PS at 6500rpm. It had twin Weber 45 DCOE carburettors, a 10.0:1 compression ratio and a 300-degree fast road camshaft. In place of the standard four-speed gearbox, customers got a five-speed type. Anti-roll bars front and rear worked with Koni dampers to deliver tauter handling, and the cars could also have lightweight aluminium wheels made by Borrani in Italy to an Alpina design. It is likely that racing-style bucket seats, a three-spoke steering wheel and a rev counter were all part of the interior specification. There are no records to show how many of these cars were built, but the probability is that they remained very rare indeed. Most would have been built between 1966 and 1968, as it is hard to imagine anyone paying to convert a 2000 CS after the six-cylinder E9 coupés reached the market, in 1968.

175

■ TUNED AND MODIFIED COUPÉS

The Alpina E9s

After the M30 six-cylinder engine became available, Alpina naturally made that the primary focus of its attention. In addition, the company began to make its products available through licensees outside Germany. In Britain, for example, Alpina tuning parts were available during 1970 from Crayford Engineering of Westerham; by about 1972 the distributor was touring-car racer Brain Muir, who operated from premises at Brentford in Middlesex and later from Pershore in Wiltshire as Alpina Automotive Ltd. These were the companies that would have handled the Alpina conversions for the E9 coupés.

The E120 2000 CS and E9 2800 CS coupés had a great deal in common, and so Alpina was able to carry over many of the items it had developed for the older cars and offer them for the new ones. Bilstein gas dampers and adjustable anti-roll bars were made available for the E9 coupés, and a limited-slip differential was usually fitted. Alpina now had its own very distinctive new style of wheel – a multi-spoke alloy in a 7J x 14 size. New for the Alpina E9s, and now a mandatory requirement in Germany on cars with more than 200PS, were ventilated front disc brakes.

A front apron spoiler became available; made of either aluminium or GRP to the customer's choice, it was derived from racing experience with the company's own 2800 CS. Large Alpina side lettering was used on the company's demonstrators, but was probably not standard on customer cars. Inside the cabin, Scheel bucket seats could replace the standard front pair, there was a rosewood shift grip with the Alpina logo, and the standard steering wheel could be exchanged for an Alpina-branded item with drilled metal spokes and a leather-trimmed rim.

All this was part of the standard Alpina conversion for the 2800 CS, which seems to have become available in early 1969. Most of it remained in place throughout the lifetime of the Alpina E9s, but there were several different engines on offer, and every one of them gave performance gains that were simply astonishing for the time.

In the beginning, Alpina offered its B1 engine, the 'B' code being used for all the Alpina versions of the M30 six-cylinder. This engine was also available for the E3 saloons of the time. At its heart was the standard 2.8-litre block with bore and stroke dimensions unchanged from their production sizes, but Alpina had re-worked the cylinder head to give conventional hemispherical combustion chambers

Alpina brought this E9 coupé to the UK as a demonstrator. Like all Alpina cars of the time, it carries racing-style stripes, and the tuner's name is prominently displayed on each front wing. Note the bonnet pins, which hint at the car's racing heritage.

TUNED AND MODIFIED COUPÉS

Another Alpina E9, pictured at the company's headquarters in Buchloe. Many of the same characteristics are in evidence, although this car lacks the front air dam. Note the black-painted bumpers, which were almost certainly made of GRP to save weight.

instead of BMW's triple-hemispherical design. Pistons, too, were changed for lightweight types that raised the compression ratio to 10.8:1. In place of the standard camshaft came a 300-degree fast road type, and the carburettors were swapped for a pair of Solex 40/45 DDH instruments.

All this delivered 200PS at 6000rpm and 260Nm at 4500rpm; the figures for the factory-standard 2800 CS, which was considered powerful in the late 1960s, were 170PS at 6000rpm and 236Nm at 4500rpm. A B1-engined coupé could reach 60mph from rest in 8 seconds; the standard car needed 10 seconds. The Alpina car's top speed also rose from 206km/h (128mph) to 220km/h (137mph). These figures made it a very fast car for its day, but it was expensive, too. A fully converted car from Buchloe cost around 38,000 DM as against the 24,510 DM asked for a standard car in November 1969.

When BMW bored out the M30 block to achieve a 3.0-litre capacity, in 1971, Alpina turned its attention to the new engine. Buchloe's take on the 3.0-litre carburettor engine was introduced with the B2 name in September 1972. Between then and July 1976, Alpina made 142 examples of the engine, although that total would have been divided between E3 saloons and E9 coupés.

The B2 shared its twin-Solex carburettors and 300-degree camshaft with the B1 engine, and the combustion chambers in its cylinder head were re-worked in the same way. New pistons raised the compression ratio to 10.0:1 from the standard 9.5:1. Power went up to 230PS at 6750rpm and torque to 270Nm at 5000rpm, so that a fully extended Alpina 3.0 CS with the B2 engine could reach 100km/h from rest in 7.3 seconds and peaked at 235km/h (146mph). Compared to the standard car's 9.0 seconds and 213km/h (132mph), these were simply fabulous figures for a road car. Only a lucky few could afford the asking price. A standard 3.0 CS was already expensive at 28,950 DM in June 1972; the Alpina B2 conversion put that figure up by more than a third, to an eye-watering 39,800 DM.

Yet even the B2 conversion was not the ultimate road-going Alpina derivative of the E9 coupé. That was the B2S, released at the same time in September 1972 and designed as an upgrade for the lightweight CSL. For this engine, Alpina bored the 3.0-litre block out by 0.25mm to give a new swept volume that was claimed to be 3020cc – although BMW claimed (see Chapter 4) that a bore increase of the same size for the racing CSLs gave just 3003cc! The usual head re-work and 300-degree camshaft were added, and new pistons raised the compression ratio to 10.5:1 from the standard 9.5:1. The factory-standard fuel-injection system gave way to a Kugelfischer mechanical injection system, which Alpina found easier to tune

■ TUNED AND MODIFIED COUPÉS

This was Alpina's take on a late 3.0 CSL. Despite the UK registration, the car has left-hand drive.

than the standard Bosch type. To release the extra exhaust gases more efficiently, a big-bore exhaust system was added on to the standard manifold. In case onlookers could not recognize what the car was from the distinctive noise of that exhaust, buyers could choose to replace the CSL's side stripes with new ones to the same pattern, but this time reading 'Alpina 3.0 CSL'.

The performance figures for an Alpina CSL are still impressive today, more than 40 years later. The car could rocket to 100km/h from rest in 6.4 seconds and keep on going until it reached 245km/h (152mph). All this was available from an engine that sounds positively puny by modern standards, although it was hugely powerful by the standards of the early 1970s. The B2S promised 250PS at 6800rpm and 302Nm at 5000rpm. Alpina brought their development car to the UK towards the end of 1972, and both *Motor* and *Motor Sport* seized the opportunity to try it out. This car had a five-speed overdrive gearbox and changed axle gearing to suit, although the standard fare was a five-speed gearbox with direct top gear. *Motor* matched the factory acceleration claim with a 0–60mph time of 6.3 seconds, and *Motor Sport* emulated the 152mph top speed.

Just one more Alpina engine was specifically intended for the E9 coupés – the B3 type that was introduced early in 1973 to give a 3.0 CSi performance similar to that of an Alpina CSL. It had the same re-worked cylinder head and 10.5:1 pistons, with the 300-degree camshaft and Kugelfischer fuel injection, and promised 250PS as against the 200PS of the standard car.

It is not impossible that some E9 coupés may have been fitted with later versions of the Alpina-developed 'big six'. Available from 1973 was the B4, a 3.0-litre with 230PS and 265Nm that was intended for another BMW model but would certainly have fitted the E9. Following that, from 1975, there was the B6, a 200PS upgrade of the 2.8-litre engine in the 528i that had Pierburg fuel injection and could, at least in theory, have been fitted into an older 2800 CS.

E24 Aftermarket Conversions

By the time of the E24 coupés, the conversions scene had begun to change. While it had been concentrated in Europe, it had been all about performance enhancement, with additions such as sports seats that gave better support in hard driving and sometimes decals or badges that advertised the car's additional performance.

After the 1973–1974 Oil Crisis, there was huge new wealth in the Middle East, and with it came a desire for the finer things in life. Arab culture tended to favour ostentation of a type quite alien to European tastes, and the ultra-rich began to vie with one another to acquire the best. Among the most desirable possessions were cars that not only had high performance but had also been custom-built with features that were not available on showroom models of any kind.

As a result, many of the performance specialists in Germany expanded their horizons to include custom coachwork, while several new companies sprang up to focus on this aspect of the conversions business. By the 1980s, the Middle East market was taking large numbers of extensively modified German cars (and others) that had been built to individual order and at enormous cost. Some of the features developed for Middle Eastern clients also became available on cars for Europe and the USA. It was axiomatic that the host car for any of these extravagant conversions would be a top-of-the-range version of an expensive car; among the more popular hosts was, inevitably, BMW's E24 6 Series.

None of that, however, detracted from demand for straightforward performance conversions of the E24 coupés in Europe, sometimes with a dash of added luxury. In the USA, where emissions-control equipment had stifled the performance of the big coupés, there was also a demand for more power, and on that side of the Atlantic it was achieved in a quite different way.

The Alpina E24s

Alpina built a bewildering number of E24 variants between 1977 and 1989, and its total of 432 cars makes it by far the most prolific modifier of the cars. All those it built after 1983 carried its own VINs, as the company was recognized as an independent vehicle manufacturer by the German authorities during that year. Typically, the original BMW VIN remained on the car but was struck through, and the new Alpina VIN (with a WAP prefix code) was stamped into the metalwork next to it.

1977–1978: The First Cars

At the start of E24 production, Alpina marketing still allowed customers to design the cars they wanted by choosing from a menu of upgrades. The E24 models built

■ TUNED AND MODIFIED COUPÉS

The stylized Alpina Deko Set of stripes seems faintly at odds with the svelte lines of this E24 coupé, rather like a glamour model wearing warpaint.

in this first year would have featured many variations on a core theme. Exactly how many there were is not known.

There were two Alpina engine options from 1977, the B8 conversion for the 633 CSi being introduced just before the B2 conversion for the 630 CS. Both delivered performance that was far better than that of the later factory-standard 635 CSi.

The B2 engine offered 230PS at 6750rpm and 265Nm at 4000rpm, with a compression ratio raised to 9.5:1 from the standard 9.3:1. With the re-shaped combustion chambers and special camshaft common to most Alpina derivatives of the M30 engine, it offered acceleration from 0–100km/h in 6.9 seconds (the standard 630 CS needed 9.0 seconds) and a maximum speed of 230km/h (143mph) as against the standard car's 210km/h (130mph).

The B8 engine also had the usual cylinder head work and special camshaft, and was only marginally quicker, even though it was based on the larger-capacity 3210cc engine. Power was 240PS and torque peaked at 308Nm, and the 0–100km/h time was 6.8 seconds with a top speed of 231km/h (143.5mph).

When Alpina could persuade its customers to take the full package, cars with these engines also had shorter and stiffer road springs, Bilstein gas dampers (the rear pair being adjustable), thicker anti-roll bars (the rear one again being adjustable), and Alpina's own 16-inch one-piece alloy wheels. As had been racing practice for some time, the rear wheels had wider rims and fatter tyres than those at the front. There were 205/55 VR 16 tyres on 7-inch rims at the front, and 225/50 VR 16s on 8-inch rims at the rear.

Inside the cabin, an Alpina-branded speedometer and rev counter could be had, together with Scheel front seats and an all-over fabric upholstery featuring Alpina's trademark blue and green stripes. The steering wheel had a leather-bound rim and the shift knob was made of rosewood. On the outside, a deep front air dam accompanied the characteristic and somewhat flamboyant Alpina Deko Set of branded decals on the flanks.

1978–1982: The First Turbocharged Cars

Turbocharging had become a popular way of extracting more power from an engine during the 1970s, but Alpina had initially avoided it because of the difficulty of eliminating turbo lag (the delay between pressure on the accelerator and a response from the turbocharger). However, by 1978 the company had that lag down to acceptable levels, and introduced its first turbocharged engines. These coincided with the arrival of a new marketing approach. In future, Alpina would sell only complete cars rather than offer its traditional menu of tuning items.

TUNED AND MODIFIED COUPÉS

Mounted low down on the left is the turbocharger of this Alpina engine for the company's B7 Turbo Coupé. The turbocharger was not ideally placed for easy maintenance, but it is unlikely that many of the owners of these expensive and astonishingly quick cars cared too much...

The inside of an Alpina B7 Turbo Coupé. The wooden gearshift grip is an Alpina item, and next to the handbrake is the circular turbo boost control. The car carries a plaque with its individual number; this one is number 098.

From November 1978, customers who wanted an Alpina E24 were offered the B7 Turbo Coupé. Although always based on the contemporary 635 CSi, its engine was actually derived from the older 3.0-litre type that had been current while it was being developed. The engine retained its standard valves and 272-degree camshaft, and Alpina re-worked the cylinder head in its usual way to give hemispherical combustion chambers. Mahle lightweight pistons lowered the compression ratio to 8.0:1 to prevent the detonation associated with turbochargers in high-compression engines.

The KKK turbocharger had an air-to-air intercooler, and the fuel mixture was delivered by a Pierburg continuous-flow injection system through a resonance-type manifold. An advanced Hartig electronic ignition system with computer control replaced the standard distributor, and there was an additional special feature: a turbo boost control operated from inside the car. This could be used to reduce boost and protect the engine if poor-quality fuel was being used, or simply to give a more relaxed drive. On minimum boost of 0.5 bar, the B7 Turbo engine gave 240PS at 5800rpm, but with full boost of 0.9 bar it gave 300PS at the same engine speed. This was good for a 5.7-second 0–100km/h time and for a top speed of 260km/h (161mph).

The B7 Turbo Coupé used the same suspension set-up and the same wheels and tyres as its Alpina predecessors, but added ventilated and cross-drilled front brake discs. The gearbox was a close-ratio Getrag five-speed, and there was a tall final drive of 2.56:1. The battery had been relocated in the boot, ostensibly to improve weight distribution, and the cars all had an auxiliary fuel tank that added 32 litres (7 gallons) to the standard capacity. The front spoiler was matched by a rubber spoiler on the boot lid, of Alpina's own design and not the same as the one on the 635 CSi. These cars went on to become a big success for Alpina, selling 153 copies – all with left-hand drive – before production ended in 1982.

The next stage on from the B7 Turbo Coupé was the B7S Turbo Coupé, announced in March 1982. Alpina was again caught out by BMW's production changes, having based its new engine on the 3453cc M90 when BMW was

TUNED AND MODIFIED COUPÉS

just about to go over (in the autumn) to the 3430cc M30. The official Alpina line at the time was that they preferred the shorter stroke of the older engine for use with a turbocharger, but that was simply whistling to keep their spirits up. Not that it mattered, because they were able to sell 60 examples of the car during 1982, all with left-hand drive and all with the suggestion that this was a limited edition.

The B7S Turbo Coupé was yet another astonishing achievement. It was also the most expensive Alpina there had ever been, with a basic cost of just under 100,000 DM. The Buchloe development engineers had found another 10 per cent of power to put the maximum up to 330PS at 5800rpm, while torque went up to 500Nm at 3000rpm. Acceleration was breathtaking for such a big and heavy car: on maximum boost, a B7S Turbo Coupé could reach 100km/h from rest in 5.4 seconds. Top speed was probably the same 260km/h (161mph) as for the B7 Turbo Coupé, although the German magazine *Sport Auto* could not better 259km/h (160mph) when it tested one.

Every B7S Turbo Coupé came in the Alpina 'house' colour of dark green metallic, with a gold Deko Set of side stripes that incorporated the 'B7S Turbo' name on each rear wing. Upholstery was in unique blue and green tartan fabric with black leather bolsters and – a sign of the times – the expensive Fischer stereo system came with a stalk-mounted remote control.

Just one other variant of the E24 was available from Alpina in this period. This was the B9 3.5, a model introduced in 1982 to provide a lower-cost Alpina coupé. Just two cars were built with the 3453cc version of the B9 engine before Alpina was obliged to switch to the 3430cc engine that arrived later in the year. These engines delivered 245PS at 5000rpm and 319Nm of torque at 4000rpm on a 10.2:1 compression ratio. Acceleration was quoted as 6.9 seconds from 0–100km/h with a maximum speed of 245km/h (152mph) – still very much faster than the standard 635 CSi of 1982, which needed 8.5 seconds to reach 100km/h and had a 225km/h (140mph) maximum.

1983–1985: The First Facelift Models

When BMW revised the E24 range in autumn 1982, Alpina changed its models to suit the new specification. Cars built from the start of 1983 or thereabouts were all based on the E24/1 models.

The revisions took a little time, but the first new model ready for production was a B9 3.5 that now used the 3430cc engine, which had become standard for the 635 CSi. It had exactly the same power and torque figures, and exactly the same performance as the B9 3.5 that had made a brief appearance in 1982 with the earlier engine, and it proved very popular, with a total of 33 cars sold during

The effect of the Deko Set depended to a large extent on the colours involved. This is a B9 3.5 coupé, and the silver-grey stripes sit rather well with the white bodywork.

TUNED AND MODIFIED COUPÉS

1983 alone. During 1984, when another 40 examples were sold, the car took on Alpina's latest Digital Cockpit Display. This digital read-out of oil pressure, oil temperature, final-drive oil temperature and inlet manifold pressure replaced one of the air vents on the dashboard.

However, there were now two new issues to be addressed. The first was that BMW had developed its own high-performance E24, which became available in early 1984 as the M635 CSi. As this was priced considerably lower than the typical Alpina conversion, Alpina needed to maintain its uniqueness and justify its higher prices by offering an even higher level of performance. The second issue was that the German government was planning to introduce legislation requiring catalytic converters on all new cars. Alpina had to be ready to meet that challenge as well.

The first new model revived the old B7 Turbo Coupé name, although it was a very different car. Staying with the standard Bosch injection system, which had been designed to be relatively easy to tune for emissions control with a catalytic converter, Alpina used its existing KKK turbocharger set-up with variable boost control to create an engine (called B9/1) that gave 330PS at 5700rpm and 512Nm at 2400rpm on an 8.0:1 compression ratio. With the five-speed close-ratio gearbox and 2.56:1 final drive, this translated into 5.8 seconds for the 0–100km/h sprint and a maximum speed of 267km/h (166mph).

E24 models came no faster, and nor did they come any more expensive. The new B7 Turbo Coupé trumped the B7S Turbo Coupé as the most expensive Alpina model yet. None of that deterred the buyers, and Alpina sold 110 examples before the car was withdrawn in 1987. Some of the later examples had 17-inch wheels instead of the original 16-inch type, with 8.5J rims and 235/45 VR 17 tyres front and rear.

1985–1989: The KAT Era

Alpina was able to continue selling examples of its models without catalytic converters into 1987, but in Germany the incentives to switch to KAT cars were quite persuasive. From 1985, a B10 3.5 Coupé replaced the B9 3.5, switching to a KAT engine in 1988. That in turn gave way to a B11 3.5. The B7 Turbo Coupé also remained in production until 1988, having switched to a KAT engine (for Germany, at least) in October 1986.

Only 20 B7 Turbo KAT Coupés were built, between 1986 and June 1988, and it looks as if customers chose the

Fairly typical of Alpina's work on the E24 is this interior. The branded four-spoke steering wheel and gearshift grip, the tasteful check upholstery and the checker-plate footrest are all obvious features.

non-KAT cars as long as they remained legally available. In fact, the KAT version of the engine did not lose too much in comparison with the earlier type. Thanks largely to a special low-restriction catalytic converter that Alpina had developed, it had 320PS instead of 330PS and 509Nm instead of 512Nm. A lowered compression ratio and less valve overlap accounted for much of the difference. Buyers had to settle for 265km/h (165mph) instead of the unrestricted car's 270km/h (168mph). It was a small difference, but it mattered to people with enough money to insist on the best.

The M635 CSi was getting uncomfortably close to offering B9 3.5 performance at a considerably lower cost. So Alpina developed the more powerful B10 3.5 as its 'entry-level' model, with a 3430cc engine further massaged to deliver 261PS at 5800rpm and 346Nm at 4000rpm. That gave 0–100km/h in 6.4 seconds and a top speed of 250km/h (155mph). In the UK, where the Sytner dealership in Nottingham had a licence to build right-hand-drive cars to Alpina specifications, the car was actually made available with an automatic gearbox option that was not on offer from Buchloe. That made it slightly slower, but 0–100km/h in 6.8 seconds and a top speed of 241km/h (150mph) made the car a viable alternative to the exclusively manual M635 CSi of the time. A total of 44 B10 3.5 cars of all kinds were constructed between 1985 and 1987.

183

■ TUNED AND MODIFIED COUPÉS

Rare UK-market Alpina B10 3.5, photographed by its owner Craig Pusey.

TUNED AND MODIFIED COUPÉS

By the time of the B11 3.5 Coupé, the Alpina Deko Set had been tamed and consisted of gold outlines rather than solid stripes.

The very last Alpina version of the E24 coupé was the B11 3.5, which was introduced in 1988 as a replacement for the B10 3.5. Based on a 635 CSi and equipped with a KAT, the car came with 250PS at 5700rpm and 330Nm at 4000rpm, and used the 3.73:1 final drive from the M635 CSi. It had the latest BMW specification with the 'universal' bumpers, and Alpina's latest 17-inch alloy wheels on 235/45 ZR 17 tyres. Unfortunately, neither production nor performance figures for the model are available.

Hartge and Schnitzer

Hartge Motorsport was a specialist tuning company that was founded in 1971 and focused particularly on BMW cars. There were Hartge E24s on the race tracks in the first half of the 1980s to promote the company's products, and from 1985 the company was granted manufacturer status in Germany so that the cars it built after that date carried its own VINs.

Hartge offered a menu of performance options for the 635 CSi, as well as some cosmetic changes. Central to its work was the H6 engine, based on the 3430cc M30 and developing 240PS at 5000rpm in standard road trim, with 335Nm at 4000rpm. The power increase came from work on the cylinder head (which was ported, and had larger valves and a 10.0:1 compression ratio), from a new camshaft and from a special exhaust manifold that fed into a free-flow exhaust system. Later versions of the engine had 254PS at 6100rpm and 340Nm at 4000rpm. Hartge also made its own version of the 24-valve engine in the M635 CSi, which was rated at 330PS at 6800rpm with 355Nm of torque at 4000rpm.

Suspension work typically involved uprated springs and dampers, thicker anti-roll bars, and a strut brace across the engine bay to stiffen the car. A bodykit with ribbed rear apron spoiler was available, and various decal seats were also on offer. From 1984 there were 17-inch multi-spoke wheels to Hartge's own design; earlier cars often had BBS wheels. The front grille often carried the Hartge name or a stylised H logo. Interiors typically had a special steering wheel and shift grip, and a 280km/h speedometer. There were right-hand-drive cars, too, and in the UK these were prepared by Bird's of Uxbridge, who held a Hartge franchise.

■ TUNED AND MODIFIED COUPÉS

The problem of obtaining the odd-sized tyres for the TRX wheels available on the M635 CSi has led many owners to fit aftermarket wheels with a more standard size. These wheels were made by Schnitzer, and are wearing 235/45 ZR 17 tyres.

AC Schnitzer in Aachen, which ran the racing E24s for BMW in the early 1980s, also offered its own roadgoing conversion: the S6. Its engine produced 246PS at 6000rpm and 322Nm of torque at 4500rpm.

Tuned E24s in the USA

Performance of the US-specification E24 coupés was always disappointing before the M6 became available in 1987, and a number of tuning shops did their best to produce cars that delivered the performance at which showroom models only hinted.

Some of these companies had spent time as importers of Alpina and other German tuning parts, and in some cases they no doubt used the knowledge they had gained to good effect when developing their own high-performance E24s. However, this was the age of the turbocharger, and a number of US-specification 633 CSi models were turbocharged to order.

Motor Trend magazine tested such a car in its September 1982 issue, a 1981 automatic model that had been uprated by Century BMW in Alhambra, California. Central to the conversion was a turbocharger from BAE in Torrance. With an 8.4:1 compression ratio, the engine made 260bhp at 6700rpm and 196lb ft of torque at 4000rpm, while retaining its three-way catalytic converter, California-specification oxygen sensor and exhaust gas recirculation equipment. The magazine recorded a 0–60mph time of 7.04 seconds, but did not publish the maximum speed – as was the practice at a time when new cars in the USA had speedometers that did not go beyond 85mph. Needless to say, suspension and tyres had been uprated to handle the additional performance.

Convertibles

No convertible version had been considered during the planning stages of the E24. One very obvious reason was that BMW, like every other car manufacturer that wanted to sell its products in the USA, was fearful that future safety legislation would outlaw convertibles altogether. That never happened, but by the time the direction of US legislation had become clear it was too late for the cars that had been designed for the 1970s.

All this led to the 6 Series becoming an obvious target for the German conversion specialists who thrived in the 1980s. Convertible 6 Series were never very numerous, and perhaps fewer than 100 were built in all; a small number of companies managed to build their designs in quantity, and there may have been several others who tried their hand with a single car and then did no more. Always costly, the 6 Series convertibles remained rare in Europe but found a ready market among wealthy buyers in the Middle East, for whom they were often modified further. Prompted by these conversions, BMW looked at producing such a car itself, but in the end rejected the idea.

The story of the 6 Series convertibles seems to have begun at some time around 1980 with an entrepreneur named Jürgen Weber, who returned from the USA where he had learned the art of converting closed cars into convertibles. It was probably in 1981 that he established Tropic Automobildesign GmbH in the town of Crailsheim in Baden-Württemberg, a company that gained contracts to create several hundred convertibles from Honda Prelude, Opel Ascona and Toyota Celica cars for the German market.

Weber saw the opportunity to create a convertible BMW 6 Series, and in drawing up the design appears to have had some assistance from Friedrich-Peter Lorenz

TUNED AND MODIFIED COUPÉS

(later of Lorenz & Rankel) and from Günter Benneman of BCS, who was already doing cabriolet conversions on other cars for companies such as Koenig and Gemballa. A prototype was built from a red 1979 635 CSi, and appeared at the Geneva Show in March 1982 with a price tag of 89,405 DM. Associated publicity suggested that production would begin that September, and that Tropic envisaged converting 400 cars a year.

However, the project never really got off the ground. BMW themselves showed an interest in the project and examined the prototype with a view to talks about a co-operative venture. However, they supposedly wanted changes that Tropic were unwilling to accommodate. German sales were then forbidden when the car failed to gain TÜV approval. In the wake of some quality problems with its Honda Prelude conversions, Tropic closed down, probably in 1983.

This experience seems to have persuaded BMW to look at the possibility of building a convertible 6 Series themselves. Most sources agree that two prototypes were built, probably during 1982, although there have been suggestions that there were three cars. Quite logically, one of the BMW prototypes was built as a full convertible and one as a targa-type cabriolet with a sturdy central rollover bar. This broadly followed the pattern of the Baur 'Top Cabriolet' originally drawn up for the E14 2002 models and continued into the E21 3 Series era. It may even be that Baur were contracted to build the targa-top car. However, the project was taken no further. Rumour suggests that these cars – or, at least, some of them – were presented to distinguished senior members of the company on their retirement.

Jürgen Weber, meanwhile, was still pursuing the idea of a 6 Series convertible. During 1983 he joined Hammond & Thiede in Sulzbach am Main (which also had a branch in Dover in the UK), a company already involved in converting Opel Ascona saloons to cabriolets. A single prototype was built from a red 628 CSi and was announced to the press in summer 1983, but no production followed and Weber left the company. By June that year, Weber was with Hy-Tech in Stuttgart, and the company was advertising the availability of a convertible 6 Series – the car in its publicity pictures was actually the red Tropic prototype. No production followed, although Hy-Tec did later market a 6 Series convertible by EBS.

Germany was not the only country with an interest in 6 Series convertibles. The Piet Oldenhof company in the Dutch town of Enschede, also known as PO after the ini-

RIGHT AND OVERLEAF: *The best-known cabriolet conversions came from Schulz Tuning. It must be said that the lines of the cabriolet top and the shortened rear side window were not wholly successful, even if the car looked good when open.*

187

■ TUNED AND MODIFIED COUPÉS

TUNED AND MODIFIED COUPÉS

tials of its owner, developed a design with a power-operated convertible top. They sold this in the Netherlands under the Oldenhof name, and also licensed the design to Schulz-Tuning in Germany, a company better known for its Mercedes-Benz conversions. The German-built cars, which carried the Schulz name, were sold through BMW dealer Faltz in Essen. Total production is thought to have been around 10 cars. Schulz may have been responsible for the bodywork of the only 6 Series convertible to bear the Gemballa name, although Gemballa certainly carried out the interior re-trim.

Somewhat later than Schulz, and probably around 1985, ABC-Exclusive of Bonn announced the availability of a 6 Series convertible that could be had in three styles. These were Classic (essentially unadorned), Prestige (with a bodykit of sills and spoilers), and Sport Breit ('sports wide'), which had widened tracks and bulging wheel arches to cover them. It is likely that this company's products were sold mainly in the Middle East.

There were also 6 Series convertibles from Belgium and the UK, the Belgian cars coming from EBS and the UK examples possibly from Crayford. EBS was Ernst Berg Styling, established as a coachwork-conversion business at Tervuren in Belgium in 1981. Berg was a Dutch racing driver, and EBS were always better known for their Mercedes-Benz convertibles. Nevertheless, they are believed to have built as many as 30 convertible 6 Series BMWs. Crayford was a long-established conversions company which appears to have adapted Baur E21 'Top Cabriolet' components to create a targa-roof derivative of the 6 Series for the UK market. It is not clear how many were made.

Two specialist coachbuilders in the USA also created 6 Series convertibles. One car is known to have been built by the American Sunroof Corporation in San Diego, and between 1983 and 1987 there were small numbers from Coach Builders Ltd, based at High Springs in Florida.

The Gemballa Wide-Body E24

The 1984 Ferrari Testarossa introduced a striking new element to car design, with air intakes in the rear wings that were blended into the body sides and doors with long, stylish strakes. The idea was seized upon by custom builder Koenig-Specials of Munich, which developed what became known as the 'wide-body' look for the big Mercedes SEC coupés of the time.

The idea caught on and some customers, mostly from the Middle East, showed an interest in a 'wide-body' style for the big BMW coupé. Gemballa, based at Leonberg, may have been the only specialist to respond to this interest, and was certainly responsible for one particularly striking car that was ordered in 1985 by a customer in the UAE. This car was rediscovered in Iraq in 2003, when it was thought to have become part of the car collection owned by Uday Hussein, son of the deposed dictator Saddam Hussein.

The car was finished in bright yellow (apparently the colour used on German postal service vehicles), had four exhaust tips instead of the standard two, and rode on stiffened suspension with 15-inch Ronal alloy wheels that were painted to match the body. The interior had been re-fitted with four power-adjustable Recaro seats and a TV screen in the dashboard. The Gemballa car is said to have cost a total of 240,000 DM when new.

Zender Bodykits

The fashion for body modifications spread right across the aftermarket in the 1980s, but most buyers could not afford hugely expensive conversions like those built to

ABOVE AND OVERLEAF: *These sills were part of a bodykit produced for the E24 by Zender, and are very much a 1980s period piece.*

189

■ TUNED AND MODIFIED COUPÉS

order for the Middle East. German specialist Zender GmbH of Mülheim offered a number of much more affordable add-on aerodynamic accessories for the 6 Series cars during the 1980s. These included several designs of front apron spoiler and also a rear apron extension, sill extensions, and a variety of rear spoilers that included a low 'wing' type. Zender also offered side decal sets and marketed wheels from a number of other manufacturers. All these items have their own period charm today.

INDEX

ABC-Exclusive 189
Active Check Control 104, 130
Airbags, for E24 141
Allison, Bobby 80
Alpina 64, 78, 80, 89, 174
Alpina E9 176
Alpina E24 179
Alpina E120 174
Alpina wheels 118
American Sunroof Corporation 189
Amon, Chris 77, 79
Art Cars 81, 90, 115, 145
Atlas Racing Team 81
Autenrieth 10
Automatic gearbox, first in a BMW 29

Baur 10
BBS alloy wheels, M635 CSi 148
BMW-Glas 3000 V8 17
BMW models:
  2.5 CS 58
  3.0 CS 48
  3.0 CSi 53
  3.0 CSL, first series 67
  3.0 CSL, second series 67
  3.0 CSL, third series 73
  8 Series 154
  331 9
  501 9, 10, 15
  502 10
  503 Coupé 10
  1500 15, 23
  2000 C and 2000 CS (E120), overview 17
  2800 CS 41
  3200S cabriolet prototype 15
  3200 CS coupé 14
  3200L and 3200S 14
  E3 saloons 41, 96
  E9 coupés (overview) 18
  E12 5 Series 100, 102
  E21 3 Series 103
  E24 coupés (overview) 20
  E28 5 Series 126
  M1 133
  M3 131
  M5 131
  Turbo concept car 102

'Batmobiles' 73, 79
Benneman, Günter
Berger, Gerhard 171
Bertone 14, 99
Betzler, Thomas 80
Bönsch, Helmut Werner 14
Borgward Isabella coupé 24
Borg Warner automatic gearbox 48
Bovensiepen, Burkard 174
Bracq, Paul 20, 100, 102
Brambilla, Ernesto 78
Brambilla, Vittorio 78, 80
Brancatelli, Gianfranco 170
Braungart, Martin 76
Broadspeed 75

Cabriolet prototype, E120 32
Calder, Alexander 81
Catalytic converter 123, 142, 183
Cecotto, Johnny 171
Cheylesmore Motorsport 169
'City-spec' 3.0 CSL 69

Coach Builders Ltd 189
Convertible E24s 186
Crayford Engineering 176, 189
CSL Turbo, 1976 81

Dashboard, E24 103
De Fierlant, Hughes 80, 81
Demol, Marc 80, 81
Designing the E9 models 38
  E24 models 99
Dieudonné, Pierre 80, 82, 89, 94
Digital Cockpit Display (Alpina) 183
Dingolfing 17, 112
Drag coefficients 102
Duez, Marc 169

E24 1980 model-year changes 116
  1981 and 1982 model-years 118
  1984 mainstream models 131
  1985 models 140
  1986 models 142
  1987 models 147
  1988 models 150
  1989 models 154
E24 aftermarket conversions 179
E120 models 22
EBS 187, 189
Ederer, Georg 105
Eggenberger Racing 164, 169, 170, 171
Ertl, Harald 80
Extras (for 2000 C and 2000 CS) 31

Facetti, Carlo 89, 94
Faltz (team) 81, 82
Federal 85mph speedometers 123
Fiedler, Fritz 14
Finotto, Martino 89, 94
Fitzpatrick, John 82
Fontaine, Yvette 81
'Francorchamps' car 80
Frua 17
Fuchs, Ernst 115
Fuel Crisis, 1973 58, 80
Fuel injection and M30 engine 53
'Full leather' interior 149, 153
Furtmayer, Ernst 67

Gardner, Frank 171
Garmisch concept car 99
Gearboxes, E24 105
Gemballa 189
Getrag manual gearboxes 48, 77, 82, 107, 114, 133
Giugiaro, Georgio 99
Glas 17, 96
Goertz, Albrecht 10
Gösser Beer (sponsor) 86, 87
Grace International Racing Partnership 169
Grano, Umberto 89, 94, 164, 169
Gregg, Peter 81, 82
Grewenig, Hanns 9, 10
Grohs, Harald 81, 82
Group A 635 CSi 166
Gubin Sport 170
Guichet, Jean 81

Hahne, Armin 169
Hahnemann, Paul 99, 174
'Halfline' interior option 154
Hammond & Thiede 187
Hanover Trade Fair 8

Hartge (team) 165, 169
Hartge (tuning) 185
Hermetite (team) 82
Heyer, Hans 76, 169
Hezemans, Toine 77, 79, 89
Highline option 153
Hoffmann, Max 10
Hofmeister, Wilhelm 17, 18, 24, 38, 100
Hurler, Karl 164
Hy-Tec 187

IAA Frankfurt, 1951 8, 9
Ickx, Jacky 80
Identification numbers, E120 models 35
  E9 models 62
  E24 models 158
IMSA 80, 82
Interior design, E24 models 103
ItalDesign 99

Japanese 635 CSi 141
Jolly Club (team) 89, 94
Joosen, Eddy 89, 94, 164
Juma (team) 169, 170

Karmann 17, 18, 28, 43, 47, 49, 57, 107, 108, 112, 120
Kelleners, Helmut 164, 169, 170
Kirkpatrick, John 76
Krebs, Albrecht 82
Kugelfischer injection 67, 80, 82, 177

L6 version of E24 for USA 154
Lancia Flaminia coupé 14
Last E24s 154
Lauda, Niki 78
Lok-o-Matic differential 43
Lorenz, Friedrich-Peter 186
Luigi (Team) 80, 81, 82, 86, 89, 94
Lutz, Bob 67, 99

M6 model for Japan 150
M6 model for USA 153
M10 engine 17, 174
M30 engine 36, 129, 177, 180
M30 2.8-litre engine 117
M49 engine 80
M88 engine 114, 133
M90 engine 114
M635 CSi 131
M635 CSi for UK 142
Mercedes-Benz 9, 144
Michelin TRX tyres 119, 137, 150
Michelotti 15
Moffat, Alan 81
Mohr (driver) 89
Motorsport division 75, 131
Motorsport Edition, of E24 156
M Technic spoiler 144
Muir, Brian 78, 176
Müller, Siggi 81

Nappa leather 149
Neerpash, Jochen 76, 81, 82
Neger, Harald 164
Neue Klasse saloons 24, 41, 96
Nève, Patrick 89
Nilsson, Gunnar 89

Oestreich, Markus 171

191

INDEX

Oldenhof, Piet 187
On Board Computer 117, 130
Osswald, Berhnhard 100

Paint and Trim Options, E24 156
Palmer, Jonathan 169
Peltier, Alain 81
Performance figures, E120 models 35
    E9 models 61
    E24 models 125, 158
Pescarolo, Henri 80
Peterson, Ronnie 80, 81, 82
Pininfarina 14
Piquet, Nelson 137
Posey, Sam 80, 81, 82
Poulain, Hervé 81, 90
Production figures, E120 models 35
    E9 models 59
    E24, 1976-1982 122
    E24, 1983-1989 155

Quandt family 22
Quester, Dieter 78, 79, 81, 82, 89, 165, 169, 171, 172

Racing Corporation Vienna 164
Racing E9s 75
Racing seasons:
    1973 76
    1974 80
    1975 80
    1976 81
    1977 82
    1978 89
    1979 94
    1980 164
    1981 and 1982 164
    1983 164
    1984 169
    1985 170
    1986 172

Rauschenberg, Robert 145
Ravaglia, Roberto 170, 171, 172
Rear air conditioning, E24 147
Rech, Horst 131
Redman, Brian 80, 81, 82
Replica Gösser Beer car 89
RHD conversions, 2000 CS 31
    2800 CS 43
    3.0 CS 49
RHD factory-built cars 54, 109
Richards, Jim 171
Road test reports, E120 range 32
    2800 CS 48
    3.0 CS 53
    3.0 CSi 57
    E24, early models 111, 116, 118, 119, 121
    M635 CSi 138, 144
Rollover bar, E24 101
Rosche, Paul 77, 79
Rossi, Carlo 169

S38 B35 engine 148
Schmid, Dieter 164
Schnitzer, Josef 81, 82
Schnitzer (team) 67, 78, 80, 81, 82, 165, 169, 170, 171, 172
Schnitzer (tuning) 186
Schulz-Tuning 189
Service Interval Indicator 130
Shadowline trim 147
Spicup concept car 99
Sport and Economy gearbox settings 131
Sports gearbox option for E24 118, 129
Stella, Frank 81
Stommelen, Rolf 76
Stork, Walter 100
Strycek, Volker 170
Stuck, Hans 77, 78, 79, 80, 81, 169, 170
Surer, Marc 171
Swedish 635 CSi 141
Sytner, Frank 169

Talbot Berlin wing mirror 43
Tassin, Thierry 169
Technical Specifications, E120 models 34
    E9 models 60
    E24, 1976-1982 124
    E24, 1983-1989 156
Thiele, Georg 131
Triple-hemispherical swirl combustion chamber 38
Tropic Automobildesign 186
Turbocharged E24s (Alpina) 180
TWR Hallmark Edition 111
Tyres, 70-section 41, 49

US bumpers for E24 102
US crash tests, and E9 49
US headlamps for 2000 CS 31
US-model 630 CSi 118
US-model 633 CSi 120, 130
US-model 635 CSi 140
US version of 2800 CS 47

Van Assche, Pedro 81
Van Hove (driver) 94
Variable-ratio power steering 105
Von Falkenhausen, Alex 23, 36
Von Kuehnheim, Eberhard 99
Von Opel, Rikky 80

Walkinshaw, Tom 82, 89
Weber, Jürgen 186, 187
Werginz, Heribert 164
Winkelhock, Manfred 169
Wollek, Bob 78, 80

Xhenceval, Jean 81, 82, 94

Zender bodykits 189
ZF 3 HP 12 gearbox 29
    3 HP 22 gearbox 107
    four-speed automatic 129